Neurodevelopment
Therapy

FOR

Cerebral Palsy

Rajesh Padnani

TABLE OF CONTENTS

LIST OF TABLE

LIST OF ABBREVIATION

CP	CEREBRAL PALSY
NDT	NEURO DEVELOPMENT TREATMENT
GMFCS	GROSS MOTOR FUNCTIONAL CLASSIFICATION SCALE
ADL	ACTIVITIES OF DAILY LIRING
AK.PS	ANTERIOR KNEE PAIN SCALE
PEDI	PEADIATRIC EEVALUATION OF DISABILITY INVENTARY
SATC	SEGMENAL ASSESSMENT OF TRUNK CONTROL
ICF	INTERNATIONAL CLASSIFICATION OF FUNCTIONING
TCMS	TRUNK CONTRAL MEASUREMENT SCALE
MACS	MANUAL ABILITY CLASSIFICATION SYSTEM
NICE	NATIONAL INSTITUTE FOR HEALTH AND CARE EXCELLECES
GMFM	GROSS MOTOR FUNCTIONAL MEASURES

LIST OF GRAPHS

CHAPTER-I

INTRODUCTION

Cerebral palsy (CP) is a group of non-progressive movement and posture development disorders that is caused due to injury to the brain. CP results in limitation of activity due to the occurrence damage to developing brain of the foetus. Though CP as such is a non-progressive disorder but the symptoms caused due to the brain damages progresses. The disorders of cerebral palsy are often due to disturbances of sensation, cognition, communication, perception, behavior, or by a seizure disorder (Bax M, 2005; Rosenbaum P, 2006).

CP is an umbrella term that includes multiple diagnoses based upon the type of symptom presentation, severity of the condition, and topographical distribution of primary motor impairment which is associated with neurological and behavioral impairments, functional deficits, and cerebral pathology. CP can be classified based upon the severity, muscle tone, topographical distribution and functional classification. Based upon the severity CP can be termed as Mild CP, Moderate CP and severe CP. CP based on muscle tone is categorized into athetoid, spastic, dyskinetic and atonic.

Diplegic, monoplegic, hemiplegic and quadriplegic CP are the types of CP classified based upon the topographical distribution. According to functional classification, CP is categorized as Grade 1, Grade 2, Grade 3, Grade 4 and Grade 5. The child is diagnosed as CP only after 2 years of age, even though the symptoms associated to motor activity show up from 6 months of age, due to brain development duration(Hack M et al, 2008).

Cerebral palsy is a condition that changes the course of a child' development in majority of the aspects which causes severe disability. An estimation of 7,64,000 Adults and children in USA manifest CP symptoms among which around 10,000 babies develop CP annually (United Cerebral Palsy, 2011).

Globally it has been reported that this condition contributes to be an economic burden because of loss of effective productivity, progressive loss of movements, utilization of recurrent rehabilitation assistances which results in deterioration of life expectancy (Wang B et al, 2008). In 2003,921,000 dollars was the estimated expenditure for the lifetime of a CP person found by the Centres for Disease Control and Prevention. 11.5 billion dollars was the estimated expenditure for the children and adults born in the year 2000(Office **CDC**, 2004).

A brief meaning of cerebral paralysis has been demonstrated because of the intricacy of the condition, and attribution of other neurological problems. The term "Cerebral Palsies" were first portrayed 150 years back, however many terms have been made in regards to manifestations of the condition and pathology ought to be thought about while depicting the term (Morris et al, 2007), from that point forward.

The condition itself is accepted to be perceived for a longer period since the Old Egyptian landmarks and figures had shown signs of such significance (Panteliadis et al, 2004). Slowly a few researchers attempted to clarify the relationship between cerebral damage and inborn loss of motion in the mid nineteenth century (Morris et al, 2007; Panteliadis et al, 2004), it was not before the English specialist William Little closed the connection of joint contractures resulting frohl long-standing spasticity and loss of motion. These are the most valuable points of what we today know as cerebral paralysis. In his work Mr.Little with no doubt expressed that the reason for spasticity and loss of motion was mostly damage to the cerebrum, and particularly in instances of preterm birth and perinatal asphyxia.

Little at that point expressed: "in numerous cases the uncontrollable warmth is delivered right now of birth or inside a couple of hours or days of that occasion. The subjects were given birth at the seventh month, or preceding the finish of the eighth month of utero incubation. In two cases the birth happened at the full time of incubation, yet attributable to the trouble and gradualness of parturition with a condition of asphyxia.

Following these announcements, the advanced ideas of cerebral paralysis was broadly found on disclosures, and despite the fact that diverse researchers in the meantime had a large number of similar views, cerebral paralysis was beforehand otherwise called Little's disease, as a praise to the individual who previously gave in a satisfactory portrayal, a depiction which was carried out from that point forward was intensely discussed.

In the late nineteenth century, the principal discoveries of an arrangement of cerebral paralysis dependent on clinical discoveries was begun. It was made by Sigmund Freud, and despite the fact that he had considerable experience with neuropathology, he demanded in just utilizing clinical discoveries in arrangement and diagnosing cerebral paralysis on the foundation that the body's own fix would carry an order dependent on the underlying injury. He at that point proposed that the reason for cerebral paralysis was pre-natal and peri-natal cause was just to be viewed as an indication that impacts the improvement of the embryo. Sigmund Freud later lost enthusiasm for the field of cerebral paralysis, and later built up his hypothesis of analysis. (Benson et al, 2009)

In view of previously mentioned Little's theory of the movement of the condition, a U.K. based assembly, known as "the Little Club", shaped a definition to coordinate his hypothesis, expressing that:

> *"Cerebral palsy is a permanent but progressive disorder of movement and posture appearing in early years of life caused due to a non-progressive disorder of the brain as a result of interference during its development".*

This definition met huge amount of analysis, particularly on the grounds that it endeavored to subdivide diverse gatherings prompting a need to change between the gatherings as the side effects of the ailment advanced. An overall accepted definition was thusly offered by the individuals from the Little's club as:

> *"Cerebral Palsy is a disorder of posture and movement due to a defect or lesion of the immature brain ".*

This definition was as often as possibly utilized in the next years, prompting a further correction in an endeavour to make a solitary globally acknowledged definition by a worldwide multidisciplinary assemble in 2004, refreshing the definition to   perceive that the key motor impairment is regularly joined by other neurological hindrances, which later has filled in as the nearest thing to an all-around acknowledged definition to the idea of cerebral paralysis, and is depicted into more subtleties.

Over the next years huge number of analysts researched further into cerebral paralysis, and endeavored to partition it into a few subgroups dependent on, clinical depiction, aetiology , pathology, mental and physical capacity, anatomical site of the cerebrum injury, level of muscle tone, geography, prerequisite, severity of the condition and the study of disease transmission.

The fundamental issue was separating it into a few subgroups did not offer an proper meaning for the condition, and the arrangement did not give clear widespread inclusion and exclusion criteria which was utilized for indicative and restorative purposes. In view of the accessible data at that time the main worldwide definition was endeavored as following:

> *"Cerebral palsy is a symptom complex arising from non-progressive brain lesion. "*

As this definition did not consider the heterogeneity of the condition a further changed definition that underlined the past one was performed from 1987-1990 expressing that:

> *"Cerebral palsy is an umbrella term covering a group of non-progressive, but often changing, motor impairment syndromes secondary to lesions or abnormalities of the brain arising in the early stages of development. "*

Following this last endeavored definition, the Surveillance of Cerebral Palsy in Europe (SCPE) influenced institutionalized symptomatic devices so as to legitimately to determine children to have cerebral paralysis. Their definition was to a great extent dependent on the definition expressed by Mutch et al., and included 5 key-focuses.

1. An umbrella term

2. Is permanent and not changing

3. Involves a disorder of movement and/or posture and motor functions

4. Is due to a non-progressive interference, lesion, or abnormality

5. The interference, lesion, or abnormality is in the immature brain.

Because of more than 150 years of discussions and debate, widespread definition acknowledged by researchers and social insurance laborers worldwide does not yet exist. In this theory the updated definition by Bax et al., and later reconsidered and clarified by an Executive Committee in April 2006; "with the purpose of giving a typical conceptualization of CP for use by an expansive worldwide group of audiences", gathered over alongside the five key focuses set by SCPE dependent on the previously mentioned definition for simplified purposes.

> *"Cerebral palsy (CP) describes a group of permanent disorders of the development of movement and posture, causing activity limitation, that are attributed to nonprogressive disturbances that occurred in the developing fetal or infant brain. The motor disorders of cerebral palsy are often accompanied by disturbances of sensation, perception, cognition, communication, and behaviour, by epilepsy, and by secondary musculoskeletal problems. "*

It is likewise critical to take note of that a child has cerebral paralysis just infers that there is a motor weakness from a static brain lesion, and says nothing regarding the etiology of the condition. That is the reason a few researchers refer the conditions in the plural type of cerebral paralyses. (Miller et al, 2005)

An estimation of 2.11 per 1000 live birth was found to be the overall prevalence of CP among them children weighing between 1000 to 1499g at birth had high prevalence of CP. High prevalence of CP was found in Children who were born before the gestational period of 28 weeks.

There was a recent increase within the overall prevalence of non-heritable CP from 1.7 to 2.0 per 1000 in 1-year survivors throughout the year from 1975-1991. This trend was primarily due to a small increase in infant CP of traditional birth weight-CP rates in moderately low and really low birth weight infants failed to show consistent trends. There was a rise within the proportion of youngster's who had CP and no different disabilities that was most common in infants with normal birth weight from 17 percentage in 1975-1977 to 39 percentage in 1986-1991. For youngsters weighing <1500 g, the proportion of youngsters with spastic diplegic CP had significantly doubled over time (7% of cases in 1975-1977, one year in 1985-1988, and thirty second in 1986-1991).

Abundant attention has been given to change in situation to prevalence of CP due to twenty-five percentage to thirty-five percentage of CP children have been born with a birth weight of 1500g. For the span of duration from 1967 to the first to mid 1980's, information from, England, Western Australia, and Scandinavian country showed a rise within the live birth prevalence of children with CP who had low birth weight. Prevalence of CP children survivors in a recent hospital-based US country study showed no change over a period of time from 1982-1988 and thereafter had a slow decrease through 1994. (Miller et al, 2005; Odding et al, 2006; Puscavage et al, 2005; Reddihough et al 2007; David et al 2005; Levitt and Sophie, 2010).

A recent documented report from American state showed a decrease within prevalence of CP child survivors born weighing 1500g over three periods: 1983-1985, 1988-1989 and 1990-1994.19 CP prevalence trends supported live births in low and very low birth weight classes, as shown during a study, could also be lost by changes in infant death rate over time. In addition, changes in medical practice like the utilization of surface-active agent might make a case for some of the discordant findings. The North geographical area and American state studies embrace within the most up-to-date birth cohorts, kids **WHO** might are treated with surface-active agent.

Surface-active agent has improved survival although its impact on disability is unsure. Recent studies recommend that severe CP is also decreasing, though the prevalence of CP has been stable as incontestable by studies of youngsters United Nations agency had CP born at term from Iceland and Sweden showing a major decrease within the proportion that had 2 or additional associated impairments. Affected Icelandic children born at term from 1997 to 2003 had higher gross motor abilities, were less doubtless to suffer from brain disorder, and were more doubtless to possess the diplegic type of CP when compared to children born from born between 1990 and 1996.

Data from the reports of cerebral palsy in Europe network, a population-based CP register representing the largest international collaboration of CP registers in the world, incontestable important changes within the prevalence of spastic CP subtypes in children born with birthweights of a minimum of 2,500 g born between 1980 and 1998. (Puscavage et al, 2005).

The wide scope of various causes and changing definitions, sub-classifications and exclusion or inclusion criteria, as examined in the past part, the outcomes found in different epidemiological studies about fluctuate to a specific degree, and any correct decision was difficult to make. Purposes behind these slight contrasts may shift standard of social insurance, challenges in finding gentle cases, and diverse elucidations of definitions. In an article Odding et al., expressed that: "It must be reasoned that a vital part of scientific knowledge about CP is absent in rehabilitation literature", while talking about the study of disease transmission of cerebral paralysis.

In view of that, clear signs recommend that the prevalence of the condition is surprisingly comparable worldwide with the distinctions clarified by a defective counting and diverse elucidations of inclusion and exclusion criteria. In view of the various findings, an expected prevalence of cerebral paralysis is accepted to be 2 in each 1000 live births, with a slight less similarity in China, contrasted with Europe and America. This makes it the most predominant of the chronic childhood motor disability disorders. (Miller et al, 2005, Morris et al, 2007; Panteliadis et al, 2004; Levitt and Sophie, 2010)

Following the arrangement made by SCPE in the late 1990's prevalence rates for six European nations were distributed, demonstrating a predominance of below 2 for each 1000 live births in the 1970's to a prevalence over 2 for every 1000 live births in the 1990's in the taking part European countries, however for this situation it is critical to remember the distinctive definitions in the diagnostics and the movement of the paediatrics restorative consideration amid the last piece of a century ago, together with the trusted increase when all is said in done medicinal services to by far most of the populace, amid a similar time length.

Another interesting finding with regards to this timeframe is that despite the fact that the general all out predominance of liveborn with cerebral paralysis has been much stable in the course of recent decades, an exceptional increment of enduring babies with low and low birth weight prompting cerebral paralysis has been discovered. This prompts another remarkable and normal finding in ongoing literature, proposing a higher pervasiveness of cerebral paralysis in preterm births joined by a low birth weight.

A Swedish research made on 241 kids determined to have cerebral paralysis demonstrates that 36% were conceived at a gestational age (GA) of under 28 weeks. A much-detailed data extricated even demonstrated a 25% prevalence of births of 28-32 weeks of GA, 2.5% of 32-38 weeks of GA, and 28.5% of non-preterm births. The moderately high level of cerebral paralysis among term new-born children found in this investigation must be found regarding the higher prevalence of term deliveries among the 241 new-born children were included for examination.

Joseph et al. thought about two huge populace-based investigations without uncertainty. With a GA of under 28 weeks the proportion was 63.9 per 1000 live born, with the proportion of live born with a GA of over 37 weeks were 0.9 per 1000 instead of the gathered proportion of 2: 1000. (Odding et al, 2006; Puscavage et al, 2005; Reddihough et al 2007; David et al 2005;Joseph, K.S., et al. 2003)

A substantial, population-based investigation from Norway helps further fascinating information in regards to the length of GA and prevalence of cerebral paralysis. It demonstrates that neonates who were born following 40 weeks of GA have the least prevalence of cerebral paralysis with 0.99 per 1000 live born. Neonates who were born on or after 41, 42 and 43 weeks of GA demonstrated a progressive increment of prevalence with 1.08, 1.36 and 1.44 per 1000 live born individually. (Moster, Dag, et al 2010).

While considering birth weight, studies show that babies weighing less than 2500 grams during childbirth comprise 50 % of all causes for cerebral paralysis. A few examinations conclude with a higher prevalence of cerebral paralysis among low birth weight children, contrasted with normal birth weight children. Researchers have been performed to study and compare the normal birth weight (NBW >2500 g), low birth weight (LBW 1500-2499 g) and very low birth weight (VLBW < 1500 g). The discussion of live born with a birth weight underneath 2500 g (LBW and VLBW) demonstrates a prevalence of 16.85 per 1000 live born.

The assembly generally discussed about the prevalence of cerebral paralysis in this investigation and stated that the prevalence was 2.51 per 1000 births, excluding the prevalence of NBW to 1.55 per 1000 births. In that event a was more detailed investigated was done, it demonstrates that there was a higher prevalence of babies with low birth weight, 57.45 per 1000 live born, than infants with low birth weight, 10. 77 per 1000 live born, in this UK based examination.

An expansion of predominance of cerebral paralysis with VLBW ascended from 29.8 per 1000 live born in 1964 to 74.2 per 1000 live born in 1993 and the rate of neonatal survivors ascended from 3.9 to 11.5 per 1000 in the gathering of children with LBW inside a similar time length, showing, in addition to other things, an expansion of neonatal consideration in this timeframe.

Adding to the propensity of a superior neonatal consideration is showed by a few sources recommending a move toward diplegia and spastic quadriplegia and far from hemiplegia and athetosis in the period between nineteen 70's to the nineteen 90's. Clarifications for this move was somewhat expanded in terms of prevalence which was explained on restorative consideration and consideration including better obstetric consideration and a higher survival rate of preterm births (Dolk et al, 2001, Odding et al, 2006; Millerand Freeman, 2005; Tecklin et al, 2008; Odding, 2006; Dolk et al, 2001).

A higher rate of an expanded or diminished maternal age is similarly present. Children born to mothers with a maternal age of 12-19, or 35+ have an wide range of chances to give birth to children with cerebral paralysis. Different births are known to expand the rate of cerebral paralysis with a prevalence for each pregnancy for singles at 0.2%, twins 1.5%, triplets 8.0%, and quadruplets 43%. (Miller et al, 2005; Tecklin et al, 2008;Hjem et al, 2008)
It is additionally discovered that an expanded prevalence with a lower social and social-financial class in examines made on epidemiological examinations in Great Britain and in the US. In the American examination 54,000 pregnant ladies from 12 urban health care centres were contemplated somewhere in the range of 1959 and 1966. Among the 38,533children who came to urban health care centres, 202 met the criteria of cerebral paralysis, or a proportion of 5.2: 1000 children, instead of around 2: 1000 in the all-inclusive community.

Patients in these urban regions, approaching private clinics, had a lower financial status than the normal populace. Extraordinary contention emerges when looking at connection between a financial angle and the frequency rate of cerebral paralysis. A substantial populace-based investigation from Sweden arranged by Hjern et al. includes vital data in this epidemiologic field, and backs the discoveries in the British and American looks into. It finished up with a higher rate of occurrence of cerebral paralysis in localities contrasted with other metropolitan or urban zones.

Children who were born with a lower maternal lower financial status had a noteworthy higher rate of occurrence contrasted with moms characterized to have a higher financial status. A similar propensity was found, not surprisingly, with a lower dimension of maternal training. It additionally finished up with a huge increment of cerebral paralysis in children naturally introduced to families that got social welfare, however the exploration does not close whether the family was getting social welfare before the delivery of children with cerebral paralysis, or if the difference in word related status was because of the new family circumstance.

Children born to Adolescents have a higher proportion of cerebral paralysis all in all, with a child born to young women with a proportion of 2.05: 1.50 per 1000 live-borns. Discoveries likewise finish up with higher rate for cerebral paralysis in births in the mid-year months, clarified by the impact of paediatric specialists, which may change occasionally. Every one of these variables examined the vital data, and could be utilized in arranging treatment, yet in addition to a specific degree keep the prevalence where intercession is conceivable. (Hjern et al,2008, Tecklin et al, 2008, Odding et al, 2006).

While talking about the term of aetiology in cerebral paralysis, it is essential to remember that the meaning of cerebral paralysis expressing that it is an umbrella term dependent on clinical signs, and that diagnosing a child with cerebral paralysis is just showing some type of motor problems and does not contemplate the aetiology. As it was, deciding the aetiology does not help the genuine administration of treatment of the weakness as the first reason for advancement of the condition does not make a difference (Miller and Freeman ,2005; Alberman et al, 2007).

For a large of cerebral paralysis, just the complications of the pre-natal, perinatal or postnatal period can be distinguished, and much of the time, there are more than one causative factor prompting the condition. This particular arrangement was offered as of now in the late nineteenth century, by Sigmund Freud, when he recognized three separate gatherings of causal factors as [1] maternal or idiopathic inherent; [2] perinatal causes; and [3] post-natal causes.

Etiology is anyway of extraordinary significance when diagnosing and for a visualization, so as to decide if the child is following the normal course of development and advancement, and it helps with imperative data to take care for future pregnancies. It is even said to help with diminishing parental blame. The author ought to notwithstanding, in all cases, be comfortable with the child's medicinal history, if information is accessible.

It is likewise imperative to focus on the way that not all instances of cerebral paralysis have any unmistakable etiology. Distinctive investigates have been made on this specific field, and figures of cerebral paralysis with no particular, recognizable, aetiological reason change between 42-44%. (Panteliadis et al, 2004; Gilman and Sid, 2007; Morris et al, 2007).

Despite the fact that any correct aetiological information has ended up being difficult to remove, figures generally propose that 30% of instances of cerebral paralysis are related with mind mutation, 40% with rashness, 20 % with neonatal encephalopathy, and 10% of
various postnatal causes. Another approach to arrange the aetiology recommend pre-birth occasions to be in charge of 75% of the cases, perinatal causes 6-8% and postnatal causes are believed to be in charge of the rest of the 10-18% of the cases. Once more different sources gauge the level of pre-birth occasions to comprise for 70-80 % of the cases, and postnatal causes to 10-25% of the cases (Wu et al, 2000; Tecklin et al, 2008; Gilman and Sid, 2007; Miller,2005).

Overall in general most predominant hazard factors for cerebral paralysis incorporate; low birth weight, intrauterine diseases and different development. Having said that, it is essential to specify that as per view into, 60 % of children determined to have cerebral paralysis were not grouped as having a particularly high hazard profile, and 97% of youngsters arranged with a high hazard profile were never determined to have cerebral paralysis (Odding et al, 2006; Guzzetta and Francesco, 2009).

As it was discussed previously the internal variables are a portion of the key segments utilized so as to decide the etiology of the motor problems seen in cerebral paralysis. As for what is as of now discussed already, it is important to investigate the particular hazard factors associated with cerebral paralysis. Risk factors were discussed in 3 separate headings, in particular the pre-birth, perinatal, and postnatal period. It is critical to remember that few risk factors correspond, expanding the likelihood of the rate of cerebral paralysis.
From the pre-birth period the maternal variables are clearly turned out to be of incredible significance while talking about the subject of cerebral paralysis. In the event that the mother has abnormalities

of the menstrual cycle, for example, delaying of menstrual cycle, unpredictable menstrual cycle, or long inter menstrual period, it is accepted to expand the odds of cerebral paralysis.

In the event that the mother's period between pregnancies are either unusually short or anomalous long, in the event that she has an equality of at least three, or has encounters with at least three unsuccessful labors, the danger of cerebral paralysis is expanded. Maternal risk factors at the time of pregnancies could likewise be medication and liquor misuse, smoking, hyperthyroidism, epilepsy, or innate diseases in the first or second trimester, for example, herpes simplex, toxoplasma gondii, rubella or cytomegalovirus (Tecklin et al, 2008; Panteliadis et al, 2004).

Other pre-birth causal factors include maternal utilization of other tetratogenicusers, maternal iodine deficiency, and a vascular occlusion, for example, hypoxia, ischemia and thrombosis, particularly in central cerebral vein. Conditions, for example, pre-eclampsia and poor intrauterine development are additionally considered as real hazard factors amid the pregnancy.

Paternal causes, for example, increased age, and motor problems in at least one sibling likewise increment prevalence of cerebral paralysis. Other pre-natal risk factors incorporate chorioamnionitis, which is seen in half of women's who are about to deliver babies. Intrauterine diseases are the most imperative risk factor of cerebral paralysis in VLBW babies, and are additionally a vital risk factor in full term newborn children with NBW (Panteliadis et al, 2004; Tecklin et al, 2008; Odding et al 2006; Wu et al, 2000).

In the perinatal period, the history of delivery is of extraordinary significance. On the off chance that intricacies happen, for example, a difficult delivery, ante partum discharge or an umbilical line prolapsed, the neonate may create neonatal encephalopathy, which incredibly builds the danger of cerebral paralysis. Other hazard factors in the perinatal period happen of an untimely birth, CNS contaminations, hypoglycaemia, untreated jaundice, and neonatal stroke of the centre cerebral course.

A standout amongst the most widely recognized hazard elements of cerebral paralysis in this period is over the top neonatal anoxia or asphyxia. This would immediately prompt a diminished oxygen dimension of the course, causing a cerebrum sore due to hypoxic-ischemic encephalopathy. Other hazard factors thought to trigger a cytokine course bringing about harm to the creating mind are passing of co-twin, placental suddenness and cerebral ischemia (Tecklin et al, 2008;Panteliadis et al, 2004; Levitt and Sophie, 2010; Odding et al 2006).

The postnatal period incorporates the recorded cases happening after the neonatal period where the child is believed to grow regularly before the occasion, and incorporates frequencies, for example, close suffocating mishaps, encephalitis and inconveniences after medical procedure. In created nations postnatal contaminations are accepted to be in charge of most instances of cerebral paralysis in the post-natal period. Despite the fact that the postnatal hazard factors make up the littlest gathering of hazard factors, they are vital because of the way that these are the most effortless to anticipate. (Stanley, Fiona J et al, 1994; Roberton et al, 2007; Creasy et al, 2004; Piek et al, 2006; Peacock et al, 2000; Clover et al, 2007).

Metabolic encephalopathy is one of the significant hazard variables of cerebral paralysis in the postnatal period, together with diseases, for example, meningitis, septicaemia and jungle fever, particularly in creating nations. The prevalence of cerebral paralysis is multiple times higher in term newborn children with encephalopathy with an extra birth deformity, then of those with encephalopathy with no extra birth abandons. Wounds, for example, hypoxia because of a close suffocating rate or different kinds of suffocation, heart failure, for example, "shaken infant syndrome", or an unpolished injury prompting a skull break are likewise among the hazard elements of the postnatal period. (Miller et al, 2005; Tecklin et al, 2008; Panteliadis et al, 2004; Odding et al, 2006).

Like the meaning of cerebral paralysis, a characterization of the condition has been discussed about since researchers originally got enthusiasm of the point in the mid nineteenth century, with various endeavors to arrange the few indications of the disability. Through history a few unmistakable individuals have finished up with the challenges in such an undertaking, with Bax expressing that: "It is difficult to continue certainly with characterizing cerebral paralysis, and Sigmund Freud reasoning that the errand of isolating innate from gained causes inconceivable, and in some cases even unhelpful.

The last proclamation has later been tested by the innovative improvement of exact analytic measures, for example, ultrasound and MRI. It has been evaluated that 70-90% of all babies determined to have cerebral paralysis has some sort of mind variations from the norm found in MRI checks (Morris et al, 2007;Tecklin et al, 2008).

The main endeavour to make any solid characterization pursued William Little's first meaning of cerebral paralysis in 1843, recognized as the primary logical meaning of cerebral paralysis. Little looked at the clinical introduction and the birth history of an expansive segment of his patients, and assembled the clinical introductions found to coordinate his recently shaped meaning of cerebral paralysis as either (1) hemiplegic rigidity affecting one side only, although a lesser impairment of the uninvolved limb was often seen, (2) paraplegia affecting lower extremities more than the upper extremities, and (3) generalized rigidity (4). (Morris et al, 2007).
Towards the end of the nineteenth century, further discussion took place with respect to the orders of cerebral paralysis emerged. On one side a gathering of researchers, led by Sachs and Peterson, expressed that a grouping ought to incorporate unique reference to the pathology of the infection. This depended on after death examinations of chose examples to decide the etiology of the condition, and essentially reasoned that in Little's arrangement, each of the three gatherings could be a consequence of an assortment of causes, and along these lines thinking about the order as pointless.

Saying as much, they didn't build some other grouping framework to back up their announcement. On the opposite side a youthful Sigmund Freund rejected the hypothesis by Sachs and Peterson, with the clarification that in an after-death examination the discoveries would not be absolutely identified with the clinical introduction of the cerebral paralysis itself, as the discoveries would in all likelihood be an after effect of the underlying injury, and the fix procedure further down the road, making such posthumous examination pointless and deceiving.

Rather he needed a characterization framework dependent on clinical discoveries. His order was straightforward and incorporated the term diplegia for the past sorted reciprocal issue, and hemiplegia for one-sided disarranges. He even distinguished three separate gatherings of causative factors as maternal and idiopathic inherent, perinatal causes, and post natal causes, however said it was hard to decide if later issues came about because of birth injury, or whether it in truth were inclining factors that may have made these newborn children have a troublesome birth (Morris et al, 2007).

In the 1920's another perspective of the grouping framework was distributed, this time by the American orthopedic specialist Winthrop Phelps. Regardless of his calling he was traditionalist with the methodology of medical procedure as the foundation of treatment and needed a grouping dependent on a practical premise, including both mental and physical capacities. Because of this he finished an arrangement framework where he assembled all development issue under the term dyskinesia with sub-classes gathered into spasticity, athetosis, flood or synkinesia, incoordination or ataxia, and tremor.

Despite the fact that he made an unmistakable partition ordered in five sub-classifications he noticed that these assortments once in a while showed themselves in an unadulterated shape. This was the main grouping made, like the most much of the time utilized in the present practice.(Morris et al, 2007)

In spite of the various endeavours of characterizing cerebral paralysis for around 100 years, extraordinary disarray held on with respect to the subject in the 1940's and 1950's. Myer Perlstein then built up a framework characterizing kids as indicated by anatomical site of the mind sore, clinical manifestations, level of muscle tone, severity of inclusion, and etiology. This framework was later supported by Minear, in light of a study of the individuals from the American Academy of Cerebral Palsy in 1953. Minear arranged the impedance as a posting of the clinical side effects with classes for engine hindrance, geography, aetiology, neuro anatomical variables, useful limit and remedial necessities. A comparable framework was likewise created in the UK, by Evans, Asher and Schonell (Morris et al, 2007).

Later on, in the 1950's the previously mentioned Little Club arranged cerebral paralysis by utilization of the term spastic, with subcategories of hemiplegia, twofold hemiplegia, and diplegia, joined by 5 different classes, in particular dystonic, choreo-athetoid, mixed, ataxic and atonic, which is a reason for the classification utilized later in this theory. Nonetheless, around then the term spastic was utilized conflicting all through different nations, prompting the gathering finishing up with that it is difficult to continue completely with arranging cerebral paralysis.

Because of the dire need of a worldwide characterization framework in the late 1980's for epidemiological purposes, Evans built up a framework that picked up a great deal of notoriety because of its straightforwardness. He classified cerebral paralysis after recorded subtleties of focal motor disability regarding the neurological sort to hypotonia, hypertonia dyskinesia and ataxia. He at that point subdivided the gatherings as indicated by where the impedances were noticeable, with subtleties for every control of head and neck independently.

From various perspectives this framework is like the one created by individuals from the Little Club a few decades already, yet it has barred a portion of the gatherings, and it is particularly essential to take note of that the blended gathering is expelled, and fairly remunerated by portrayals of numerous gatherings when required, prompting a superior depiction in every individual case. (Bax et al, 1964; Morris et al, 2007)

With respect to the meaning of cerebral paralysis, there still is no all-around acknowledged technique for characterizing cerebral paralysis. The accompanying rundown of sub-bunches depend on work by the Little's discussion, and by Evans, and is by all accounts the most utilized characterization as far as subgroups of cerebral paralysis. This grouping of kind of motor disorder with attribution of a portrayal of anatomical circulation is believed to be the most ideal method for arranging from a physiotherapeutic perspective, and is accepted to be the order framework most as often as possible utilized in productions incorporated into the consideration criteria for this proposal.

Such an anatomical order incorporates the types of spastic kind, ataxic sort, athetoid/dyskinetic type, and hypotonic kind of cerebral paralysis, which will be portrayed into further detail in the accompanying sections. The blended gathering is forgotten, despite the fact that the event of more than one sub-assemble in a solitary individual is regarded. In those cases, the dominating sub-gather wins.

The clarification on the accompanying pages serves to depict the portrayals of the distinctive subtypes of cerebral paralysis, subsequently a different depiction of the blended type of cerebral paralysis appears to be pointless. Normal for all these diverse arrangements is the subdivision of which part of the body is being influenced. This topographic characterization is accepted to be helpful so as to.

Premature infants are at greater risk of brain dysfunction. There are many causes of the brain damage, including abnormal development of the brain, anoxia, intracranial bleeding, excessive neonatal asphyxia (hypoxic ischaemic neonatal encephalopathy), trauma, hypoglycemia and virus and other infections. These have been extensively discussed in the medical literature (Stanley & Alberman 1984; Gordon & McKinlay 1986; Rosenbloom 1995; Hagberg et al. 1996). The therapist is, however, rarely guided by the aetiology in her treatment planning.

In some cases, the cause is not certain and in many cases knowing the cause does not necessarily indicate a specific diagnosis or specific treatment. Nevertheless, the therapist should acquaint herself with the history of the case. Many of these children have been affected from infancy and have been difficult to feed and handle. Many hospitalizations and separations of babies from parents may happen in the early period. This may easily have influenced the parent-child relationships. Furthermore, the history may sometimes give an indication of the prognosis, e.g. with marked microcephaly with severe multiple impairments the prognosis would be poor.

The brain damage results in disorganized and delayed development of the neurological mechanisms of postural control or balance and movement. The muscles activated for these motor aspects are therefore inefficient and in coordinated. Individuals have hypertonic or hypotonic muscles with weakness. Besides neuromuscular components the motor dysfunction has muscular-skeletal components. Therapy aims to improve postural control and movement as well as provide for specific abnormal muscles and joints.

The motor components change both with growth and a child's development. Change also depends on how an individual uses his body. However, the brain damage is not progressive, though the motor behaviour changes. What matters most to a child and his family is the overall functional delay and abnormal performance. Therapists need to address these daily functional difficulties together with a child and his parents or directly with an older person with cerebral palsy.

There are different views as to which abnormal motor components are responsible for the total motor dysfunction and what correlation exists between various components. The underlying motor dyscontrol is controversial. This is not surprising as not all the normal and abnormal neurological mechanisms are fully understood. Additional biomechanical problems result from these abnormal mechanisms which also provide controversies. Research continues on the basic dyscontrol and biomechanics.

As a child does not 'move by neurophysiology alone', various ideas on learning motor control have been integrated into the general therapy framework so that 'what to do' is combined with 'how to do it'. The associated impairments and disabilities influence the motor function and the learning of motor control. Motor learning and learning daily functions need to be considered in the context of a child's whole development, which takes place in his home, school and community.

Brain damage in cerebral palsy may also be responsible for special sense defects of vision and hearing, abnormalities of speech and language and aberrations of perception. Perceptual defects or agnosias are difficulties in recognizing objects or symbols, even though sensation as such is not impaired, and the patient can prove by other means to know or have known what the object or symbol is. There may also be dyspraxias, some of which are also called visuomotor defects. This means that the child is unable to perform certain movements even though there is no paralysis, because the patterns or engrams have been lost or have not developed.

Dyspraxia can involve movements of the limbs, face, eyes, tongue or be specifically restricted to such acts as writing, drawing, and construction or even dressing. In other words, there seems to be a problem in 'motor planning' in those children who are dyspraxic.

Some children may also have various behavioral problems such as distractibility and hyperkinesis which are based on the brain damage. All these defects result in various learning problems and difficulties in communication. In addition, there may also be various epilepsies or intellectual impairment (Foley 1977b; Hall 1984; Neville 2000).

Not every child has some or all of these associated impairments. Even if the impairment were only motor, the resulting paucity of movement would prevent the child from fully exploring the environment. He is therefore limited in the acquisition of sensations and perceptions of everyday things.

A child may then appear to have defects of perception, but these may not be due to the brain damage but caused by lack of experience. The same lack of everyday experiences retards the development of language and affects the child's speech. His general understanding may suffers that he appears to be intellectually retarded. This can go so far that normal intelligence has been camouflaged by severe physical disability.

Furthermore, the lack of movement can affect the general behavior of the child. Thus, some abnormal behavior may be due to the lack of satisfying emotional and social experiences for which movement is necessary. It is therefore important for any therapist to recognize that motor function cannot be isolated from other functions and that she is treating a child who is not solely physically but multiply disabled.

Motor problems create difficulties for a child in social activities and in being able to access educational activities. A therapist needs to address the motor problems in these situations. In order to manage the multiple disabilities and lack of related learning experiences which interfere with a child's development, a physiotherapist or occupational therapist needs to be part of a team. The teamwork varies in different places such as community centers, child development centers, units in hospitals or within educational settings.

It is important to recognize that the causes of cerebral palsy take place in the prenatal, perinatal, and postnatal periods. In all cases, it is an immature nervous system which suffers the insult and the nervous system afterwards continues to develop in the presence of the damage.

The therapist must therefore not think of herself as treating an upper motor neuron lesion in a 'little adult' nor can she regard the problem solely as one of retardation in development. What the therapist faces is a complex situation of pathological symptoms within the context of a developing child (Twitchell 1961, 1965; McGraw 1989; Griffiths 1967; Sheridan 1973, 1975; Egan 1990; Holt 1975; Van Blankenstein et al. 1975; Illingworth 1975, 1983; Drillien & Drummond 1977, 1983). There are three main aspects to the clinical picture:

(1) Retardation in the development of new skills expected at the child's chronological age.

(2) Persistence of infantile behaviour in all functions, including infantile reflex reactions.

(3) Performance of various functions in patterns never seen in normal babies and children. This is
    because of the pathological symptoms or impairments due to upper
    motor neurone lesions such as hypertonus, hypotonus, involuntary movements and
    biomechanical difficulties confronting children with cerebral palsy.

Although normal child development is the basis on which the abnormal development is appreciated, it does not follow that assessment and treatment should rely upon a strict adherence to normal developmental schedules. Even 'normal' children show many variations from the 'normal' developmental sequences and patterns of development which have been derived from the average child.

The cerebral palsies child will show additional variations due to neurological and mechanical difficulties. If one considers, say, the normal developmental scales of gross motor development, the cerebral palsied child has frequently achieved abilities (components) and motor functions at one level of development, omitted abilities at another level and only partially achieved motor abilities and functions at still other levels. There is thus a scatter of abilities and whole motor functions.

If the gross motor development is generally considered to be around a given age, the development of hand function, speech and language, social and emotional and intellectual levels may all be at different ages. None of these ages may necessarily coincide with the child's chronological age.

Therefore, the developmental schedules in normal child development should only be used as guidelines in treatment and adaptation should be made for each child's disabilities and individuality. More attention is usually given to motor development rather than other avenues of development, as it is the motor dysfunction which characterizes cerebral palsy.

Whilst aiming at the maximum function possible, the therapists concerned must take account of the damaged nervous system and adjust their expectations of achievements by the child which involve:

(1)   Late acquisition of motor skills and slow rate of progress from one stage to the next.

(2)   A smaller variety of skills than in the normal child.

(3)   Variations in normal sequences of skills.

(4)   Abnormal and unusual patterns of some of the skills.

As the lesion is in a developing nervous system the clinical picture is clearly not a static set of signs and symptoms for treatment. But whilst the lesion itself is non-progressive its manifestations change as the nervous system matures. As more is demanded of the nervous system the degree of the handicap appears to be greater.

For example, a 3-year-old is expected to do more than a baby, and therefore his difficulties are greater for the same lesion.

In addition, the pathological symptoms may develop with the years. Spasticity may increase, involuntary movements may only appear at the age of 2 or 3 years, and ataxia may only be diagnosed when the child walks or when grasp is expected to become more accurate. Diagnoses may change as the baby develops to childhood, and especially as the child becomes more active. For example, a monoplegia reveals itself as a hemiplegia. Later a triplegia reveals itself as a tetraplegia. Cerebral palsies have an evolving diagnosis. Later, especially in adolescence, growth and increase in weight contribute to apparent deterioration as the child matures.

Hypertonus of the clasp-knife variety. If the spastic muscles are stretched at a particular speed they respond in an exaggerated fashion. They contract, blocking the movement. This hyperactive stretch reflex may occur at the beginning, middle or near the end of the range of movement. There is increased tendon jerks, occasional clonus and other signs of upper motor neurone lesions.

Abnormal postures. These are usually associated with the antigravity muscles which are extensors in the leg and the flexors in the arm. The therapist will find many variations on this especially when the child reaches different levels of development (Bobath & Bobath 1972). Common abnormal postures in supine, prone, sitting, standing, walking and in hand function are described in.

The abnormal postures are held by tight shorter spastic muscle groups whose antagonists are weak, or apparently weak in that they cannot overcome the tight pull of the spastic muscles and so correct the abnormal postures.

There are various other causes of abnormal postures which are discussed in relation to abnormal postural mechanisms of control. Spasticity is therefore not over-emphasized as a cause. Abnormal postures appear as unfixed deformities which may become fixed deformities or contractures.

Changes in spasticity and postures may occur with excitement, fear or anxiety and pain which increase muscle tension. Shifts in spasticity occur in the same affected parts of the body or from one part of the body to another in, say, stimulation of abnormal reactions such as 'associated reactions' or remnants of tonic reflex activity. Changes in spasticity are seen with changes of position in some children. Position of the head and neck may affect the distribution of spasticity. The latter are due to abnormal reflexes which may sometimes be found in these children. Sudden or fast movements, rather than slow movements, increase spasticity.

Hypertonus may be either spasticity or rigidity (dystonia). The overlap between the two is almost impossible to differentiate when severe. Rigidity is recognized by a plastic or continuous resistance to passive stretch throughout the full range of motion. This lead-pipe rigidity differs from spasticity as spasticity offers resistance at a point or small part of the passive range of motion. For treatment planning the type of hypertonus is rarely important and techniques for motor development and prevention of deformity are the same.

Voluntary movement. Spasticity does not necessarily mean paralysis. Voluntary motion is present and may be laboured. There may be weakness in the initiation of motion or during movement at different parts of its range. If spasticity is decreased or removed by treatment or drugs, the spastic muscles may be found to be strong, or may be weak. Spastic muscles may have specific structural changes due to adaptability to abnormal use or disuse (Tabary et al. 1981). Initially spastic muscles are however structurally normal though not normally extensible (Tardieu et al. 1982).

Once spasticity is decreased the antagonists may also be stronger once they no longer have to overcome the resistance of tight spastic muscles. However, in time these antagonists may have become weak with disuse.

The groups of muscles or chains of muscles used in the movement patterns are different from those used in normal children of the same age. Either the muscles which work in association with each other are stereotyped and are occasionally seen in the normal child, usually at an infantile level of movement, or the association of muscles is abnormal.

For example, hip extension-adduction-internal rotation is used in creeping movements or in the push-off in walking but many other combinations must be used during the full execution of creeping and walking. This may be impossible and a child only uses the same pattern at all times in the motor skill. One example of a' normal arm pattern is shoulder flexion-adduction with some external rotation for feeding or combing one's hair. In the case of the child with spasticity, the arm pattern is usually flexion adduction with internal rotation and pronation of the elbow.

Co-contraction of the agonist with the antagonist instead of the normal reciprocal relaxation persists in the spastic type. Normal co-contraction is also evident in any person attempting a new and difficult skill. Before the postural control develops in normal infants there is co-contraction of a positive supporting response in weight-bearing and co-contraction features in early stages of walking. These patterns persist in cerebral palsy (Leonard et al. 1991; Foley 1998; Lin 2000) so that training of postural control is essential. Voluntary movements are directly affected as poor postural control interferes with their efficiency creating weakness of both postural muscles and voluntary synergies (movement patterns).

Lack of isolated or discrete movements and fine motor coordination are also delayed in younger able-bodied children as well as in older children with this type of cerebral palsy. Treatment is therefore needed for abnormalities of voluntary movement such as weakness, abnormal movement patterns (synergies), lack of isolated (discrete, selective) movements and abnormal co-contractions. Deformities develop due to abnormal postures and abnormal repetition of a few stereotyped movements which are only available to a child with this condition.

Associated impairments

(1) Intelligence varies and IS usually more impaired in tetraplegia.

(2) Sensory loss occasionally occurs in hemiplegia with visual field loss and lack of sensation in the hand (Tizard et al. 1954). Sensory dysfunction such as sensory discrimination and sensory integration rather than sensory loss is present in individuals (Lesny 1993; Yekutiel et al. 1994). Children may be hyposensitive or hypersensitive to sensory input so that sensory-motor therapy needs to be carefully assessed.

(3) Perceptual problems especially of body and spatial relationships are more common in the spastic type. They relate to sensory dysfunction and cognitive problems as well as to poor sensory-motor experiences.

(4) Poor respiration with later rib cage abnormalities may exist. Feeding problems exist.

(5) Growth of hemiplegic limbs or severely affected lower limbs in bilateral cases can be less than the other limbs.

(6) Epilepsies are more common in tetraplegia and hemiplegia but minimal in diplegia (Neville 2000).

(7) A congenital suprabulbar palsy is found in some tetraplegias with mild spasticity (eville 2000) or severe involvement.

Cerebral palsy consists of both motor delay and motor disorder. There are many other conditions which present similar problems of motor delay or of delay and disorder. All these conditions are also called the developmental disabilities (Pearson & Williams 1972). They may be due to: Intellectual impairment which is caused by various metabolic disorders, chromosome anomalies, leucodystrophies, microcephaly and other abnormalities of the skull and brain, endocrine disorders and the causes of brain damage given for the cerebral palsies. Down's syndrome also creates motor delay.

Deprivation of normal stimulation associated with social, economic and emotional problems, including maternal depression. Malnutrition alone, but usually together with deprived environments. Once malnutrition is treated, lack of normal stimulation may still retard the child's development. The presence of non-motor impairments which may lead to motor delay, e.g. severe visual impairments, severe perceptual defects, apraxias, as well as intellectual disabilities mentioned above. Children with delay in any developmental area may have an associated delay in motor development

Presence of motor impairments other than the cerebral palsies. For example spina bifida, the myopathies, myelopathies and various progressive neurological diseases and congenital deformities may obviously delay development, e.g. hand function has been delayed in children with spina bifida (Holt 1975) as well as gross motor development.

Karl Bobath, a neuropsychiatrist, and Berta Bobath, a physiotherapist, base assessment and treatment on the premise that the fundamental difficulty in cerebral palsy is lack of inhibition of reflex patterns of posture and movement (Bobath, B. 1965, 1971; Bobath, K. 1971, 1980; Bobath & Bobath 1972, 1975, 1984).

The Bobaths associate these abnormal patterns with abnormal tone due to overaction of tonic reflex activity. These tonic reflexes, such as the tonic labyrinthine reflex, symmetrical tonic neck reflexes and asymmetrical tonic neck reflexes, have to be inhibited. They are not used in a reflex chart today, but are fundamental in treatment which 'counteracts the abnormal patterns of released postural reflex activity, and at the same time facilitates normal reactions by special techniques of handling'. Once the reflex patterns of abnormal tone are inhibited the child is said to have been prepared for movement.

In addition, various primitive reflexes of infancy should also be inhibited. The main features of their work are currently being modified, but the focus on treatment of tone continues (Mayston 1992). Features of the approach are: Reflex inhibitory patterns specifically selected to inhibit abnormal tone associated with abnormal movement patterns and abnormal posture.

Sensory motor experience. The reversal or 'break down' of these abnormalities gives the child the sensation of more normal tone and movements. This sensory experience is believed to 'feedback' and guide more normal motion. Sensory stimuli are also used for inhibition and facilitation and voluntary movement. Facilitation techniques for mature postural reflexes.

Abnormal tone is the cornerstone of this approach, which tries to 'normalize' it. Developmental sequences were more strictly followed in the past, but are now greatly modified according to each child (Mayston 1992). All-day management should supplement treatment sessions. Parents and others are advised on daily management and trained to treat the children.

Diplegia depicts the situations where the two furthest points are included symmetrical, with the essential inclusion of the lower limits, despite the fact that warmth of the furthest points may happen. Hemiplegia portrays youngsters with inclusion of a large portion of the body, with one arm and one leg on a similar side being influenced. Finally, quadriplegia, now and again alluded to as tetraplegia, includes every one of the four appendages and now and again even the storage compartment, with the contribution progressively articulated in the lower limits contrasted with the furthest points.

As a rule, one can say that kids displaying diplegic and hemiplegic designs can play out an autonomous movement with assistive gadgets when required, though kids with a quadriplegic design are wheelchair bound. This may obviously fluctuate. (Miller et al, 2005; Tecklin et al, 2007; Panteliadis et al, 2004; Peacock et al, 2000).

In a few children the clinical appearance does not entirely fit in under the orders of diplegia, hemiplegia or quadriplegia. Other name proposals, for example, bilateral hemiplegia, triplegia, monoplegia and pentaplegia has been incited to depict these uncommon rates, which includes a considerable amount of disarray in the writing as the terms does not appear to have any reasonable all-inclusive definition. It is, notwithstanding, trusted that twofold hemiplegia depicts the people with upper and lower furthest point contribution of both sides, with a striking higher association on one side.

Triplegia has hemiplegic example of the furthest point and diplegic example of the lower limit. Monoplegia would be, as the name recommends, inclusion of one single appendage, either on the upper or the lower furthest point. At last, people that are depicted as pentaplegic are utilized for the most extreme cases. It shows itself in indistinguishable way from quadriplegia, however in these cases, the individual isn't even ready to control the head or neck. (Miller et al; 2005)

To evaluate a child with a suspected neuro developmental disorder or CP 4 criterions are usually assessed, such as motor, speech and language, social-emotional and cognitive abilities. Further, the motor development of infant and developmental biomechanics is viewed at in specific, to the main aim of a physiotherapeutic management treating in CP children. The infant motor development is of a surprisingly specific nature as a human infant is one of the most immature new-boms on the earth.

When compared to new-boms of other species, the human infant requires 1-12 months of development in order to achieve a skill, the normally developing child undergoes a set of motor milestones on a way to acquire walking and running skill to reach an erect locomotion erect bipedally, but other species start walking and running within a few hours after birth. These motor milestones are, of obviously the primary developmental domain that could be found in a child and are further it plays a vital role in paediatric care and early diagnostics of CP.

A child acquires specific motor milestones at specific ages, and a hindrance in achieving these motor milestones at a respective age might indicate a motor delay. A delay in achieving motor milestones is also a typical finding in CP children. Characteristics of infant development are determined by different principles. Development of a human is subjected to continuous process of change during the life span. This development also involves a consecutive change, where one skill is achieved and the next skill is followed by.(Patel and Dilip R, 2011; Kolar and Pavel, 2007; Dodge and Nancy N, 2011; Haywood et al,2009; Martin et al, 2007; Payne et al, 2011; Hinchcliffe and Archie, 2007; Sieglman et al ,2012; Thelen and Esther et al, 1995;)

Few other principles that are vitalto consider when evaluating human infant motor development that includes: (i) Gross motor development takes places cephalo-caudal direction, whilst fine motor development takes place from the midline to lateral, also known as proximo-distal development. (ii) The primitive reflexes should be lost at a respective time. (iii) The development must progress as the child gets grows, from generalized and reflexive and local responses to more of voluntary and purposeful movements. Having discussed that, the evaluation of the individual child is of more importance than just labelling or classifying a child with cerebral palsy, as the signs and symptoms and motor functions vary at a wider range in each individual child. Some even views those even motor milestones at certain ages. (Thelenand Esther, 1995)

Throughout the early stages ofnormal and CP children have a complicated nature ofthe trunk control that induces vulnerability for dysfunctions. In general, children with CP develop direction-specific activity in postural muscles, and therefore the initial level of Hirschfeldt and Forsberg's Functional model of organization ofpostural control is connected. Severe CP children (GMFCS Level V), who are unable to sit without support, completely lack these changes.

In GMFCS Level IV and Level III CP children, parietal loss was found in direction-specific changes. However, the foremost frequent dysfunctions in CP children was associated with the second level, which implies that they had issues with adaption ofactivity of postura Muscles (fine-tuning of the   fundamental direction-specific changes to   environmental   conditions, that is predicated on expertise and sensory info from sensory system, visual, and proprioception systems).

One study assessed the influence of two totally different sitting positions on adaption of postural muscles in CP children compared to children who were typically developing and revealed that CP children had deficient reconciling capability was a lot pronounced within the erect position than within the unerect position. A detailed description about NDT prinicples, basic techniques and its evolution over the period of time is being elaborated in Appendix-I (Gurfinkel VS,1981; Brogren E et al, 1996; Brogren E et al, 1998; van der Heide JC et al, 2004 and 2005; Molenaers G, et al 2013).

A study of 100 CP children was done to find out the differences in trunk control according to topography and therefore the severity of motor impairments between 8-15 years. The maximum scores obtained from hemiplegic type of CP, spastic and diplegic CP and Quadriplegic CP obtained the minimum score for trunk control which was reduced considerably with increase in GMFCS level.

The finding regarding the trunk control score in relevancy with GMFCS level was in accordance with findings in earlier study by Field DA in 2011, a study to find out the trunk control using trunk impairment scale. Moreover, many studies have delineated typical characteristics of trunk control in CP children, and of those the foremost typical may be a cephalic to caudal enlisting of muscles of posture, excessive degree of antagonist co-activation, and an absence of modulation to task-specific. Several studies that compared CP children with normal children showed that anticipatory movements with compensation was less than anticipatory movements without compensation. (Carlberg EB et al, 2005; Hadders-Algra,2008; Brogren E et al,2001).

More than 100 studies were done to find out trunk control patterns and reaching activity in sitting position among CP children and compared them with typically developing children. The results of these studies were similar and showed that the CP children had low adaptability to direction-specific activity, and therefore the degree of their pathology was associated with the severity of CP. Stereo type characteristics of movements with a top-down enlisting of muscles of posture and excessive degree of antagonist co-activation were as deliberately higher in CP children.

However, there was lack of co-contraction of antagonist muscles, showing that the co-contraction in CP children is specific to situation. A study by van der Heide and colleagues with CP children showed incontestable ability to adapt or fine-tune their activity of postural muscles. This was based mostly on information from trunk position. The authors argue that this finding fits with the rising concept that sensory information from the trunk may well be a serious supply of input for posture regulation.

In an exceedingly separate study, van der Heide and colleagues assessed the kinematic characteristics of trunk control throughout reaching in CP children who were born preterm and showed that the sitting position and onset of reaching in CP Children differed from typically developing children. (Heyrman L, Desloovere K, Molenaers G, et al 2013; Brogren E et al, 1996; Brogren E et al, 1998; van der Heide JC et al, 2004; Gurfinkel VS,1981; van der Heide JC et al, 2005). As Campbell states, "Functioning information of motor development is the basis of the application for paediatric physiotherapy". Data of motor development (MD) is equally important for activity and speech-language pathologists in operating with children as a result of motor development changes the approach children manipulate and move in their environments. Motor development provides norms for (1) distinguishing competencies and impairments in developing body systems, (2) developing effective plans of care, (3) establishing age-appropriate skills as practical outcomes, (4) structuring intervention methods to facilitate learning and motor control, and (5) choosing play and activities of daily living and discourse factors to improve participation in real-life settings.

Therapists World Health Organization work with adults understand that changes within the expression of motor milestones continue across the lifetime. These changes influence social development and quality of life, as well as education, employment, and independent living. For older adults, the aging method might need new motor strategies and adaptation of motor skills to a stiffer joints, weaker muscles, and changes in vision, hearing, and balance. (Campbell P et al 2006; Oudgenoeg-Paz O et al 2014, Vogtle LK2012, Park CH, 2014, Shaffer SW, et al 2007)

Neuro-Developmental Treatment (NDT) has invariably had a powerful foundation in MD. Nearly since the origination of their approach, the Bobaths wrote and educated that understanding the event of posture and movement, and also the changes that occur over time, provided the suggestion for recognizing variations in typical movement and movement pathology. In an NDT framework, MD is taken into account a method that happens throughout the lifetime. In children, movement repertoires develop, are refined, and adapt as a toddler grows, and responds to and learns from the strain of recent contexts.

Totally different movements are required to deal with typical aging processes. Older adults might shorten their step and stride length, use hand support to ascend and descend stairs, extend their neck to accommodate bifocals, and tilt or flip their head to concentrate with an improved ear.

Throughout life, expertise and learning among specific environmental contexts strengthen bound motor behaviours, and at identical time offer opportunities for amendment. Therefore, within the NDT framework, MD is viewed as a long method that explains unambiguously individual motor characteristics whereas holding identical general style of motor behaviour at any purpose in time. (Bobath K et al,1984).

Over time, researchers have offered totally different views in MD. From the Nineteen Twenties through the Forties, MD was viewed as a neural-maturational process; genetic directions were viewed because the thrust. Reflexes were thought of the inspiration of movement, and MD was thought to proceed from reflexive movement to extremely skill ful movement because the levels of the central system (CNS) matured.

The inhibition of reflexive movement caused an orderly and planned progression of postural property reactions and motor milestones that every child skill full on the thanks to adulthood. When maturity, the adult CNS was hardwired and stuck, and any substantial recovery of operate was not possible in spite of what intervention was used. Health care practitioners adopted a "wait and see" perspective. Though this observe persisted for several years, the Bobaths insisted that it absolutely was attainable to supply changes in MD with specific intervention methods.

An initial shift of paradigm came from activity theories that stressed interactions between the child and also the surroundings. Skinner and Jean Piaget emphasized the importance of environmental opportunities and also the importance of learning and reinforcement on motor behaviour. (Gesell A, 1928; Arnold Lucius Gesell A et al, 1940; Taub E et al, 2014; coach M,1963).

The above scenario did lead to paralleled changes in considering motor control explained. The effect this had on the NDT approach was to move the focal point of consideration from encouraging motor movement to incorporate exploratory developments and critical thinking exercises for inspiration and an emphasis on the significance of a steady domain to cultivate and shape Motor Development (MD). The following movement in speculation has been the presentation of dynamic theories in motor control set forth by

Bernstein and Edelman and connected to Motor Development advancement by Thelen, and Hadders-Algra, among others.

This new perspective put motor milestones as the final result of a perplexing and variable outline. Today, MD is thought to rise up out of the collaboration and dynamic associations of numerous subsystems-inborn and outward-in assignment explicit settings. Improvement of explicit motor functioning relies upon a fair mix of neural and body frameworks, including the biomechanical, kinematic, and anthropometric changes; psychological and perceptual variables; and the individual hereditary code (nature) and a situation that gives a setting to involvement and learning (support).

The current NDT practice underlines inconstancy-the manner by which youngsters complete a specific engine capacity, and consistency-the movement of MD. These ideas underlie NDT suppositions in MD. As NDT advisors observe stances and developments in children, they perceive toddlers lean toward one stance over another, or one development design over another; however this isn't really an indication of atypical advancement. Families may firmly stick to the standards of Safe to Sleep programs, and the newborn child may have had little chance to invest energy in inclined.

Or then again, the newborn child's room might be set up so improvement originates from one side, or the baby might adjust the guardians' solid inclination for holding and conveying. Specialists consider outside imperatives just as inside framework weaknesses while dissecting inclinations and varieties in stance and development. For whatever length of time that the normal challenge among engine designs does not repress the newborn child's accomplishment in achieving the objective (e.g., turning over, conveying hand to mouth, nourishing, or vocal play), variety is profitable in the scan for numerous approaches to draw in with the world.

For this reason, the NDT specialist watches development in each position accessible to decide if an inclination for a stance or development is (1) a statement of run of the mill rivalry among entrenched development and recently creating ones, (2) an endeavor to boost open doors for investigation, (3) a component of the tyke creating body frameworks, or (4) a pointer of atypical improvement. (Gewirtz JL et al, 1992; Piaget J et al, 1952; Thelen E, 1998; Smith LB, 2003; Hadders-Algra M, 2000; Edelman GM, 1987; Fetters L,1991; Vereijken B, 2010; Heineman KR, 2010; Dusing SC, 2014).

Postural control is a basic improvement of the body's development in and through space, talented manipulation, velocity, discourse, introduction, and attention. Postural control relies upon contributions from visual, vestibular, and somatosensory receptors, just as the capacity of the CNS to decipher each information. The neural framework must initiate, time, and execute synergistic muscles at mechanically related joints to guarantee steadiness while allowing portability at different joints, at the same time contrasting the executed development and the expected action.

Postural control incorporates the accompanying: 1. Arrangement and weight bearing. 2 Proactive or postural introduction that envisions the suitable relationship among body sections in an assignment explicit setting. 3. Postural strength or enduring state balance, which is the capacity to keep up the COM inside the points of confinement of the base of help (BOS). 4. Postural modifications or harmony responses, which are adaptable, variable reactions to bothers from nature, self-initiated developments, or a moving help surface.

The slow advancement of postural control compels formative achievements requiring body control against the power of gravity and upgrades engine aptitudes that involve situating body fragments to one another and with the impacts of gravity. For instance, as postural control creates in inclined, the 4-month-old baby changes from moving as a unit to moving with separation between the pelvis and shoulder supports.

In an alternate precedent, child can take full body load on the legs at 4 months of age however can't stand unsupported until 11 months, when postural control creates in standing. The improvement of postural control requires the incorporation of tangible data to survey the position and movement of the body in space and the engine capacity to create powers for controlling body position and to plan for the responsive powers of development.

For the most part, the improvement of postural control in newborn children and kids pursues a cephalocaudal movement-control of the head and neck going before that of the storage compartment, which goes before the hips and lower furthest points (LEs). This movement results from the connection of numerous neural subsystems and the biomechanical parts of the musculoskeletal framework to meet the objectives of introduction and balance as newborn children create ideal approaches to alter their body over their BOS.

Various segments add to the development of postural control for autonomous position and headway, including (1) tangible subsystems that incorporate visual, vestibular, and somatosensory frameworks for recognizing impending (or compromised) loss of parity; (2) engine components, including postural tone and muscle cooperative energies, for controlling equalization; (3) versatile frameworks for adjusting tactile and engine frameworks to changes in undertaking or condition; and (4) biomechanical and kinesiological powers and body morphology for arrangement and weight bearing.(Heineman KR, 2010; Dusing SC, 2014; Campbell SK, 2012; Bly L, 1994; Adolph KE et al 2006; Alexander R, 1993, Bly L, 2011, Lobo MA, 2014; Thelen E et al, 1993; Wallace PS et al, 2003;Sacrey LA et al, 2010; d a Costa CS, 2013; Thelen E et al, 1985; Dusing SC, 2010; de Graaf-Peters VB, 2007; Brogren Carlberg E, 2008; Oberg GK, 2012; Arndt SW, 2008; Flatters I, 2014; Shumway-Cook A, 2011, Adolph KE,2011; Butterworth G et al, 1977; Bertenthal B et al,1998; Woollacott M et al, 1987; Hedberg A et al, 2005).

Several researchers have examined the impacts of vision on postural control in sitting and standing. Despite the fact that outcomes have fluctuated to some degree, most specialists concur that recently sitting newborn children depend vigorously on visual contributions to control body influence. This reliance on the visual framework diminishes with understanding and with the arrangement and control of postural muscle collaborations. As babies develop, they tum out to be less subject to vision and depend more on the quicker transmission of vestibular and body proprioceptors to control postural action. By the time a newborn child can sit freely, postural reactions are heading explicit and controlled principally by somatosensory data sources and associated with unconstrained objective situated engine behavior.

Shortly after they start to walk, if babies are stood up to with clashing tactile data, they can disregard misdirecting visual data and utilize somatosensory data to control equilibrium. Grown-up like reactions with insignificant influence, be that as it may, are not obvious until early school years. These versatile abilities demonstrate that the kid can adjust tangible data and frame new engine methodologies as per changing assignment and ecological conditions, despite the fact that this limit isn't refined until the point when the children is ~ 7 years old.

Periods of stability in postural control can likewise result from changes in skeletal development and the children's endeavour to adjust body arrangement to new skeletal length and morphological connections among body fragments. Musculoskeletal changes advance quickly in the initial couple of long periods of life and are affected by interior muscle and skeletal improvement and outer mechanical and gravitational power. Postural control requires age and coordination of powers that adequately control the situation of the body in space. Hedberg et al revealed that babies as adolescent as aged child show a fundamental dimension of association of postural acclimations to outer annoyances. In any case, exact muscle energies that control unconstrained influence to stay
upstanding keep on creating after some time.

Newborn children without related knowledge at first show inconsistency and different procedures toward the start of sitting, and after some time they create reliable, directionally suitable reactions to perturbations. As neuromuscular reactions turn out to be better sorted out, babies exhibit a decline in influence speed, a decline in beginning inertness, enhancement in timing and excessive muscle reactions, and a decline in inconstancy of muscle reactions. For instance, the development of free sitting is portrayed by the newborn child's capacity to control unconstrained influence of the head and trunk with front/back and side-to-side annoyances.

When the newborn child can sit autonomously, postural muscle cooperative energies relating the head and trunk sections for postural control actuate immediately, and the baby is stable. Stable stance is influenced by the advancement of tangible and neuromuscular components and by the arrangement of body fragments that add to soundness in the upstanding position. Arrangement alludes to the course of action of body fragments as for each other just as the situation of the body with reference to the power of gravity and the BOS.

In perfect arrangement, the different parts of the body are kept up in a condition of balance with minimal consumption of vitality. Expectant parts of stance build up a balancing out structure that bolsters deliberate development. This feed-forward framework happens when an individual envisions and starts the postural and development necessities of an undertaking proactively, ahead of time of the engine demonstration.

From the underlying beginning of sitting, newborn children indicate changes in stance ahead of time of most coming to movements. Van Balen et al found that achieving developments are joined by heading explicit postural modifications 100% of the time somewhere in the range of 10 and year and a half of age. A similar initiation relationship happens in children in standing at a later age. (Butterworth G et al, 1977; Bertenthal B et al, 1998; Woollacott M et al, 1987; Hedberg A et al, 2005; Sundermier L, 1998; Assaiante C et al, 2005; Foster EC et al, 1996; Lowes LP et al, 2011; Hedberg A et al, 2004; Cignetti F et al, 2011; Van Balen LC et al, 2012; Harboume RT et al, 2009; Adolph KE et al, 2008; Hasson CJ et al, 2014)
A generally acknowledged technique for estimating the general circumstance of motor function is the Gross Motor Function Classification System (GMFCS). It is generally utilized globally, and it is a unique framework, at first created by Palisano et al. in 1997, and later extended and reconsidered in 2007, to order children from birth to 18 years old, with the point of arranging cerebral paralysis children into 5 clinically significant dimensions.

The GMFCS depends on self-started developments, accentuating on trunk. Criteria for grouping of the dimension of engine capacities depend on useful restrictions, with the need of extra assistive tools for motion, for example, walkers, supports, sticks and wheelchairs. It additionally, to a lesser degree, takes the nature of the development into thought. (Rosenbaum, Peter L et al, 2008; Palisano, Robert et al, 1997 and 2007)

It was produced by Palisano et al. over some stretch of time in the 1990's, and depended on parts from effectively existing characterization frameworks for youngsters with cerebral paralysis, from tapes of cerebral paralysis children officially arranged by their separate physiotherapist and after broad discussion with different authors. At first being made as an enhancement for ill-defined wording of the GMFM, it has later filled in as building obstructs for other characterization frameworks, for example, the Manual Ability Classification System (MACS)and the Communication Function Classification System (CFCS). The GMFCS means to arrange children into 5 dimensions of severity in various age gatherings. It regards the way that the gross motor function is subject to age, particularly in the beginning periods of the engine improvement.

The focal point of the GMFCS is on figuring out which level is best speaking to the child's present capacities and constraints in motor function. That is the reason accentuation is typically put on execution in a home, or school condition, or other every day life settings, instead of in a settled setting at a physiotherapy facility, with a steady and settled floor and an even surface. (Rosenbaum, Peter L et al, 2008; Palisano, Robert et al, 1997 and 2007).

As per the researchers of the arrangement framework, accentuation is to be put on the child's capacities and not the restrictions. This ought to be remembered while recovering a child's gross motor work utilizing the GMFCS. A child does not really satisfy every one of the criteria for the separate dimension, in this manner in all actuality making the child's dimension of motor work more regrettable in a few spaces.

The clinical criticalness of GMFCS has been demonstrated through various distinctive research programs amid the most recent decades, and has for the most part been utilized in observational research or test examine. In observational views into contrasting bigger gatherings of cerebral paralysis children, in view of their GMFCS score has been valuable in investigates in the field of practical confinements. It has been demonstrated that condition of versatility, skill, discourse, vision, hearing and discernment is related with the dimension of GMFCS.

GMFCS levels have likewise been related with the conclusion, etiology, scholarly limit, epilepsy and visual impedance. As far as test inquires about, the GMFCS has been demonstrated an essential gadget in surveying either advance in treatment, or in looking at viability of two remedial strategies. Numerous examinations have effectively utilized GMFCS as a method for making homogeneity between two randomized gatherings. Being such a moderately new order framework, a requirement for proof of the unwavering quality, strength and legitimacy before long happened.

Presently, right around 15 years after the underlying production of the GMFCS we can see some long haul lines after the utilization of the characterization framework, and in this manner talk about the unwavering quality. Above all else, the overall utilization of the framework could be a decent marker of the nature of the framework. The far reaching use and quick extension of the framework was exhibited by a little portion of the underlying engineers.

Morris et al. expressed that in 2004, 7 years after the underlying distribution of the arrangement framework, GMFCS was found in 102 references in different dialects, with an expanding recurrence consistently, showing an expanding notoriety. Studies have been made to approve the GMFCS's capacity to anticipate future gross engine work. A similar report even demonstrated high test retest unwavering quality and a high inter-rater dependability.

A multicenter consider was accumulated in 2004 with the principle point of researching the connection among GMFCS and other understood and all around dependable strategies for setting up the dimension of seriousness, closing with a moderate to solid connection among GMFCS and other existing result instruments. So as to decide the security, and along these lines additionally the legitimacy of the GMFCS, Palisano et al. gathered a report expressing that: "The aftereffects of this investigation give proof of the solidness of the GMFCS in youngsters with CP".

The point of this report was by the creators to survey the dependability of the GMFCS by inspecting whether the kids with cerebral paralysis remained in a similar dimension of engine work after some time. The legitimacy of this report must be considered cautiously, as it was incorporated by the designers of the framework, henceforth the creators may be one-sided, however by the manner in which the outcomes were found and by connecting to other evaluation devices evaluating engine capacities like the Gross Motor Function Measure **(GMFM),** the discoveries are deserving of consideration. In the wake of testing the aggregate sum of 610 kids determined to have cerebral paralysis with a mean testing recurrence of 4.3 occasions over a long-haul testing period a sum of 73% remained in at a similar dimension all through the entire testing time frame. Intriguing sub discoveries were additionally found in this exploration.

CP children at first characterized in level I or V had the least changing rate all through the testing time frame. Conceivable clarifications offered for this finding is that youngsters in these gatherings have the most particular portrayals, making appraisal simpler for the specialist. Another conceivable clarification is that these gatherings are on the two closures of the scale, making it conceivable to alter bunches in a single course just, thus bringing down the shot of any change whatsoever.

Then again, CP children at first characterized in the dimensions II-IV had a higher rate of exchanging between the dimensions all through the testing time frame. Conceivable purposes behind these discoveries may be clarified by the more prominent inconstancy as far as potential outcomes in versatility of children in these gatherings. The portrayal are neither that particular, making the evaluation by the analyst moderately harder. (Palisano, Robert, et al, 1997 and 2007; Eliasson, Ann-Christin, et al 2006, Morris et al ,2004; Kennes, Janneke, et al, 2002; Nordmark, E., et al, 2001; Wood et al, 2000; Oeffinger, D.J., et al, 2004; Palisano, Robert J., et al , 2006; Gorter, Jan Willem, et al, 2008).

Different discoveries show that newborn children and kids younger than two years have a generally higher shot of changing gatherings than more seasoned kids. Gorter et al. consequently prescribes grouping kids less than 2 years, however expresses a need of renaming at 2 years old, to maintain a strategic distance from any brokenness in the order. Be that as it may, notwithstanding some little contrasts in discoveries, the consistency of 73% of the youngsters all through the testing time frame demonstrates a wonderful dependability mulling over all the distinctive components of which can meddle with the improvement.

It additionally demonstrates the precision of the grouping framework, yet perhaps above all, it is a critical device so as to compute a forecast and the normal dimension of gross engine work later on, which must be a much looked for after plausibility for social insurance specialists, guardians and other overseers. Some even case that: "The GMFCS has unmistakably settled itself as the primary order arrangement of practical capacity for CP children. (Gorter, Jan Willem, et al, 2008)

The Paediatric Evaluation of Disability Inventory (PEDI) was initially created for a clinical appraisal of chose key capacity abilities and execution of children, and is approved to gauge versatile capacities among children from a half year to 7 years old. It was planned in an approach to both portray the child's present execution, and so as to think about changes of execution after some time. The designers proposed that

PEDI could be utilized to: (an) identify whether an utilitarian shortfall or deferral exists,(b) decide the degree and substance region of a recognized postponement or deficiency, (c) screen individual or gathering progress in pediatric restoration projects, and (d) assess pediatric recovery administrations or helpful projects in instructive settings. Constrained data exists upon regardless of whether it is in reality a solid testing apparatus for estimating its total and expected reason. (Campbell et al,2007; Brashear et al, 2011).

PEDI measures the capacity of performing exercises of day by day living (ADL) through institutionalized organized meetings. Despite the fact that the test isn't particularly intended for cerebral paralysis or some other condition with formative postponement so far as that is concerned, usually utilized as an evaluator in testing the useful capacity in these youngsters. It has likewise been approved to recognize incapacities in bigger populaces, and is a valuable instrument to do as such, as it is conceivable to gather date for the framework by meetings with guardians, coordinate perception by a parental figure, educator or advisor, or by expert judgment by the psychologist and additionally instructor. (Burton, Allen William and Miller, Daryl E, 1998).

PEDI measures the versatile elements of youngsters in three areas, to be specific: self consideration, portability and social capacities. A Functional Skill Scale is then delivered from these 3 areas. What's more, a Caregiver Assistance Scale is delivered from a lot of 20, complex utilitarian exercises, and a Modification Scale is determined from the dimension of adjustment expected to play out the tests performed in the Caregiver Assistance Scale.

These scores are again determined into purported regulating standard scores, where the age of the children is thought about, and scaled scores, where the exertion is scaled on a scale from 0-100 without thought to the child's age, in this manner giving the likelihood to assess the growth of child with correlation with the age of his friends, and to assess the relative capacity level free of age Several preliminaries have been led so as to check the unwavering quality and legitimacy of the evaluative measure appearing exceptional high between questioner dependability.

Studies have additionally presumed that PEDI adequately separates between an impaired and a nondisabled gathering of tried kids, making it a proper evaluation instrument for youngsters with cerebral paralysis. It is likewise said to be a valuable device while portraying practical deferral in kids with cerebral paralysis and was discovered delicate to useful change. (Feldman, Amy bet al, 1990; Dumas et al, 2001).

The Segmental Assessment of Trunk Control (SATCo) was developed by The Movement Centre, which is an internationally validated and recognizedtool to measure trunk control. The SATCo results clearly show there was an improvement in trunk control throughout Levels of ability which further provides a basis for progress in functional activities. A study of 498 children was introduced to assess control when sitting and includes static (steady state), active (or anticipatory) and reactive control tests. The SATCo assesses child's trunk control to progressively note the changes at the level of trunk support from a level of high support at the shoulder girdle to test cervical control, through support at the axillae (upper thoracic control), lower scapula (mid thoracic control), lower ribs (lower thoracic control), below ribs (upper lumbar control), pelvis (lower lumbar control), and finally, no support, in order to measure full trunk control. (Butler PB et al, 2010).

The SATCo is a clinical assessment tool that tests a child's trunk postural control as the assessor steadily stage by stage reduces the trunk support from complete supported sitting to unsupported sitting. Evidence has shown that the SATCo is a reliable and valid tool that can clinically measure trunk control for infants with Typical development **(TD)** or children who have neuromotor disabilities. The administration and scoring instructions of the tool are so clear and constant so that it confirms the level of reliability.

The advantages of SATCo are that it allows documentation of trunk control independent sitting children as well as those who are able to sit without dependence. It has excellent reliability in TD infants and in neuromotor disability children. As this tool has a high correlation for validity which strengthens the results proving that the SATCo corresponds to function and ability. For each level of trunk segmental static, active and reactive control are noted as present, absent or not tested (NT).

Static control is scored if a child maintains a neutral trunk posture above the level of hand support; active control is scored if the child maintains a neutral posture during head movement; reactive control is scored if the trunk above the support remains stable during an external perturbation or push. It should be taken into consideration that, there are various aspects of control which may or may not be present at the same or even at adjacent levels as it completely depended on the child to be evaluated.

The ability of the child to maintain or regain an erect position of the independent trunk in all planes as soon as possible is evaluated during static, active and reactive testing and control accordingly scored as present or absent. The perturbation is applied once from each front, back, left and right direction and the point of perturbation application must remain at the same horizontal level throughout. In cases when erect collapse of the trunk is observed during administration of the evaluation a sagittal view is further advised.

Although the SATCo does not correspond to 'real-life' situation of sitting ability nor does it take into consideration the environmental or contextual factors, it only corresponds to the finding the child's specific disability. Current functional evaluations of static and dynamic capacity to sit give some derivation of trunk control while progressively explicit trial of sitting stance report static and dynamic trunk arrangement. None of these tests has straightforwardly evaluated the level of control within the trunk.

The SATCo supplements and broadens at present accessible tests by permitting discrete appraisal of static, dynamic and responsive trunk control in child with and without the capacity to sit autonomously. Also, the SATCo permits solid evaluation of trunk control in exceptionally youthful youngsters as well as child with psychological disabilities since little is expected from the child as far as cooperation is concerned. (Pountney TE et al, 2004; White MA et al, 1992; Fife SE et al, 1991; Bartlett D et al, 2005)

With regards to the International Classification of Functioning, Disability and Health (ICF) the SATCo is a Body Function measure. A shortage in trunk control, characterized by the SATCo, is probably going to impact Activity Limitations and Participation Restriction. It will influence all Activities of Mobility and will stretch out to Major Life Areas, for example, training since poor trunk control will influence steadiness of the head in space in this manner influencing visual abilities, eye-hand coordination, reach and hand work. Poor trunk control may likewise meddle with eye to eye connection and proficient respiratory help for verbalization and along these lines may unfavorably impact social collaboration.

Despite the fact that compensatory techniques, for example, trunk crumple or hand support can be of an incentive in day by day working, the SATCo tries to characterize the genuine dimension of trunk control. This will clarify a portion of the practical confinements seen. For instance, a tyke with control issues in the lower lumbar dimension is probably going to have the capacity to sit freely, assuming unreliably, though a tyke with control issues in the upper thoracic dimension will have a lot more noteworthy utilitarian misfortune and be notable sit autonomously.

The more itemized data about control of the storage compartment furnished by the SATCo assists with treatment arranging which would then be able to be coordinated at enhancing control in the particular zone of shortage as opposed to regarding the storage compartment as a solitary unit. When control has been gained at the highest dimension of misfortune, treatment would then be able to be coordinated at the following dimension of control misfortune a caudal way. This has been appeared to be a successful procedure for increasing autonomous sitting capacity in the extremely neuromotor impaired child. The SATCo additionally permits a better grained documentation of advancement, especially if advance is moderate. Subject

The subject is situated on a seat, feet bolstered on the ground or on a steady surface and pelvis/thigh position controlled by the lashing framework. The pelvis is orientated to unbiased with respect to vertical. The subject is bolstered in an upstanding stance "sitting up tall" with the nearness of typical cervical, thoracic and lumbar bends. The head is upstanding. The subject's hands and arms ought to be free of all outside contact incorporating with possess trunk, thighs, seat or the analyzer's arms/hands all through the test aside from as showed.
The subject's hands ought not be combined. The analyzer applies firm manual help on a level plane around the storage compartment at every one of the assigned dimensions thus. The help given ought to be adequate to guarantee that the storage compartment is in an impartial vertical stance and that any crumple of the storage compartment is wiped out. The subject's hands/arms ought to be lifted so they there is no contact with the subject's body or legs, the seat or the analyzer's hands.

Toys can be utilized to rouse a youngster guaranteeing that the child extends/turns towards the toy yet does not get a handle on it. At each help level the analyzer urges the subject to sit up tall and lift the hands/arms amid testing of a) static control, b) dynamic control, by turning the go to each side (>45° or to impediment of range) and c) receptive control by staying stable amid pokes. This requires a right hand to apply a solitary energetic bump from front (manubrium/sternum), from behind (-C7), and from each side (acromion) utilizing the fingertips, adequate to quickly aggravate balance. On the off chance that a subject has negligible parity impedances they influence exorbitantly yet can come back to vertical.

Toys can be utilized to rouse a youngster guaranteeing that the child extends/turns towards the toy yet does not get a handle on it. At each help level the analyzer urges the subject to sit up tall and lift the hands/arms amid testing of a) static control, b) dynamic control, by turning the go to each side (>45° or to impediment of range) and c) receptive control by staying stable amid pokes. This requires a right hand to apply a solitary energetic bump from front (manubrium/sternum), from behind (-C7), and from each side (acromion) utilizing the fingertips, adequate to quickly aggravate balance. On the off chance that a subject has negligible parity impedances they influence exorbitantly yet can come back to vertical.

Assuming, in any case, they have moderate to extreme equalization impedances they lose balance and go to the furthest reaches of their scope of movement. The test proceeds with bringing down of help level until the point when the subject unmistakably can't keep up or rapidly come back to the beginning stance. The analyzer ought to be behind the subject, as a rule in stooping relying upon the extent of the subject and tallness of the seat and the right hand in a perfect world out of line of the subject's vision.

The Gross Motor Function Measure (GMFM) is an assessment tool that has been created to test the change in gross motor function in cerebral palsy children from the age of 5 months to 16 years of age. The GMFM measures 'activity' as defined within the International Classification of Functioning, Disability and

Health. The GMFM is administered by a trained physiotherapist who observes gross motor tasks performed by the child in a constant environment which is then measured.

This tool assesses the capacity of a child where a child is able to perform tasks in a controlled environment rather than performance of a child, where the child actually performs in his/her daily environment. The assessment usually takes 45 - 60 minutes to complete and only requires does not require any special equipment. The first GMFM version has 88 items each scored on a 4-point ordinal scale of 0 to 3, where Oindicates that the child does not do or even start any of the task; 1 indicates that the child begins performing the task (completes < 10% of the activity); 2 indicates that the child completes the half of the given task (completes from 10 to 99% of the activity); 3 indicates that the child has completed the task (100%); and NT indicates that the child was not tested.

This tool consists of 88 items which has been grouped into five dimensions: 1) lying and rolling, 2) sitting, 3) crawling and kneeling, 4) standing, and 5) walking, running and jumping. A highest of 3 trials is allowed for each item where the best trial is recorded. Scores are expressed in percentage with maximum score and the total score is obtained by averaging the percentage scores across the five dimensions.

Rasch analysis was applied to the GMFM-88 in order to improve its interpretability and clinical usefulness, which resulted in a unidimensional interval-measure hierarchical scale - the GMFM-66 - consisting of 66 items from the original 88. The GMFM-66 can be used only for cerebral palsy children, while some evidence supports the use of GMFM-88 for Down syndrome and acquired brain injury children. The GMFM-66 has a Sets number of items which uses a scoring algorithm, thereby a set of items guide the therapist toward a pre-set item relevant to the level of child function.

The GMFM- 66 Basal and Ceiling (B&C) approach establishes the 'basal' score of three successes in a row as the start of the test and testing ends when the 'ceiling' is reached, which is indicated by scoring three zeros in a row. However, if the primary goal of this evaluation is to measure the change, hence full GMFM-66 must be used. Studies have reported a great interrater and test-retest reliability and internal consistency cerebral palsy and Down syndrome children.

The Responsiveness of this tool to change has been tested using many statistical methods, including comparison of parental and clinician responses, investigating minimum clinically important difference, effect size, receiver operating curves and standardised response means. The minimum clinically important difference is 0.8 to 1.6 for medium effect size and 1.3 to 2.6 for larger effect size. Different versions of the GMFM are responsive in children with cerebral palsy, Down syndrome and traumatic brain injury.(Russell DJ et al 1989, 2000, 2013,2010; Holsbeeke L e t al, 2009, Brunton LK et al, 2011; Avery LM, et al, 2013; Adair B, et al, 2012; Harvey A, et al, 2008; Oeffinger D, et al, 2008;Vos-Vromans. et al,2005)

The Trunk control Measurement Scale (TCMS) is an objective outcome measure that scores the trunk ability in sitting and consists of two main components of trunk control during activities of daily living: (a) sitting in a stable base of support (BOS), and (b) sitting in an actively moving object and maintaining stability. Therefore, the scale consists of two sections: static sitting balance and dynamic sitting balance.

The latter section is further divided into two subscales: selective movement control and dynamic reaching. The 'static sitting balance' subscale assesses static trunk control during movements of upper and lower limbs. The subscale 'selective movement control' measures selective trunk movements in 3 planes (flexion/extension, lateral flexion, rotation) within BOS. The subscale 'dynamic reaching' evaluates the performance during three reaching tasks, requiring active trunk movements beyond the base of support. The total scale consists of 15 items, with the subscales contains five, seven and three items, respectively.

All items in this tool are scored on a 2-, 3- or 4-pointordinal scale and administered bilaterally in case of clinical relevance. The total score of the TCMS ranges from 0to 58, with a higher score indicating a better performance. This assessment tool showed a good relative reliability in spastic CP children aged between 8 and 15 years. While a study investigated the absolute measurement error of the total score (the Smallest Detectable Difference (SDD) was 4.66 for the intra-rater reliability, and 5.47 for the inter-rater reliability), such data is missing for the sub scores of the TCMS. Furthermore, the results of a study were obtained in a relatively small group of children and were restricted to spastic CP children. (Heyrman Let al, 2011).

CHAPTER2

Review of literature

Cerebral palsy is a non-progressive developmental problem associated with any insult to the brain during the time of birth. It can manifest as both severe and milder forms. The individuals usually present with mild spasticity, which is increased tone of the muscles and contracture in extremities on one side of the body, which obstruct the coordinated movement and fine manual dexterity. The individual may have sensory inattention to the affected side of the body and to that visual field. They might have associated focal epilepsy too.

Severe CP which is the other end of the spectrum, patients can present with involvement of all the four extremities with a mixed picture of spasticity and abnormal kinetics. The individual can have considerable contractures and scoliosis, hence may require a wheelchair mobility. The subjects also present with associated severe learning deficits, cortical visual problems, and are commonly prone to chest infections. CP is a syndrome of motor impairment which results following lesion occurring in child's developing brain.

The disorder varies in the temporal variables of the lesion, the clinical features, and the site and severity of the brain involvement. orthopedic surgeon William Little can be credited for the earliest description of the CP in 1862. (Little W, 1862) Several attempts to properly define and classify the CP have been made for a century.

As a result of such efforts, the International Executive Committee for the Definition of CP, came up with the following definition: which states that

"Cerebral palsy describes a group of permanent disorders of the development of movement and posture, causing activity limitation, that are attributed to non-progressive disturbances that occurred in the developing fetal or infant brain.

The motor manifestation of cerebral palsy is often associated with abnormal sensation, perception, cognition, language and communication and social and behavior problems, by epilepsy, and by secondary musculoskeletal problems". This definition is supplemented by a clear explanation of the terms utilized in the definition. (Rosenbaum P, 2007) From its various classifications one can understand the complexity of the syndrome.

CP can be defined from the anatomical perspective based on the site of the brain lesion weather its involving the cerebral cortex, pyramidal tract (cortico-spinal pathway), extrapyramidal system, or cerebellum. The clinical signs and symptoms of spasticity, dyskinesia [altered kinetics], or ataxia (abnormal coordination) time of brain insult (pre-partum, intrapartum, or post-neonatal); and classification of degree of muscle tone as hypotonicity or hypertonicity).

There is always a strong need for Standard classifications for the purpose of research and transfer of knowledge. The 9th and 10th edition of International Classifications of Disease include many categories of CP and substantial inconsistency had existed in how clinicians interpret the provided guidelines. (Colver AF, 2003) A straightforward classification is needed that can be applied reliably by clinicians and used in registers. Surveillance of CP in Europe drew such a classification (with priority to categories of unilateral spasticity, bilateral spasticity, dyskinetic, and ataxic) along with which an associated decision mapping was developed by the European network (SCPE) and is now widely practiced and adopted.

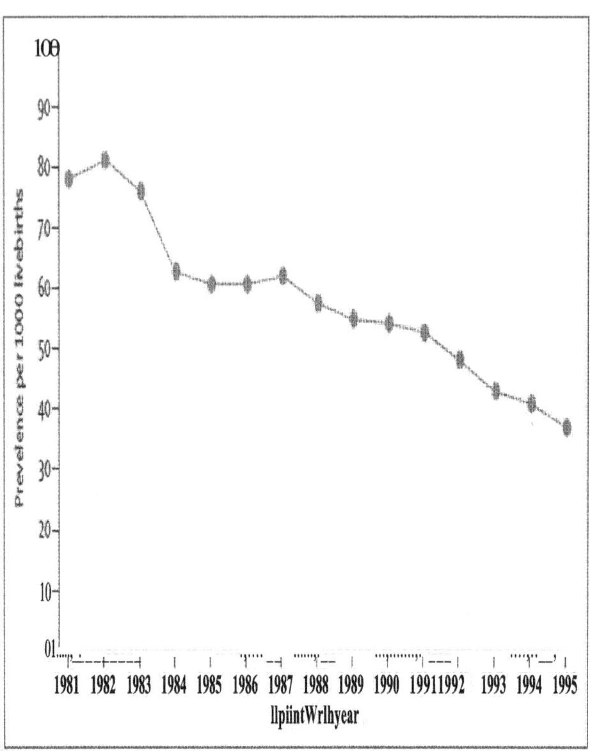

(Figure 2.1: Prevalence of cerebral palsy in infants with birthweights of 1000-1499 g from nine European countries in birth years 1980-96 (3 year moving average)
Countries are Denmark, France, Germany, Ireland, Italy, Netherlands, Norway, Sweden, and the UK
Reproduced from Platt and colleagues.

(A database study. Lancet 2007; 369: 43-50.)

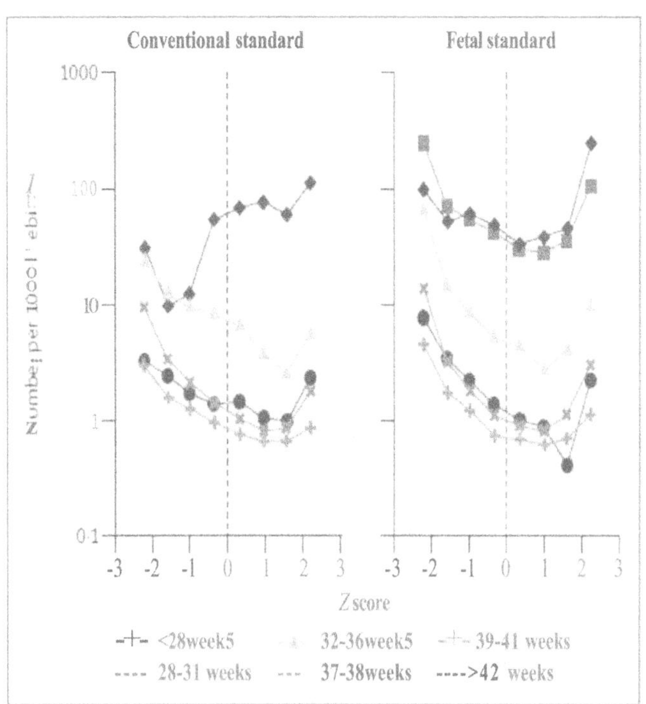

(Figure 2.2 : Prevalence of cerebral palsy by Z score of weight for gestation - reproduced from Jarvis and colleagues.)
(European collaborative study. Lancet 2003; 62: 1106-11.)

2.1 Epidemiology of CP

The prevalence of CP was more in the developed countries in the late 20th century with europian countries showing more prevalence than most of the other countries. The prevalence of cerebral palsy is 20-2.7 per 1000 livebirths during the period of 1967 to 1985. (Stanley FJ et al, 1992). Later there was a gradual rise in the prevalence during the period of 1991-1994 which inched close to 3.0 - 3.5 per 1000 live births (Hagberg B et al, 2001). The similar pattern was also seen in Scotland too in relatively the same decade. (Pharoah PO, eta la, 1998) The prevalence rate in united states was determined around 3.5 per 1000 live births in twenty first century beginning by Yeargin-Allsopp M.

Though the data sources are inconsistent and not established as far as the prevalence of CP in developing countries, there seems to be similar pattern. (Gladstone M, 2010) The prevalence of CP in Pakistan also showed the similar pattern on an survey done during 2013 by Ibrahim SH et al. Cerebral palsy prevalence is seen often associated with gestational age and birthweight. There is an inverse association with a prevalence ranging from 90/1000 neonatal kids with a weight of less than 1000 g to 1·5 cases/1000 for the kids born with a weight of 2500 g or more. (Paneth N et al, 1984, Stanley F et al, 1984 and Sellier E et al in 2010) The upper age limit considered for definition of post-neonatal CP is arbitrary, but almost in every study it is considered to be more than 5 years.

About 10 percent of all cases of CP are classified as post neonatal (Maudsley G, 1999) which are largely attributable to central nervous system infections like meningoencephalitis and traumatic and non-traumatic head injuries. The prevalence of CP in infants of normal weight (2500 g) have not changed over the period of time (Platt MJ et al, 2007) but there is a decreasing trend in prevalence is seen in Europe with low birthweight infants (figure 1) by Freud et al and a decreasing trend is also seen in and confirmed in an Australian cohort as well by Cerebral Palsy Research Institute in 2013.

As noted more than a 100n years ago by Sigmund Freud, multiple pregnancy is considered as also a risk factor for CP. Comparisons of the risk of CP in singleton and multiple births are indirectly influenced by the effect of birthweight and gestational period or age. This problem is split into two parts: firstly, there is an inverse association of the prevalence of CP with birth weight and, secondly the inflating proportion of multiple live births of decreasing body weights.

Compared with singletons, the relative risk of CP in twins is 5·6 and the rate in triplets is 12·6 according to National Perinatal Epidemiology Unit in 2002 at United Kingdom In a scenario when both twins are livebirths, there is a probability of one in 56 that one infant has CP and a probability of one in 430 that both have CP which was proved by two different studies conducted by Pharoah PO in 1996 and Burguet A, et al in 1999.

Most pregnancies are incidence where the twins share the same amniotic sac which is described as monochorionic, which is a established risk factor for CP (Grether JK, et al in 1993) even in the early preterm infants. Various studies on population suggest that there is a 50-100 times increment in the prevalence of CP in an alive co-twin of a still birth compared to that of singleton pregnancies. (Petterson B, 1993)

In case if both twins are live-births, infant death of a twin baby is associated with an increased risk (which is very significant) of CP in the survivor. The CP risk in the same-sex survivor associated with infant death of the cotwin is about 167/1000 when compared to 21/1000 in an unlike pair according to Pharoah

PO in 2001. A risk factor doesn't mean its necessarily a cause and other newly identified risk factors have derived little in the way of preventive strategies. (Blair E, Watson, 2006)

A systematic review conducted by McIntyre S, et al in 2013 reported about ten risk factors as very closely associated with CP which are as follows, placental abnormalities, major and minor birth impartments, LBW, meconium aspiration, emergency C- section, birth asphyxia, neonatal seizures, distress syndrome due to respiratory causes, hypoglycemia, and neonatal infections.

2.2. Pathogenesis of CP

There are many mechanisms that have been proposed to explain the etiology, nature, and timing of the infliction of cerebral insult. But still it's obvious that the adverse factors might have been existed for some time during pregnancy. For a given gestation and for a given type of cerebral palsy, there exist an optimum birthweight; the increased rates of CP are observed in the preterm baby birth that occur when gestational birth-weight had deviated from this optimum according to Jarvis S in 2003.

This optimum birthweight influence is especially pronounced if the fetal assessment of weights in the mother's womb are used to calculate weight standards rather than precise weights of delivered babies. Most cases of CP result from an interference of the development in brain during in-utero and Magnetic Resonance Imaging scanning has helped in understanding these processes accurately. In general, cerebral inflicts during the first trimester are associated with cerebral impaired developments such as schizencephaly; during the second trimester, the white matter of the periventricular region gets damaged; and in the third trimester, it is the cortical and deep grey matter derangement. (Krageloh-Mann I et al 2009)

Neonatal asphyxia was considered to be a key cause of brain damage associated with preterm or term babies. But still, the evidence for asphyxia was applied loosely, and frequently referred only as a mere need for administration of oxygen at or after the time of birth. Asphyxia is now considered to account for 10-20% of CP patients according to Blair E et al in 1997 and attribution of causation now requires literature evidence of encephalopathy according to MacLennan A et al in 1999.

Monochorionic can have a significant role in the pathogenesis of CP because the vascular anastomoses in the placenta supplies both fetuses and transfusion can potentially occur between the two fetuses. Embolic theory suggests that the transference of thromboplastin or thromboembolic of the dead fetus to its cotwin leads to damage to the cerebral tissues, which was observed by Moore CM, in 1969 and was ascertained by Hoyme HE in 1981. The Ischemic theory explains that some exchanges occurs between the surviving fetus into that of the low resistance dead fetus. (Fusi L, 1991)

Although these established theories do not seem to have helped in explain plaining CP in singletons or dichorionic multiple pregnancies, diagnostic procedure like obstetric ultrasound has demonstrated that one or more embryos from a multiple conception tend to be lost early in pregnancy termed as vanishing twin or triplet (Landy H,1995) and hence, this twin may be the cause of CP in some singleton births according to and Pharoah PO et al in 1997. In developed countries, particularly the western countries cause of CP are routinely prevented and are often unnoticed. For instance, marriage between close relatives are not common, mothers receive prompt attention for rhesus isoimmunization (in which severe jaundice is a striking cause of dyskinetic CP), and mainly immunizations are directed at with a motive of preventing infant infections such as meningitis. In some developing countries, deficiency of iodine causes a specific type of CP as explained by Dunn J in 1986 in America.

A RCT of iodinated oil highlighted that the disease could be prevented, if not the supplementation was provided before conception as reported earlier than Dunn J by Pharoah PO in 1971 itself. In another study done by Pharoah PO and colleagues in 1974, withdrawal of an all good source of dietary iodine precipitated an epidemic of CP. Infections such as rubella material and organisms like cytomegalovirus can result in CP. Several studies have advocated that chorioamnionitis to be a risk factor for CP, particularly in preterm babies. (Shatrov JG, 2010)

But still, enhanced identification and treatment of these infections has not been beneficial. A significant rise in the prevalence of non-cerebral origin congenital anomalies coexistent with CP has been reported by many researchers in the past. (Croen LA et al, 2001, Pharoah PO et al, 2007 and Rankin J et al, 2010) Undoubtedly, some cases of CP that have a fetal origin in combination with non-cerebral congenital abnormalities have a genetic or teratogenic cause. The transfusion issues between fetuses can also provide a unified pathogenic cause in some cases. Artificial reproductive therapies may play a vital part in the genesis of CP. Even though these associations are hard to study because of strict confidentiality and legal regulations in most of the countries. (Bahtiyar MO, et al, 2007, Pharoah POD,2005, Pharoah POD 2009 and Hvidtj0m D, 2006) In the past studies linking anonymized national calamity have been possible, a high risk was observed, but was largely due to increased risk of multiple pregnancies and preterm baby births according to Hvidtj0m D and colleagues through there researches conducted during 2006 and 2010.

2.3. Diagnosis of CP though MRI

About 85% of children with CP have an abnormal scan reports done by MRI. The role of magnetic resonance imaging in elucidating the pathogenesis of cerebral palsy was analysed using a systematic review. The results showed that an MRI scan can give information about an estimate of the timing of the insult and assist in identifying   whether the lesion is responsible for the movement impairment or it's a mere incidental finding. (Krageloh-Mann, 2007) An abnormal MRI scan finding is not a necessary for diagnosis of CP but scans are recommended to help monitor clinical management. (Ashwal S, 2003). These findings can provide families with an in-depth and complete explanation of the cause of their kid's CP or could show lesions such as polymicrogyria of bilateral side, with implications for genetic counselling. Lastly, a normal MRI scan can advocate the need for a more elaborate investigation of some genetic conditions such as hereditary hypertonic paraplegias, dopa responsive dystonia's, and metabolic abnormalities that can mimic CP.

2.4. Life expectancy of CP

Blair E, in 2001 and Hutton JL et al in 2006 studied the Life expectancy in severe CP, Strauss D in 2008 did a similar study on Life expectancy in cerebral palsy. They reported that to estimate life expectancy, there is a need for a register of all cases with dates of birth and information updates of deaths to allow precise analysis. The severities of mental, manual, mobility and visual ailments are significant considerations in survival. If all ailment domains are not so severe, survival is only marginally less than that of children without CP. If severe impairments are present, then life expectancy is reduced approximately in proportion to the number and severity of associated impairments.54 Of individuals with cerebral palsy in the UK who were alive at age 2 years with four severe impairments (IQ <50, no ambulant, partially sighted, and poor manual function), 72% lived to 10 years, 44% to 20 years, 34% to 30 years, and 27% to 40 years (JL Hutton, University of Warwick, Coventry, UK, personal communication). There doesn't seem to be any improvement in the Life expectancy, although this observation might be due to more children with severe forms impairments are now more likely to be alive at least into their early years. Quality of rehabilitation care can also be relevant. A UK report done by Michael J in 2008, noted that in adults with high intellectual impairment, components of severe physical ailments are often not have been identified; this is a important problem in those with added severe CP

Reid SM, et al in 2012 did an analysis of Survival of individuals with CP born in Victoria, Australia, between the years of 1970 and 2004. He reported that cause of death in individuals with CP in Australia was mainly due to motor deficits associated with CP in 50% of cases, next to inflict death was pneumonia at 23% and aspiration was 11% In individuals with mild and moderate impairment, CP was cited in 28%, accidents in 18%, cardiac reasons in 15%, and pneumonia in 12% of the cases. Inclusion of CP on death certificates as a secondary cause rather than the only cause of death would benefit information about cause of death and how to bring about prevention.

2.5. Quality of life of CP children

In the past ten years, studies of individuals with CP have been done within the limitations of the International Classification of Functioning, Disability and Health (ICF, 2001). The ICF address three major claws: body structure and function, activity limitation, and participation. Each one can influence the others and there is no causative progression from the impairment of structure to participation. Furthermore, the interactions of the three criteria are influenced by the environmental context in which an individual lives, and the ICF recognizes two more factors: environmental and personal factors.

Means to measure ICF concepts are been developed and revised; for children and young kids, a recent book has set out the different types of questionnaires that are available to quantify the constructs. (Majnemer A et al, 2012) Increasingly, children and youngsters are requested to complete questionnaires as well as their parents. Although CP is a lifelong disorder, many researches regard it as always, a pediatric illness. Acknowledgment that results in adulthood have been not exactly positive has demonstrated the requirement for clinical practice to embrace a long-lasting viewpoint on the turmoil.

Grown-ups with cerebral palsy have disservices in public activity and business. Fatigue, agony, and burdensome side effects are likewise normal in grown-ups with cerebral palsy and some proof proposes that physical maturing may happen more quickly than in grown-ups without the confusion. A real existence course point of view likewise features the change stage, when a youngster's social insurance exchanges from tyke to grown-up administrations in the meantime as they advance from youth to adulthood.

Results are additionally poor in this period. Pediatric administrations frequently neglect to plan youngsters for grown-up human services. Besides, a grown-up can adjust decisions between treatment, training, relief from discomfort, and business, while kids for the most part have less power over such options. In any case, as kids enter immaturity, such autonomy ought to be supported as opposed to limited by guardians and clinicians.

Agony in kids and grown-ups with cerebral palsy is significantly more typical than recently thought and is either not perceived or ineffectively overseen by clinicians. Torment in people with cerebral palsy is caused by numerous reasons, including fits, contractures, hip disengagement, gastrostomy tubes, gastric reflux, and extreme touchiness around agent scars. Besides, treatment is excruciating for some youngsters.

Helped extending has been distinguished as the everyday movement most as often as possible related with torment; which is of concern in light of the fact that, in people with neurological scatters, for example, cerebral palsy, extending does not deliver clinically huge changes in contractures or capacity. Besides, little proof exists to help postural administration however considerable proof of its disservices, including torment. The ICF characterizes investment as contribution in life circumstances and is caught crosswise over nine spaces including self-care, relational connections, tutoring, and business.

Support is reliably diminished in kids and grown-ups with cerebral palsy contrasted and the all-inclusive community and in extent to the seriousness and number of debilitations. Wellbeing related personal satisfaction of people with cerebral palsy is lower than that of the overall public. Be that as it may, the builds caught, for example, administrations required, the recurrence of treatment, and action limitations unavoidably score bring down in people with a wellbeing issue, for example, cerebral palsy. Such factors could have little effect on a person's generally speaking abstract prosperity.

In the individuals who can self-report, emotional prosperity is comprehensively like that of the all-inclusive community as indicated by quantitative and subjective investigations. Youngsters with cerebral palsy have more mental challenges than do offspring of the all-inclusive community. Such troubles can be because of disturbance of neural pathways or systems that manage feelings and conduct, along these lines rendering the brainless versatile.

On the other hand, guardians can oversee and define limits contrastingly for a handicapped kid. Societal perspectives and previously established inclinations of the guardians can blend with parental sentiments of blame and pity to in a general sense change how guardians manage a kid with cerebral palsy, in this way permitting tyke conduct that guardians would not permit in a commonly creating kid.

Moll LR and Cott CA in 2013 studied the paradox of normalization through physiotherapy in growing up and growing older with CP. He elaborated the following scenario in a practical manner. According to them the ICF and life-course frameworks suggest, a divergence exists in-between trying to make the body of the subject to function more normally and accepting the subject as they are and concentrating on the environmental adjustments. Enormous physical therapies are available, but very little evidence is present on which to choose.

Physiotherapy combined with medical and surgical management offers positive results, at least in the short term. Seeking restoration of pre-morbidity of physical impairment in childhood only provides gains in the direction of normalization; but even these improvements might not be sustained beyond the certain months of a trial or are lost as the subject grows heavier.

Adults with CP state that their participation in social activity does not correspond to being able to walk but on the ability to communicate and being able to adjust, adapt and control their environment. Instead of seeking small improvements in functional activities during childhood which are deteriorated almost, concentration on communication and technical abilities needed for the occupation might be more important, as well as the adoption of a more practical and realistic approach to what physical therapy might achieve.

Fauconnier J, et al in 2009 did a studied the participation in life situations of 8-12-year-old kids with CP using a cross sectional analysis. They concluded that after controlling for severity of CP, striking differences prevails in participation between subject from different countries or different geographical areas of the same country. The information was in line with study performed by Hammal D, et al in 2004 when they analyzed the participation of children with CP and the influenced of place where they live. These differences due to geographical boundaries suggest that environmental adjustments could be possible and few of which will need legislation to facilitate a country to the standards of other countries that best facilitate participation.

However, much environmental modification can also be delivered locally. Rosenbaum P analyzed the Family and quality of life in terms of being the key elements in intervention in children with CP. There results stated that the importance of family-based services for disabled children that aims to help a family perceive in control, be stress free, and well able to be responsive to their kids, has been emphasized.

King G, et al in 2006 came up with analyzing the various predictors of the leisure and entertainment participation of children with physical disabilities through a structural equation modeling analysis. He concluded that family lifestyle effects kids' participation as much for disabled as for normal children like the families with a greater participation in sports. Law MC, et al in 2011 studied the focus on function through a cluster, RCT comparing child- versus context-focused management for young children with CP. The first RCT in this specialty suggested that, the environmental adjustments for kids with physical impairment were equally effective as conventional therapeutic therapies that aimed to change the child.

Dr. Victor Santamaria (2017) The Impact of Segmental Trunk Support on Posture and Reaching in Children with Cerebral Palsy Seventeen children (age range 2-15y, GMFCS levels III-V) were classified with the Segmental Assessment of Trunk Control into: mild (complete trunk control/lower-lumbar deficits), moderate (thoracic/upper lumbar deficits) and severe (cervical/upper thoracic deficits). Postural and arm kinematics were measured while reaching with trunk support at axillae, mid-ribs or pelvis. Conclusion: Children with CP and trunk dysfunction demonstrate improved motor performance when the external assistance matches their intrinsic level of trunk control.

Sandra L Saavedra (2015) Segmental contributions to trunk control in children with moderate-to-severe cerebral palsy. Fifteen children (4-16 years) with moderate (Gross Motor Function Classification System (GMFCS) IV; n= 8; 4 males) or severe (GMFCS V; n= 7; 4 males) cerebral palsy. Interventions Each child participated in three data collection sessions. During each session, we evaluated postural control for sitting using kinematics and clinical assessments. Conclusions Children with GMFCS V have limited trunk control but respond to support similarly to young typically developing infants suggesting delayed postural control. Response to external support for children with GMFCS IV suggests a unique strategy for trunk control not observed in typical infants. Overall a segmental approach offers new insights into development of trunk control in children with moderate-to-severe CP.

Maria sanchez (2018) Working towards an objective segmental assessment of trunk control in children with cerebral palsy Twelve children with CP were recruited and an average of 3 (±1. 1) SATCo tests performed per child. The full SATCo was concurrently video-recorded from a sagittal view; markers were placed on specific landmarks of the head, trunk and pelvis to track and estimate head/trunk segment position. A simplified objective rule was created for control and used on videos showing no external support. This replicated the clinical parameters and enabled identification of the segmental-loss-of-control. The subjectively and objectively identified segmental-loss-of-control were compared using a Pearson Correlation Coefficient. This study showed that simple objective video-based measurements can be used to reconstruct the subjective assessment of segmental head/trunk control.

Derek John Curtis (2018) The functional effect of segmental trunk and head control training in moderate-to-severe cerebral palsy: A randomized controlled trial
To determine whether segmental training is more effective in improving gross motor function in children and young people with moderate-to-severe cerebral palsy than conventional physiotherapy. Methods: Twenty-eight participants were randomized to a segmental training or control group. Outcomes were Gross Motor Function Measure (GMFM), Pediatric Evaluation of Disability Inventory (PEDI), Segmental Assessment of Trunk Control (SATCo), and postural sway at baseline, at primary endpoint (6 months), and at follow-up (12 months). Conclusion: Segmental training was not superior to usual care in improving GMFM. Improvements in head and trunk sway were greater in the segmental training group at primary endpoint but not at follow-up.

Sina LABAF (2015) Effects of Neurodevelopmental Therapy on Gross Motor Function in Children with Cerebral Palsy. In a quasi-experimental design, 28 children with cerebral palsy were randomly divided into two groups. Neurodevelopmental therapy was given to a first group (n= 15) with a mean age of 4.9 years; and a second group with a mean age 4.4 years (n= 13) who were the control group. All children were evaluated with the Gross Motor Function Measure. Treatments were scheduled for three - one-hour sessions per week for 3 months. concluded that the neurodevelopmental treatment improved gross motor function in children with cerebral palsy in four dimensions (laying and rolling, sitting, crawling and kneeling, and standing). However, walking, running, and jumping did not improve significantly.

Sharma, Sonia (2018) Effects of NDT Treatment Based Trunk Protocol on Gross Motor Function of Spastic CP Children. study the effects of NDT treatment-based trunk protocol on gross motor function of spastic CP children. To study the effects of NDT treatment-based trunk protocol on gross motor function of spastic CP children. To compare the effects of NDT treatment-based trunk protocol with conventional therapy for spastic CP children. Children were divided in control and experimental group. Gross motor functions of all children were assessed using GMFM -88 scale prior to the protocol (NOT/Conventional) and reevaluated after treatment. Result: The study proved NDT based trunk protocol to be effective on gross motor function of spastic CP Children. Conclusion: Long duration NDT treatment-based trunk protocol focused on dynamic co-activation of trunk flexors and extensors significantly improved gross motor function in children with spastic CP (1-6 Years). Also, it was more effective than conventional therapy. hence it is suggested that trunk should be focused and it should not be overlooked while working for gross motor function of CP children.

Dorothy Russell (2018) Neuro-Developmental Therapy/Bobath Approach on children with Cerebral Palsy. The pilot study included four children with active participation of the parents during frequent intervention sessions. The children were classified on the Gross Motor Function Classification System (GMFCS) at levels IV and V with some homogeneity. All children were evaluated before intervention, directly after intervention sessions and again at eight weeks after the initial testing using the Paediatric Evaluation of Disability Inventory Computer Adaptive Test (PEDICAT) and Gross Motor Function Measure (GMFM). Goal Attainment Scaling (GAS) that involves careful prediction of expected outcomes enabled a thorough description of the children's level of performance in a target area. Concluded that Intensive task-specific training showed to be beneficial for the children, resulting in improved developmental domains for the child with CP. These findings emphasize that evidence-based treatment-intervention approaches for children with CP should be applied including traditional NDT/Bobath.

Reda S Sarhan 2012 Effect of Reciprocating Gait Orthosis on Standing Balance in Children with Spastic Diplegic Cerebral Palsy and Concluded that There were significant improvements in some measured test parameters in children of the experimental group compared to those of the control group that Reciprocating gait orthosis was effective in improving standing balance in children with spastc diplegic child.

Shamekh Mohamed El-Shamy2012 Effect of whole-body vibration (WBV) is a new type of exercise that has been increasingly tested for the ability to prevent bone fractures and osteoporosis in frail people. The purpose of this study was to examine the effects of a 6-month WBV training program on bone mineral density (BMD) in cerebral palsy children and the study revealed no significant difference was recorded between the two groups before treatment. While after 6 months, significant improvement was recorded in the two groups. There was also significant difference between the two groups in favor of the study group. Thus, whole body vibration training plays an important role in improving patients bone mineral density.

Ahmed M. Azzam 2012Efficacy of enhancement forearm supination on improvement of finger dexterity in hemiplegic cerebral palsy children. The aim of this work was to show the effect of enhancement forearm supination on improvement of finger dexterity in hemiplegic cerebral palsy children and Concluded The use of specialized treatment program for enhancement of supination plus traditional physiotherapy program are superior to traditional treatment program only for finger dexterity improvement after 12 weeks follow up.

Chandan Kumar 2013 Effect of Neuromuscular Electrical Stimulation Combined with Cryotherapy on Spasticity and Hand Function in Patients with Spastic Cerebral Palsy. To determine the effectiveness of Neuromuscular electrical stimulation combined with Cryotherapy on spasticity and hand function in patients with spastic Cerebral Palsy Children with CP often demonstrate poor hand function due to spasticity in wrist and finger Flexors and Concluded that this study suggests that NMES combined with cryotherapy is more effective as compared to cryotherapy alone in reducing spasticity and improving hand function in spastic CP patients.

Di$_{v}$$_{y}$a Gupta 2013 Reliability of Modified Ashworth Scale in Spastic Cerebral Palsy in assessment of spasticity in the pediatric population, methods used in practice are ordinal scales that lack reliability. Being a recent scale, Modified Ashworth Scale has not been used in pediatric population as yet. This study aimed to assess inter- and intra-rater reliability of MMAS in assessing children with spastic cerebral palsy and also compare results with those of AS and MAS and concluded that the MMAS is a reliable tool in assessing children with spastic CP and so are AS and MAS.

Preet Kamal Kaur 2010 Effect of single session of prolonged muscle stretch on spastic plantar flexors of children with quadriplegic and diplegic spastic cerebral palsy the control of spasticity is often a significant problem in the management of patients with cerebral palsy which hinders in achieving functional goals and mobility and purpose of this study is to evaluate the effect of prolonged muscle stretch on ankle plantar flexors spasticity and concluded that that there is no effect of the prolonged muscle stretch in reducing spasticity in patients with spastic cerebral palsy.

Dharam Pani Pandey 2011 Effect of functional strength training on functional motor performance in young children with cerebral palsy and concluded that present randomized clinical study support the view that a four week functional strength training program consisting of weight bearing exercises functional strength of muscle of lower extremity and also improves functional motor performance such as walking, running, stair climbing, sit to stand in young children with spastic diplegic cerebral palsy, the finding are in agreement with other previous studies which have shown that functional strength training in cerebral palsy is associated with improvement in motor functions.

Saleh AL-Oraibi 2011 Home based constraint-induced therapy for children with hemiplegic cerebral palsy and Constraint-induced movement therapy as implemented in this study was acceptable to mothers and their children but with some difficulties. over the intervention period, participants experienced improvements in the performance of important daily activities as determined by parents rating and concluded that Modified constraint-induced therapy which is family-focused is sufficiently promising to justify additional studies with larger sample size in the form of a randomized control trails using different types of splints.

Gagandeep Kaur 2011 Relationship Between Motor Impairments of Hand and Manual Ability in Spastic Cerebral Palsy Children and concluded that There is a significant correlation between grip strength, fine finger dexterity, gross manual dexterity and manual ability grip strength has correlation of with the manual ability, fine finger dexterity has the correlation of with the manual ability and gross manual dexterity has the correlation of with the manual ability.

Tamis W. Pin 2019 Effectiveness of interactive computer play on balance and postural control for children with cerebral palsy Interactive computer play (ICP)becomes popular in rehabilitation for children with cerebral palsy With the nature of ICP, it could be an effective intervention specifically to improve balance and postural control for children with CP and aimed to review the effectiveness of ICP on postural control and balance for children with CP and concluded that ICP seemed to be more effective than conventional therapy in improving postural control and balance, with medium to large effect sizes for children with mild to moderate severity of CP.

Sistabu m Karin (2016) Supervised V/s Unsupervised Constraint Induced Movement Therapy in Improving Upper Extremity Function in Spastic Hemiparetic Cerebral Palsy Children and Constraint Induced Movement Therapy has been found to be a promising treatment for substantially improving the use of extremities affected by neurologic injuries such as stroke and traumatic brain injury in adults. The purpose of this study was to determine the applicability of a child friendly form of CI Therapy on young children with cerebral palsy and concluded that the CI Therapy can improve motoric function among children with hemiparesis and that this efficacy is more in a therapist supervised CIMT program

Chandan Kumar, Shina Kataria (2015) Effectiveness of Task Oriented Circuit Training on Functional Mobility and Balance in Cerebral Palsy this study is to determine the efficacy of task related circuit training on functional mobility and balance in children with spastic diplegic type of cerebral palsy and concluded that this study suggests that task oriented circuit training is more effective as compared to the conventional training for the functional mobility and balance in spastic diplegic cerebral palsy children.
Y Ramya, V Sri Kumari, K Madh 2014 :- Effect of Neuro Developmental Therapy Based Trunk Protocol on Gross Motor Development of Sitting Posture and Functional Reach Ability in Cerebral palsy children trunk muscle co-activation that is necessary for development of sitting postural control is delayed in cerebral palsy children which is a common developmental disability that is caused by to brain damage before, during (or) after birth, prevalence of cerebral palsy is 3.3 per 1000 (or) 1 in 303 children are affected by C.P. Damage to Brain motor control centers, leading to impairment of abnormal posture and movement which may change as child grows resulting in developmental delay and give rise to importance of rehabilitation for correction of impairment and concluded that NDT trunk activation protocol was found to be effective in improving sitting postural control and helps in enhancing functional reach ability in cerebral palsy children.

Ruchi Kumari 2016 to Determine effectiveness of Closed-Kinetic Chain Exercise on Motor Control and Function as Compared to Open-Kinetic Chain Exercise in Children with Spastic Diplegic CP and concluded that study revealed that Progressive resisted lower limb strength training was found to be slightly (insignificant) more effective than Loaded sit-to-stand exercise. The SCALE score, GMFM Dimension D and GMFM Dimension E scores improved 1.08, 1.10 and 1.05 times more respectively in children those who received Progressive resisted lower limb.

Mohmad Ali 2017 Reciprocal Electrical Stimulation and Postural Stability in Diplegic Children received the treatment for two hours, three times weekly for three successive months. Balance and postural stability index were assessed for both groups pre and post treatment using Berg's balance scale and Biodex Balance system consequently. The result of the study showed significant improvement in all measured variables for both groups in favor for study group. It could be concluded that reciprocal electrical stimulation for dorsi and planter flexors muscles after tendon achilles tenotomy is safe and effective method of treatment, its improved balance and postural stability in spastic diplegic children.

Suvans s tealia (2018) Effects of the Neurodevelopmental Treatment (NDT) on the Mobility of Children with Cerebral Palsy children participated in an intervention that consisted of an 8-week Bobath program. GMFM-88, PEDI and TUG scores were measured across three time points during the intervention and concluded that there is strong evidence of the effectiveness of the NDT (Bobath) method in improving the mobility of children regardless of the frequency of its application.

Kizel et al 2014 The Comparison of Neurodevelopmental-Bobath Approach with Occupational Therapy Home Program on Gross Motor Function of Children with Cerebral Palsy Traditional Bobath approach (TBA) is one of the several methods which is used for the treatment of children with cerebral palsy (CP) who are referred to occupational therapy settings. In this study the effect of TBA on the gross motor function (GMF) of children with CP was compared with that of the Home Program Bobath approach (HPBA) and concluded that the results of this study showed that TBA with HPBA was more effective than the traditional ones.

Geriban et al 2015   To Study the effects of Mcimt Versus Cimt for Young Children with Spastic Hemiplegic Cerebral Palsy- A Comparative Study and the study is to find out whether restraining of the uninvolved limb and use of hand techniques will help to overcome hand function and improve functional activity in spastic hemiplegic cerebral palsy and concluded that Data collected through the study showed more improvement in the hand function and functional activities in patients with hemiplegic cerebral palsy in the group A Thus, it can be concluded that CIMT are more beneficial in improving hand function for young children with spastic hemiplegic cp. This is one reason in all the literature which emphasizes the importance of above CIMT over MCIMT.

Terms B Avanar 2016   Evaluation of the functional effects of a course of Bobath therapy in children with cerebral palsy: a preliminary study Evaluation of the functional effects of a course of Bobath therapy in children with cerebral palsy: a preliminary study spastic quadriplegia (n= 9); spastic diplegia (n= 4); athetoid quadriplegia (n= 1), and ataxia (n= 1) Participants showed a significant improvement in scores in the following areas following Bobath therapy compared with the periods before and after Bobath therapy This demonstrates that in this population, gains were made in motor function and self-care following a course of Bobath therapy.

Nikos Tsorlakis 2016   his study examined the effect of neurodevelopmental Treatment (NDT) and differences in its intensity on gross Motor function of children with cerebral palsy (CP) Children in group B performed better and showed significantly greater improvement than those in group A and concluded the effectiveness of NDT and underline the need for intensive application of the treatment.

He MX, et al. Medicine (Baltimore). 2019 The effectiveness and safety of electromyography biofeedback therapy for motor dysfunction of children with cerebral palsy This systematic review does not require formal ethical approval because all data will be analyzed anonymously. Results will provide a general overview and evidence concerning the effectiveness and safety of EMG biofeedback therapy for children with CP. The findings of this systematic review will be disseminated through peer-reviewed publications or conference presentations.

Begnoche, Denise M. PT; Pitetti, 2014 Effects of Traditional Treatment and Partial Body Weight Treadmill Training on the Motor Skills of Children with Spastic Cerebral Palsy and concluded that results indicate improvements in motor and ambulatory skills of individual children indicating positive measurable outcomes of intensive physical therapy with partial body weight treadmill training.

Saleh Al-Oraibi, Ann-Christin Eliasson 2015 Twenty children with unilateral cerebral palsy (CP) were randomized to either CIMT or neurodevelopmental treatment (NDT). NDT is the usual treatment method in Jordan for children with CP and was used in the control group and concluded that treatment effect of CIMT can be seen after a 2-day workshop in a novel environment.

Sina LABAF, MSc, Alireza 2018 Effects of Neurodevelopmental Therapy on Gross Motor Function in Children with Cerebral Palsy all children were evaluated with the Gross Motor Function Measure. Treatments were scheduled for three -one-hour sessions per week for 3 months and concluded that concluded that the neurodevelopmental treatment improved gross motor function in children with cerebral palsy in four dimensions (laying and rolling, sitting, crawling and kneeling, and standing). However, walking, running, and jumping did not improve significantly.

Mohammad Khayatzadeh Mahani, Masood Karimloo 2016 Effects of modified Adeli suit therapy on improvement of gross motor function in children with cerebral palsy six children with CP assigned by match pairs to three equal groups such as the MAST, the AST, and the Neurodevelopmental Treatment. They were treated and all children were tested by the Gross Motor Function Measure (GMFM) at baseline, immediately before and 16 weeks after treatments and concluded that The MAST was more effective than using either the AST or the neurodevelopmental treatment on improvement of gross motor function in children with CP after treatment and at follow-up.

Marj olijn Ketelaar, Adri Vermeer, Harm't Hart 2011 Effects of a functional therapy program on motor abilities of children with cerebral palsy using the Gross Motor Function Measure (GMFM) and the self-care and mobility domains of the Pediatric Evaluation of Disability Inventory (PEDI), respectively and concluded that both groups had improved GMFM and PEDI scores after treatment. No time xgroup interactions were found on the GMFM. For the PEDI, time xgroup interactions were found for the functional skills and caregiver assistance scales in both the self-care and mobility domains. The groups' improvements in basic gross motor abilities, as measured by the GMFM in a standardized environment, did not differ. When examining functional skills in daily situations, as measured by the PEDI, children in the functional physical therapy group improved more than children in the reference group.

Eileen G Fowler, Teresa W Ho, Azuka I Nwigwe 2001 The effect of quadriceps femoris muscle strengthening exercises on spasticity in children with cerebral palsy Knee muscle spasticity was assessed bilaterally using the pendulum test to elicit a stretch reflex immediately before and after 3 different forms of right quadriceps femoris muscle exercise (isometric, isotonic, and isokinetic) during a single bout of exercise training. Pendulum test outcome measures were: (1) first swing excursion, (2) number of lower leg oscillations, and (3) duration of the oscillations and concluded that there were no changes in spasticity following exercise between the 2 groups of subjects.
Catherine Morgan, Johanna Darrah, Andrew M Gordon 2016 Effectiveness of motor interventions in infants with cerebral palsy and concluded that the two interventions that had a moderate to large effect on motor outcomes had the common themes of child-initiated movement, environment modification/enrichment, and task-specific training.

Eun-Young Park, Won-Ho Kim 2017 Effect of neurodevelopmental treatment-based physical therapy on the change of muscle strength, spasticity, and gross motor function in children with spastic cerebral palsy and concluded that Spasticity was significantly reduced after 1 year of treatment. The Gross Motor Functional Classification System levels 1-11 group showed a significant increase in muscle strength compared with the Gross Motor Functional Classification System levels III-V, and the latter showed a significant decrease in spasticity compared with the former.

2.6. Outcome measures

Lieve Heyrman and Guy Molenaers in 2011, designed a clinical tool to measure trunk control in children with CP named the Trunk Control Measurement Scale, which incorporates both static and dynamic balance component of trunk control unlike the former which took only the static balance in to consideration. This study reported there was good psychometric properties which supports the use of the TCMS as an evaluative tool.

Further, the use of qualitative items in the TCMS was suggested to facilitate clinical implementation of this measurement tool because it provides an overview of the advantages and disadvantages of the child's trunk performance. Future they stated that studies in future should address responsiveness of the tool to interventions, as well as application to a much younger age group and to other types of CP. Knowing the utility of the scale the Korean form of TCMS was drafted and was tested for its reliability and validity.

This study was undertaken by Jun-Young Jeon and Won-Seob Shin in 2014. They termed the Korean TCMS scale as TCMS-K. The results of the study suggested that TCMS-K has a high reliability and validity, which was identical to the original version. Thus, they concluded that the TCMS-K is a suitable evaluation scale for assessing the qualitative performance of the trunk control and sitting balance for Cerebral palsy children, and they recommended the tool as an useful tool for clinicians and researchers.

Elena Mitteregger and Petra Marsico, found the translation and construct validity of the TCSM in children and youths' patients with brain lesion. They proved that the TCMS may also be applicable to children with acquired brain injury, but they clearly emphasized that more research is needed on a larger population. Hong Phi Pham, Anita Eidem, tried to find the Validity and Responsiveness of the TCMS Scale in Young children with Cerebral Palsy and found that construct validity of the TIS and TCMS in young individuals with CP was good whereas they were not able to document response veness.

However, the correlations between the TCMS dynamic sitting balance and reaching change score and hours spent on "trunk-targeted training" advocates that this subscale may have the real potential to be used in research particularly in the intervention studies. Petra Marsico et al in 2017 analysed the Trunk Control Measurement Scale for its reliability and discriminative validity in pediatric population with neuromotor disorders. They concluded that the reliability of the TCMS was superior in the group of children aged 5 to 19 years suffering from neuromotor impairments.

When using the TCMS they advocated a total score as an outcome measure at the same time the change should exceed six points to be considered higher than the measurement error. With this cut-off values of the TCMS, discrimination can be made between the children who are independent or mild to complete dependent in self-care activity and mobility. The creative cut-off scores were different between the TCMS sub scores, which could reflect the differences in measuring of these sub-scores.

2.7. Clinical management Overview

Two factors are vital in management of the individuals with CP. First, all interventions must be pre planned, implemented and validated by a multidisciplinary service with the option of the child and family at the centre of decision making. Next difficulties encountered are not limited to an individual's motor problem but also to the variety of co-existing morbidities. (Parkinson KN,et al, 2010)

The social model of disability was performed by Oliver M when he analysed the theories in health care and research and the theories of disability in health practice. He explained that the problems in participation are due to the failure of society to accept and accustom to the needs of the children and thus it has its limits.

Hadjipanayis A, et al, studied the epilepsy in patients with CP and came out with the fact that the successful management is the one that balances the social and clinical models of care equally; by doing so one can minimises the effect of medical difficulties at the same time maximising physical ability, environmental adaptability, child and family choice, and last but not least the much-needed social support.

Individuals with CP usually have comorbidities, particularly if they have more severe forms of CP, including epilepsy, difficulty in feeding, swallowing, and bowel function, poor nutrition and growth, vulnerability to infection, and poor hearing and vision. They gave a final verdict by confirming that in subjects with unilateral spastic CP, partial epilepsy is common. In patients with severe involvement of bilateral sides, up to 50% have generalised epilepsy in whom the seizure control can be difficult to achieve. Further, diagnostic problems can also arise if the underlying movement disorder is mistaken for epileptic events.

Fairhurst C, in 2011 came up with a study on management strategies for drooling in children and came up with the fact that problems with saliva control are managed well by drugs especially botulinum toxin to the salivary glands, or holding of salivary ducts. Sullivan P, et al questioned with their study asking does gastrostomy tube feeding facilitate the risk of respiratory morbidity and came up with an answer saying that it's the unsafe swallowing and aspiration may require gastrostomy. There are a sequence of studies performed in CP particularly the work done by Kuperminc M and Sullivan P, which explained that there are various factors, including posture, food intake, absorption, and endocrine and GI problems can result of enhance the poor growth and nutrition in subjects with CP. Kuperminc M, and Stevenson R analysed the growth and nutritional disorders in kids with CP and concluded that however, health and wellbeing, not the growth itself, are the main objectives, and a balance needs to be reached for every individual between growth, development and the complexity and invasiveness of any treatment.

Fehlings D, et al. in 2012 studied the effect of informing evidence-based clinical practice guidelines for kids with CP at risk of osteoporosis through a systematic review. They proved that osteopenia and osteoporosis are identified in some non-ambulant adults with CP, particularly when an individual is on drugs like anticonvulsants and has nutritional difficulties. Chandra R in his overview on the nutrition and immunity in CP children proved that poor nutrition can result in immune dysfunction and immobility, and the deformity can lead to infection of skin and urinary tract; aspiration of the saliva or gastric contents highly increases the risk of chest infections. (Sullivan P, et al, 2006) Reports published by Australian cerebral palsy register, for the children born in the year 1993-2006 stated that in CP postoperative infection rates, particularly after surgery to correct severe scoliosis, can be as greater as 10%. In addition, 35% of children with CP have a visual problem and hence, all children should have a compulsory ophthalmological assessment. The most common known disorders are strabismus, visual field disorder, myopia, or hypermetropia.

Dutton G,et al from their analysis on visual impairment in children due to brain damage concluded that about 8% of children with CP have severe visual impairment, mainly attributable to cortical visual disorder, and noted most often in those with severe CP and associated chronic learning difficulties. Permanent sensory neural deafness is not common and, if present, is usually realted with neonatal gentamicin therapy and/or neonatal hyperbilirubinemia. Rehabilitation of motor problems, Medical management of motor disorders has evolved substantially in the past 30 years. This change is attributed in part, to introduction of new interventions modalities or modification of others, but also due to development of appropriate measures of functional activities that allow goals for clinical intervention to be set and outcomes of trials which are to be compared.

Eliasson AC, et al studied the Manual Ability Classification System (MACS) for children with CP as a part of scale development and evidence of validity and reliability. He defended that the scale as good as any other scales in fulfilling its purpose. Palisano R, et al did a study on development and reliability of a system to classify a scale - gross motor function in children with CP and proved that Gross Motor Function Classification System is highly reliable and valid tool in various age categories in paediatric population. There are many scales devised for attesting various aspects of CP children as follows. Reid SM, et al analysed the Drooling Impact Scale which is a measure of the impact of drooling in children with disabled developmental and standardised it, Pennington L, et al tried to Develop the Viking speech scale to classify the speech of children with cerebral palsy and succeeded in do so. Hidecker MJ, et al validated the Communication Function Classification System and the Centre for Cerebral Palsy and Cerebral Palsy League of Queensland standardised the functional Communication Classification System.

Approved scales additionally exist for pain, health-related quality of life, and explicit oromotor, upper, and lower appendage capacities. Proper intercessions for cerebral palsy are managed by the patient's useful capacity, seriousness, example of engine issue, related pain and inconvenience, and age. Pediatric practice intends to lessen optional musculoskeletal distortion as opposed to treat the essential focal neurological defect. A versatile methodology is expected to encourage every formative space and lessen the impact of therapeutic issues.

Physical, word related, and discourse and dialect treatment approaches are basic; they likewise work in blend with therapeutic administration. Distinctive focuses use marginally different approaches however they share center standards. For instance, most non-intrusive treatments depend on the standards of neuroplasticity, designing, postural balance, muscle reinforcing, or extending. (Damiano DL, 2009)

Anttila H, et al in 2008 performed a focused review on finding the effectiveness of physiotherapy and conductive educational interventions in cerebral palsy population and proved it to be significantly effective. However, Reddihough DS, et al in 1998 studied the efficiency of programs based on Conductive Education for young children with CP which did not show any higher benefits in gross motor function compared with traditional physiotherapy approaches.

Motor intervention mean to change the overactive components of the upper motor neurone disorder by lessening the impact of expanded muscle tone or enhancing the ease of motor control. Their belongings may be brief, similarly as with oral drug, or lasting as in most careful intercessions. The proof for a large portion of these intercessions is powerless, mostly as a result of the scarcity of randomized controlled preliminaries yet in addition as a result of the numerous confounders to treatment, for example, the impact of co morbidities.

Clinical approach has often been based on information from case series and expert guidelines. Recently, the National Institute for Health and Care Excellence (NICE) from UK provided guidelines for spasticity management in children with CP.

Delgardo M, et al in 2010 provided the practice parameter and pharmacologic treatment of spasticity in children and adolescents with CP which is evidence-based review. They concluded that the muscle relaxants work at both the spinal and the muscle levels to diminish muscle activation by the uncontrolled spinal reflex arc and spasticity resulting due to lack of descending inhibition. The most commonly available muscle relaxant is baclofen, a y-aminobutyric acid (GABA) Bagonist which depresses the release of facilitatory neurotransmitters at the spinal level. As baclofen is very lipophilic, it will not cross the blood-brain barrier that easily.

In order to obtain useful CNS concentrations, subjects have a dose-deepen dent risk of adverse effects including sedation, hypoventilation, and high vulnerability of seizures. That the reason why patients increasingly have Baclofen provided by an intrathecal route through an implantable pump.

<u>**2.7.1 Neuro developmental therapy -Advantages and shortcomings**</u>

Neurodevelopmental treatment (NDT) is a valuable technique widely used by physiotherapists all over the world in the management of children and adults with neurological dysfunction resulting in motor deficits, such as CP, spinal cord injury, traumatic brain injury, stroke and low-birth weight children. (Bobath 1980, Bobath and Bobath 1984) But neuro developmental therapy is not an undisputed therapy procedure.

Similar to other theoretical frame work NDT also had to undergo lot of modifications due to the evolution and understanding of the neural science about how movement occurs in human body. There are good volumes of studies which support NDT at the same time their equal volumes of research which disputes its results. In 1972 Taft stated from his study that there is no solid evidence to indicate that treatment protocol which attempt to modify sensory modalities, to suppress primitive reflexes, or to modify or correct abnormal movement patterns are ever successfully included in the maturing central nervous system with the resulting development in motor function.

In 1982, Pearson conveyed from his studies that Despite this appalling scarcity of a scientific basis for much of what we do in NDT, the governments are spending a very huge portion of their national expenditure to support these same services, and very little in support of research in determining outcomes. About 20 years later Taft's remarks, the same concern had not been resolved and the competence of NDT had not been confirmed to satisfy a critical scientific and medical fraternity. NDT has few logical flaws that make research investigations difficult at best. 'Valvano JS and Long Tin 1991 performed a systematic review on Neuro developmental treatment and found out that it was no more effective than a placebo group, through some valid earlier documentations and also added that, the fundamental criticism is about the lack of operational definitions. Van Sant AF in the same year analysed the efficacy of NDT and pediatric physical therapy in the treatment of cerebral palsy and came out with the fact NDT is not the appropriate intervention due to the fact that the neuro development do not follow a top down flow or a sequential development. Later in the year 1998 Blanche and Halloway conducted a study on few controversial aspects of NDT which were evident in the published research literature for many years.

Mayo in 1991 analyzed the practical difficulties in applying neuro developmental therapy from patient as well as care takers perspective using a cross sectional analysis. He concluded that NDT is demanding for both the patient and the parent since it necessitates regular outpatient attendance for therapy along with a programme for parents to be performed at home. He further emphasized that many parents are unable to comply with the treatment regimen fully, because it is stressful and time taking both to master the recommendations and, once mastered, to steadily maintain them'. However, many physiotherapists support the initiation of therapy at the earliest and intensely as possible, this enthusiasm has not been supported by evaluation research, and so many rehabilitation professionals doubt that the benefits occur from therapy warrant the time and the effort expended by parent and kid (Mayo 1991).

Several authors like Paine in 1962, Wright and Nicholson in 1973, Scherzer et al in 1976, Kanda et al in 1984 and Keshner in 1981 have supported these ideas well before Mayo. Bly et al, Palisano et al in 1991 and Levi in 1995 expressed their views through their research work saying that NDT is a costly therapeutic procedure and demands therapeutic approach in terms of care taker's time and dedication, physiotherapists' salaried hours to enhance therapy and what the kid has to endure and experience. A study was conducted by Ottenbacher et al in 1986 which was an initial step towards enlightening pooled empirical evidence about NDT.

2.8. Outcome measures used in the study - GMFCS scale

The Gross Motor Function Classification System (GMFCS) was initially developed to classify severity of functional problems in children with CP by Palisano R, et al in 1997 when they performed a research to develop and find the reliability of a system to classify gross motor function in CP population. Russell D, et al in 1993 analysed the Gross Motor Function values in Cerebral Palsy children using GMFCS scale and reported that instrument was highly responsive to both negative and positive changes in children's motor abilities.

Wood E, et al conducted a study in 2000 to analyse the reliability and stability over time of GMFCS scale in cerebral palsy children and concluded that the scale has a good inter-rater and intra-rater reliability and also most notably it has a good stability quotient over time. Beckung E et al in 2000 Correlated ICIDH handicap code and GMFCS in children with CP and concluded that there was a striking similarity between the two scales as far as the grading of disability is concerned. In this scenario the study concluded that GMFCS is considerably easier to evaluate as it is less time consuming and it can be evaluated retrospectively.

GMFCS level has been proved to be strongly correlated with the handicap code developed by the World Health Organization in 1980, the ICIDH (International Classification of Impairment, Disabilities, and Handicap) with $r = 0.95$ and $p < 0.0001$. Bodkin et al in 2003 conducted a study to analyse the reliability and validity of the Gross Motor Function Classification System for CP children and concluded that the GMFCS scale is reliable and valid.

They also demonstrated strong inter-rater reliability by using videotape segments. Moderate correlation between the GMFCS level and established tests of the gross motor function supports that the GMFCS have a good criterion-related validity. Adding to this, they did not recommend the use of the GMFCS in other populations except cerebral palsy, except in very limited situations. They were able to demonstrate good construct validity because GMFCS levels remained stable in CP children over time more than in Down syndrome. The GMFCS aped to them to be a good clinical outcome tool for risk adjustment in outcome studies in CP children as well as a tool for predicting future function CP children.

2.9. Segmental Assessment of Trunk Control (SATCo)

Butler P and associates in 2010 designed a scale titled Segmental Assessment of Trunk Control (SATCo) to provide discrete information about the levels of trunk control in children suffering from motor disabilities. This study tried to refined the assessment method and examined the reliability and validity of the SATCo and concluded that, SATCo is a highly reliable and valid measure which allows clinicians greater specificity in the assessment of trunk control.

2.10. Trunk Control Measurement Scale (TCMS)

Lieve Heyrman et al in 2011 studied various clinical tool to measure trunk control in cerebral palsy children. This study found out that though SATCo is a reliable and valid tool, the assessment tool scores only the ability to maintain a stable sitting posture on a dichotomous scale in three conditions namely during supported sitting, when head movements and when external perturbations and with a gradually diminishing support of the trunk. Once a patient has achieved unsupported sitting in these three conditions, the maximum value on the scale is obtained. Further, the SATCo covers static (balance) trunk control only and items which evaluate the dynamic trunk control are not being included.

Lieve Heyrman and Guy Molenaers in 2011, designed a clinical tool to measure trunk control in children with CP named the Trunk Control Measurement Scale, which incorporates both static and dynamic balance component of trunk control unlike the former which took only the static balance in to consideration. This study reported there was good psychometric properties which supports the use of the TCMS as an evaluative tool. Further, the use of qualitative items in the TCMS was suggested to facilitate clinical implementation of this measurement tool because it provides an overview of the advantages and disadvantages of the child's trunk performance.

Future they stated that studies in future should address responsiveness of the tool to interventions, as well as application to a much younger age group and to other types of CP. Knowing the utility of the scale the korian form of TCMS was drafted and was tested for its reliability and validity. This study was undertaken by Jun-Young Jeon and Won-Seob Shin in 2014. They termed the Korean TCMS scale as TCMS-K. the results of the study suggested that TCMS-K has a high reliability and validity, which was identical to the original version.

Thus, they concluded that the TCMS-K is a suitable evaluation scale for assessing the qualitative performance of the trunk control and sitting balance for Cerebral palsy children, and they recommended the tool as a useful tool for clinicians and researchers. Elena Mitteregger and Petra Marsico, found the translation and construct validity of the TCSM in children and youths' patients with brain lesion.

They proved that the TCMS may also be applicable to children with acquired brain injury, but they clearly emphasized that more research is needed on a larger population. Hong Phi Pham, Anita Eidem, tried to find the Validity and Responsiveness of the TCMS Scale in Young children with Cerebral Palsy and found that construct validity of the TIS and TCMS in young individuals with CP was good whereas they were not able to document responsiveness. However, the correlations between the TCMS dynamic sitting balance and reaching change score and hours spent on "trunk-targeted training" advocates that this subscale may have the real potential to be used in research particularly in the intervention studies.

Petra marsico et al in 2017 analysed the Trunk Control Measurement Scale for its reliability and discriminative validity in pediatric population with neuromotor disorders. They concluded that the reliability of the TCMS was superior in the group of children aged 5 to 19 years suffering from neuromotor impairments. When using the TCMS they advocated a total score as an outcome measure at the same time the change should exceed six points to be considered higher than the measurement error. With this cut-off values of the TCMS, discrimination can be made between the children who are independent or mild to complete dependent in self-care activity and mobility. The relative cut-off scores were different between the TCMS sub scores, which could reflect the differences in measuring of these sub-scores.

Thus, from this review of literature its clearly seen that the study is about a real clinical problem and can be a better answer to the prevailing controversies regarding the use of NDT in the pediatric population. The hypothesis is tested using some valid outcome measures, which are already used by the predecessors which is observed from the volumes of research quoted in this section.

CHAPTER3

Aim, Objective and Hypothesis

Cerebral palsy one of the major challenges faced by any physical therapist as it involve different challenges at different stages of the child's development. As it is not a progressively deteriorating condition the expectations of the parents and the kid have to be met by the rehabilitation team But on the other hand, it's a developmental condition, characterised by different obstacles and objectives of treatment in various stages of the child development. The physical therapist should have an in-depth knowledge about normal developmental sequences for finding out the needs of the children by calculating the chronological age and developmental age mismatch and deficits. Though there are controversies regarding using developmental sequence for treatment of cerebral palsy, there are also studies which support the same.

Neuro developmental therapy has been used to correct abnormal posture and facilitate normal movement patterns for performing both gross motor function, fine motor function and skill development. Though **NDT** has been researched enough in the past, yet there are some doubts prevailing in the physical therapist weather to use **NDT** for every cerebral palsy children or for a given set of population. As there are many studies which states that CP has many stages based on the gross motor development and certain stages are well treated with NDT particularly GMFCS 1 and 2.

With the advent of task specific training and functional retraining the value for NDT has been always question. But the authors of neurodevelopment therapy have claimed that relearning may not be possible in children who have not even learnt to move. Hence the movement rehabilitation should take place in a developmental sequence rather than relearning pattern or functional task training approach which will be realistic and ideal for the given population need.

3.2 Need for the Study

In this study, an honest effort is being taken to find out whether or not NDT is effective in treating a specific set of population in Cerebral palsy. NDT as a technique has gone through many evolutionary changes in the past which have made the technique based upon the current theories of neuro science. Though NDT has been studied earlier for its effect on function and gross motor development, it's effect on trunk control and segmental trunk stability have not being studied sufficiently. Segmental trunk control is ability of doing coordinated movement of the neck and head, head and trunk, trunk and pelvis, pelvis and the lower extremities, which is inevitable for equilibrium and balance reactions.

Not only in the child population but also in the adult population trunk is an ignored part of research for a long period of time. It was in the late 1990 and 2000, when good volumes of research have emerged testing the trunk component and now we have a good volume of research done on trunk. This may be true in case of adult hemiplegia and other adult neurological conditions, but as far as child neurological rehabilitation is concerned trunk is still being unexplored part compared to functions like balance, gate, and motor activity of the extremities. Hence it is very clear that there is a strong need for finding out the effect of NDT non-segmental trunk mobility and correlate the improvement of segmental trunk mobility in improving static dynamic balance function and the quality of life of cerebral palsy children.

3.3 Aim of the study

The study aims to find the effect of NDT in improving the segmental trunk control and compare the influence of segmental trunk control on static posture, dynamic balance activity and quality of life in cerebral palsy children with GMFCS score of 3 and 4.

<u>**3.4 Objectives of the study**</u>

The objectives of the study are

1. To find the effect of NDT in improving segmental trunk control in cerebral palsy children with GMFCS score of 3 and 4.

2. To find the effect of NDT in improving static posture in cerebral palsy children with GMFCS score of 3 and 4.

3. To find the effect of NDT in improving dynamic balance activity in cerebral palsy children with GMFCS score of 3 and 4.

4. To find the effect of NDT in improving segmental trunk control in cerebral palsy children with GMFCS score of 3 and 4.

5. To find the effect of NDT in improving quality of life in cerebral palsy children with GMFCS score of 3 and 4.

6. To compare the improvement gained through NDT in segmental trunk mobility with static posture, dynamic balance activity and quality of life in cerebral palsy children with GMFCS score of 3 and 4.

<u>**3.5 Hypothesis of the study**</u>

3.5.1 Null Hypothesis

- ▶ This study hypothesis that NDT is not effective intervention tool in improving the segmental trunk control, static posture and dynamic balance activity in cerebral palsy children with GMFCS score of 3 and 4.

- ▶ This study hypothesis that improvement in segmental trunk control may not improve static posture, dynamic balance activity and quality of life in cerebral palsy children with GMFCS score of 3 and 4.

3.5.2 Alternate hypothesis

- ▶ This study hypothesise that NDT is an effective intervention tool in improving the segmental trunk control, static posture and dynamic balance activity in cerebral palsy children with GMFCS score of 3 and 4.

- ▶ This study hypothesis that improvement in segmental trunk control can improve static posture, dynamic balance activity and quality of life in cerebral palsy children with GMFCS score of 3 and 4.

CHAPTER 4

Methodology

<u>**4.1. Study design**</u>

This Single blinded Randomized control trial was carried out to evaluate the effect of NDT in children with cerebral palsy with a GMFCS score of 3 and 4. Based on selection criteria children were selected for the study. The children were selected for the study using a consecutive sampling. For allocation of the subjects into two groups namely group A and group B, simple random sampling method was performed using a random number table method.

<u>**4.2. Study center**</u>

The study was performed at a single centre at the Department of Physiotherapy, Sanjivani hospital, Rajkot.

<u>**4.3. Sample size**</u>

Sample size was calculated for the study using the below formula by Shein-Shung C,et al, recommended in 2003. The formula was also used on a previous study done on trunk intervention in spastic cerebral palsy children by Heba M Youssr El-Basatiny et al, in 2015.

$$\underline{n = [(Za/2 + Z_)^2 \times \{2(6)2\}]! \,(\mu 1 - \mu 2)^2}$$

Where

n	= sample size required in each group
$\mu 1$	= mean change in control group
$\mu 2$	= mean change in experimental group
$\mu 1-\mu 2$	= clinically significant difference
6	= standard deviation
ZaJ2:	= level of significance, for 5% this is 1.96
Z:	= power, for 80% this is 0.84
n	= 34 each group.

Based on the above formula, the sample size required per group is 34. Hence total sample size required is 68. Considering a drop-out rate (attrition rate) of 10% total sample size required is 80 (40 in each group).

<u>**4.4. Selection criteria**</u>

<u>**4.4.1. Inclusion criteria**</u>

- ► Children who were referred for physiotherapy by paediatrician.
- ► Only diplegic and herniplegic type of CP was recruited.
- ► Children with age group between 3 to 14 years with either spastic herniplegic and diplegic cerebral palsy, with GMFCS level 3 and 4.
- ► Both male and female children were recruited.

4.4.2. Exclusion criteria

- ▶ Children with other types of cerebral palsy.
- ▶ Children with spastic hemiplegic and diplegic cerebral palsy with GMFCS level 1 and 2.
- ▶ Children with poor neck control.
- ▶ Children with poor comprehension to follow simple commands.
- ▶ Children with history of cognitive deficits that may interfere with the study.
- ▶ Children with history of seizure disorder.
- ▶ Children with perceptual disorder which will interfere with motor tasks
- ▶ Children with any other co-existing morbidity that may influence the results of the study as perceived by the researcher.

4.5. Participants

Based on selection criteria using a consecutive sampling the children were selected for the study. All children's care takers/parents signed an informed consent for participation following a clear explanation of the prerequisites for participation. The children were being randomly allotted in to the two groups.

4.6. Randomization

All children after assessment were randomly allotted in any of the following two groups namely Group A (Control) and Group B (interventional). Randomization technique adopted by simple random sampling using random table method and using a concealment method.

4.7. Outcome measures

The following outcome measures was used in the 1st session (1st week) before the treatment begins as the base line value and at the end of 2nd week (post-test 1) and at the end of fourth week (post-test 2) to assess the segmental trunk control, static posture and dynamic balance and quality of life

The TCMS is an objective outcome measure is which is available to score the trunk performances of the child in sitting. The TCMS consists of static and dynamic balance from a seated posture; the latter is divided into selective movement control and dynamic reaching. The TCMS tool shows good relative reliability in CP children with age of eight to 15 years.

The Gross Motor Function Measure (GMFM) is a clinical tool designed and evaluated to measure change in the gross motor function over time or with the intervention in children with CP. It was developed in the year 1980 for use in both clinical and research avenues and has evolved through in time using advanced analytic techniques and in response to the requests for more efficient testing. There are two versions in GMFM namely GMFM-66 and GMFM-88 which is the original 88-item measure. The Items span the spectrum of gross motor activities in 5 different dimensions namely lying and rolling, in sitting, in crawling and kneeling, in standing, and in Walking, Running and Jumping.

The SATCo tests the CP child's trunk control as the evaluator progressively changes in different level of trunk support from a highest level of support at the shoulder girdle to assess cervical (head) control, through support at the axillae (upper thoracic control), lower scapula (mid thoracic control), lower ribs (lower thoracic control), below ribs (upper lumbar control), pelvis (lower lumbar control), and finally, no support, in order to measure full trunk control.

These instruments are useful for evaluating interventions designed to improve the lives of children and adolescents. The CP QOL - Child was first designed to assess the QOL of children with cerebral palsy aged 4-12 years and an adolescent version, the CP QOL - Teen has recently been developed for adolescents aged 13-18 years.

4.8. Procedure

In this phase 80 children were selected consecutively from the commencement date of the data collection. Children's who are referred to physiotherapy by pediatrician at department of Physiotherapy, Sanjivani hospital, Rajkot. The children were screened initially by the primary researcher for the inclusion criteria and exclusion criteria and who ever felt satisfied by the researcher were recruited in to the study.

Further, the children and their parents were explained regarding the importance of Physiotherapy following cerebral palsy and also the significance of the study. They were also educated about the procedures which are going to be done in the study, the duration of the intervention, the timing of intervention and the intensity of the intervention. Once the parents are completely satisfied and sign the informed consent the children were considered for randomization into the two group namely group A and group B.

Following the randomization, a concealment method was used, using a closed cover envelope. The primary researcher was responsible for the randomization and recruitment of the children into the study. Following the randomization, at the 1st session (1 st week) the evaluation was done by a blinded evaluator who is a physiotherapist and qualified person for using the outcome measures used in the study.

The blinded evaluator did not have any idea about to which group the children belong. Following the baseline analysis using the outcome measures used for the study the children underwent the intervention specific for the group allocated. The interventions were provided for the group A by the "physiotherapist A" who was a post graduate with 5 years of clinical experience in the management of pediatric subjects, who is working in the institution (study Centre). The "Physiotherapist A" is not the primary Researcher and also the blinded evaluator. The intervention for the group B was provided by the primary researcher only

4.9 Intervention tool

The intervention was provided for 60 minutes of intervention, one session per day, 5 days in a week, for four consecutive weeks. Group A was provided with voluntary control training, postural control training, muscle strengthening, mobility exercises, static and dynamic sitting balance. The outcome measures were repeated at the end of 2nd week and 4th week by the blinded evaluator after the treatment session. A brief intervention plan and basics of the intervention of NDT used for the study are furnished in table 4.1 to 4.5. A detailed description about the NDT as approach is given in the appendix.

Trunk facilitation with weight bearing (right side)

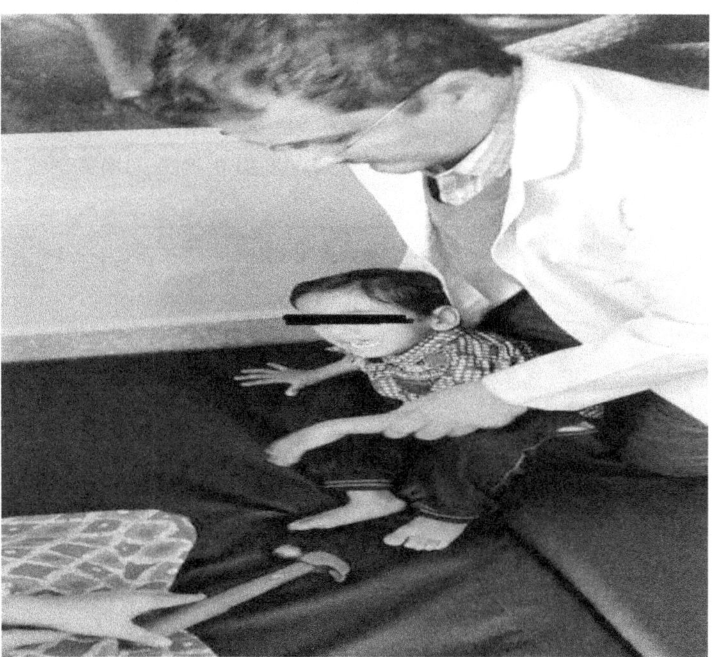

Trunk facilitation with weight bearing (left side).

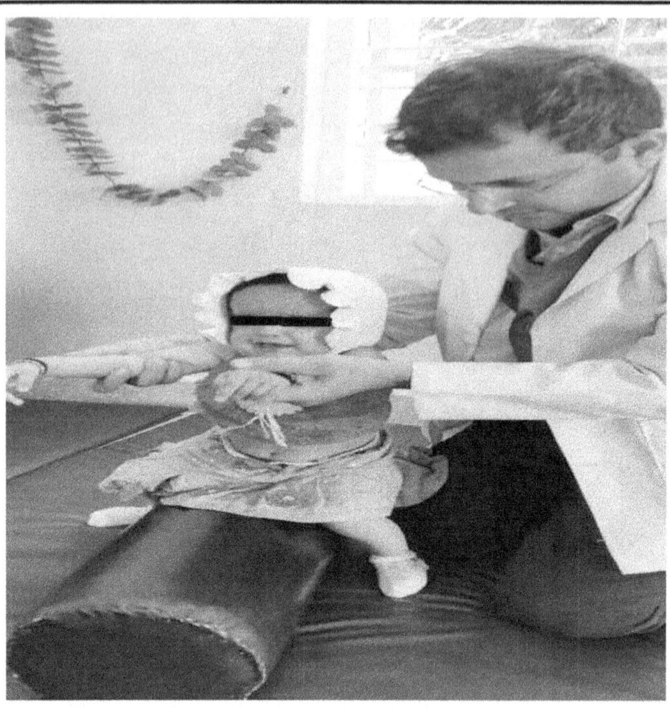

Balancing exercise for trunk control

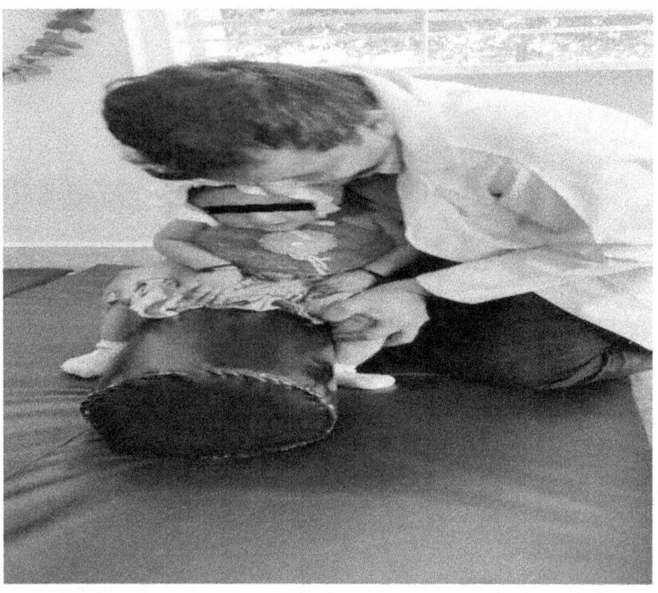

Balancing exercise for trunk control with weight shifting on left side

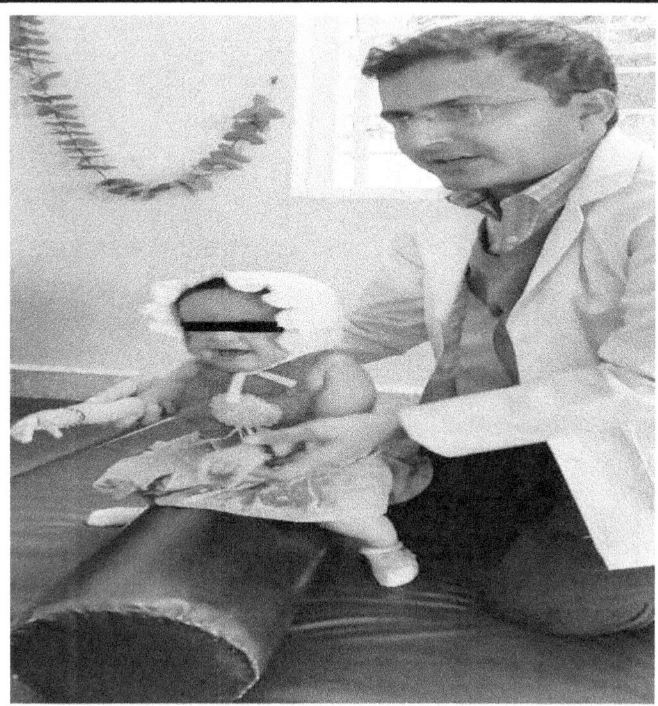

Balancing exercise for trunk control with weight shifting on right side

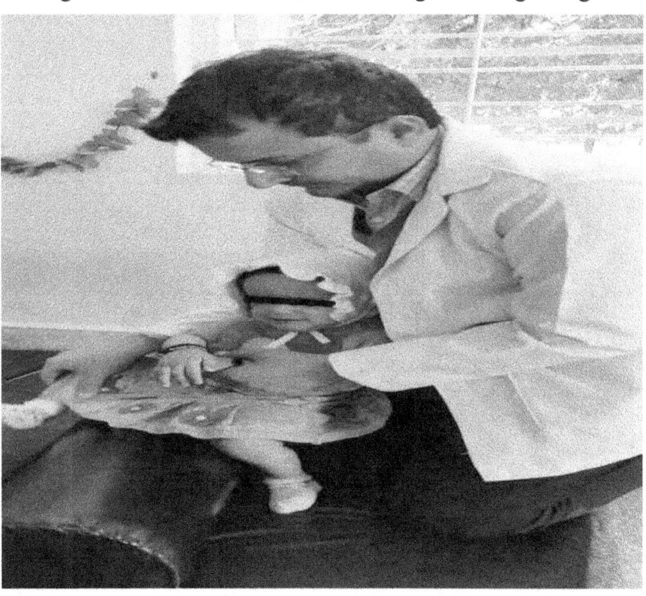

Balancing exercise for trunk control with weight shifting on left side

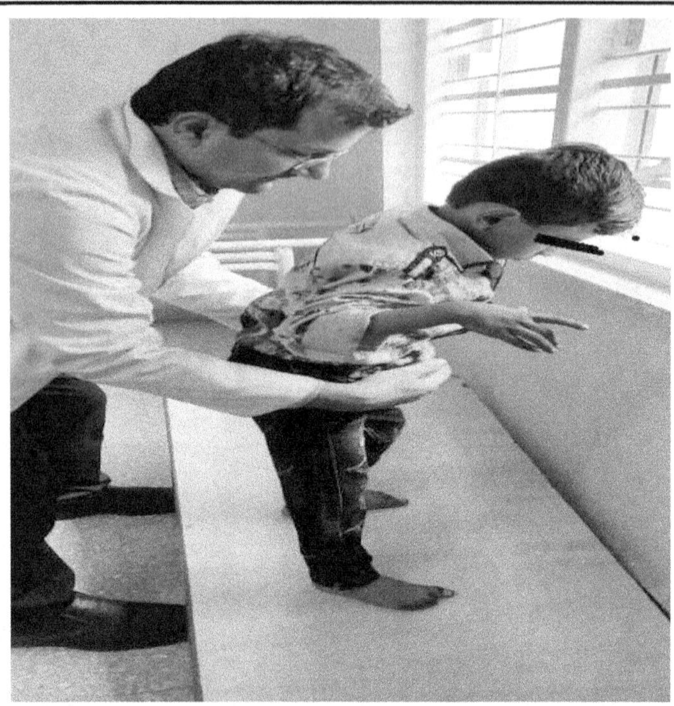

Weight shift training on balance board

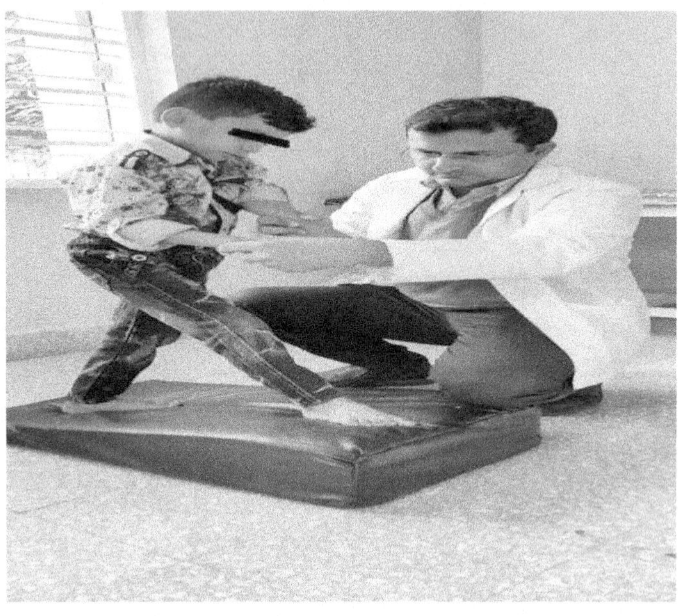

Trunk facilitation with weight bearing on wedge

Group **B** was provided with NDT designed for analysis in this study and voluntary control training, postural control training, muscle strengthening, mobility exercises, static and dynamic sitting balance. The outcome measures were repeated at the end of 2nd week and 4th week by the blinded evaluator after the treatment session. The following strategy was adopted from the school of **NDT** to be employed for the study.

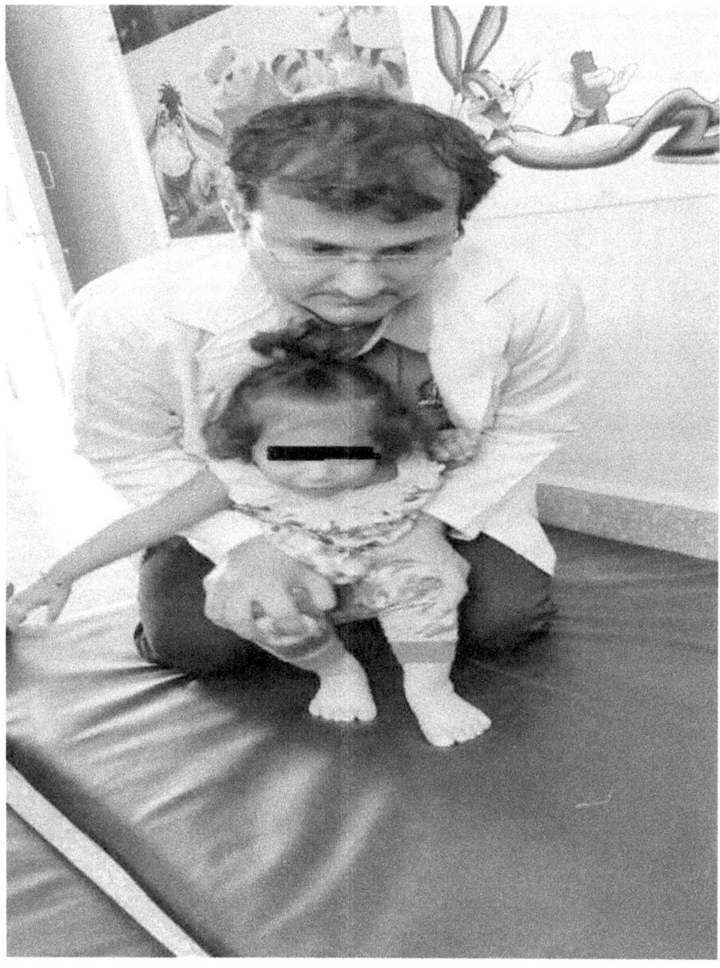

Squatting training for trunk control

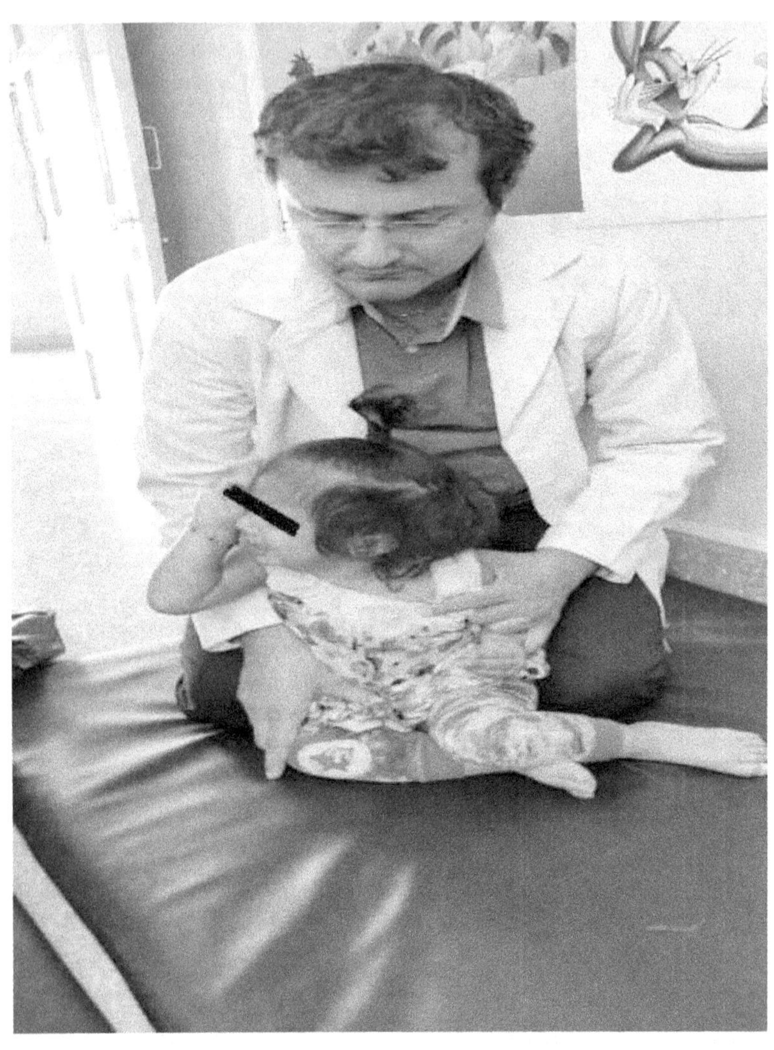

Side sitting with head and trunk control training

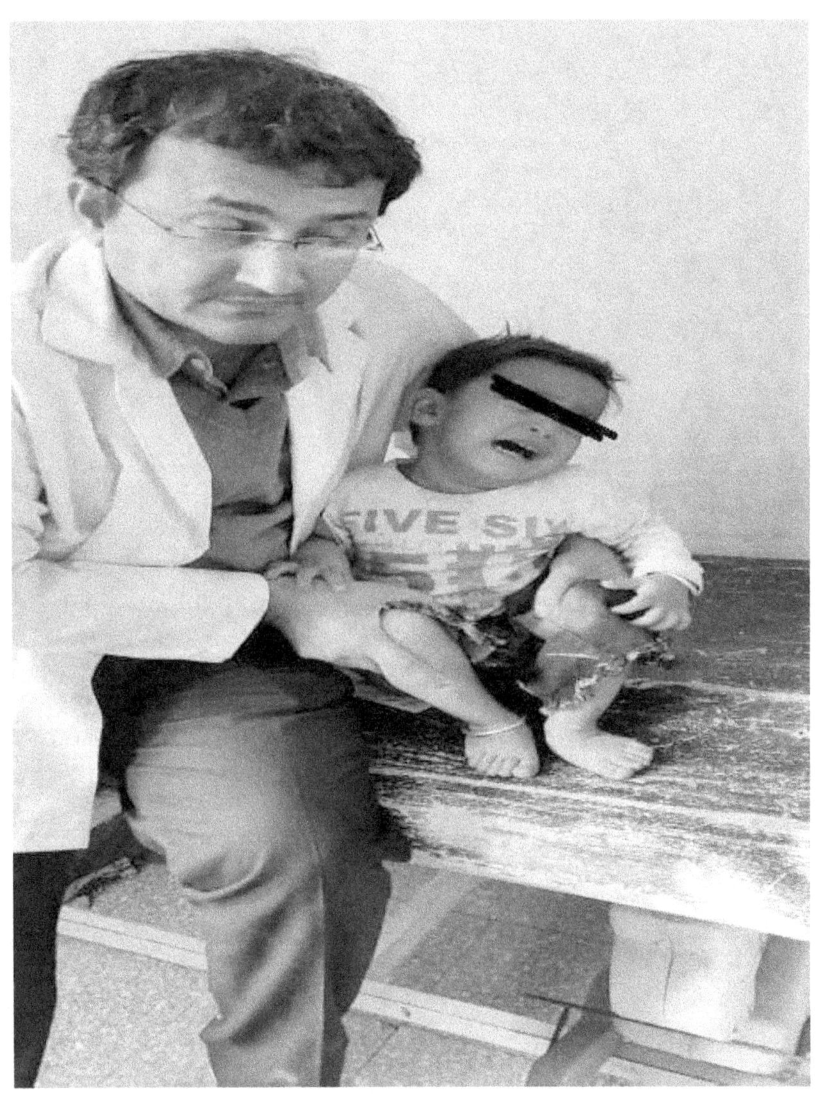

Squatting with head and trunk control

Trunk facilitation

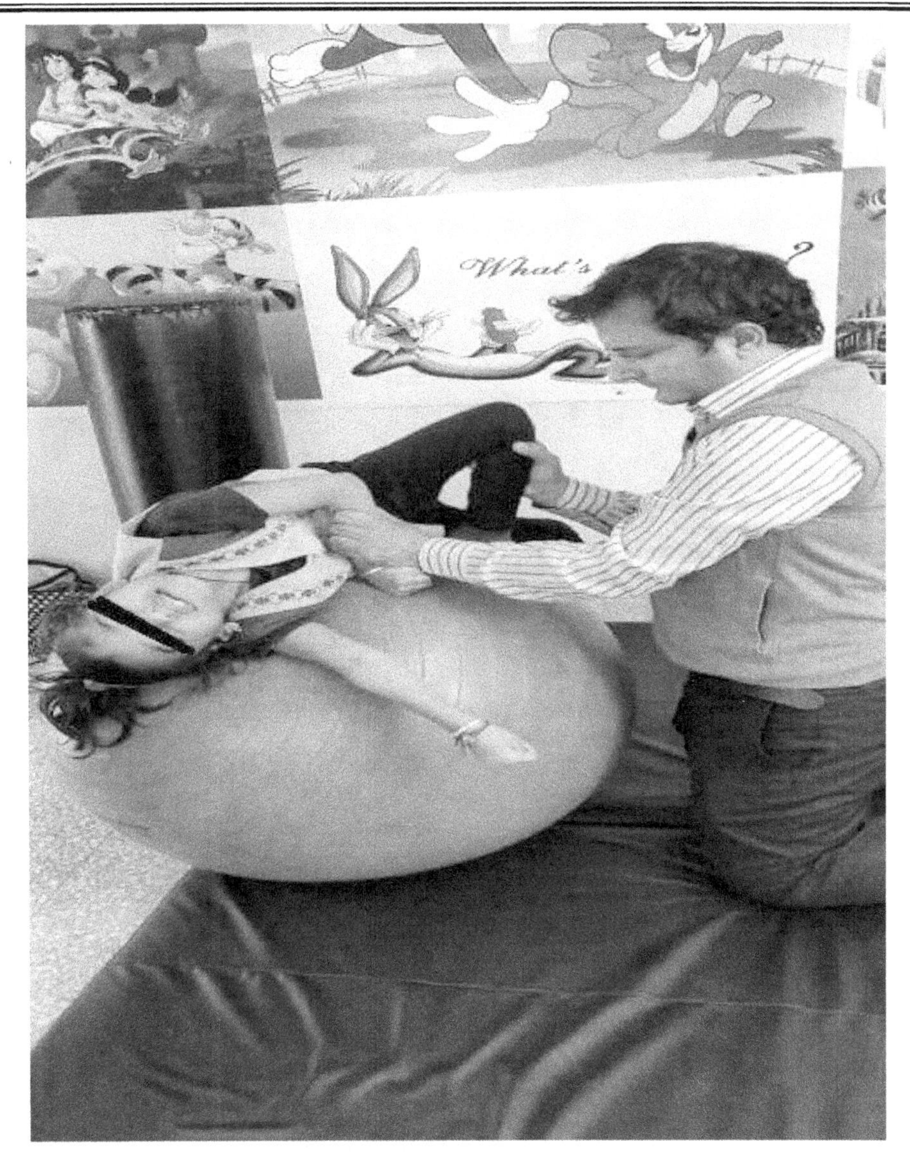

Head and trunk control on vestibular ball

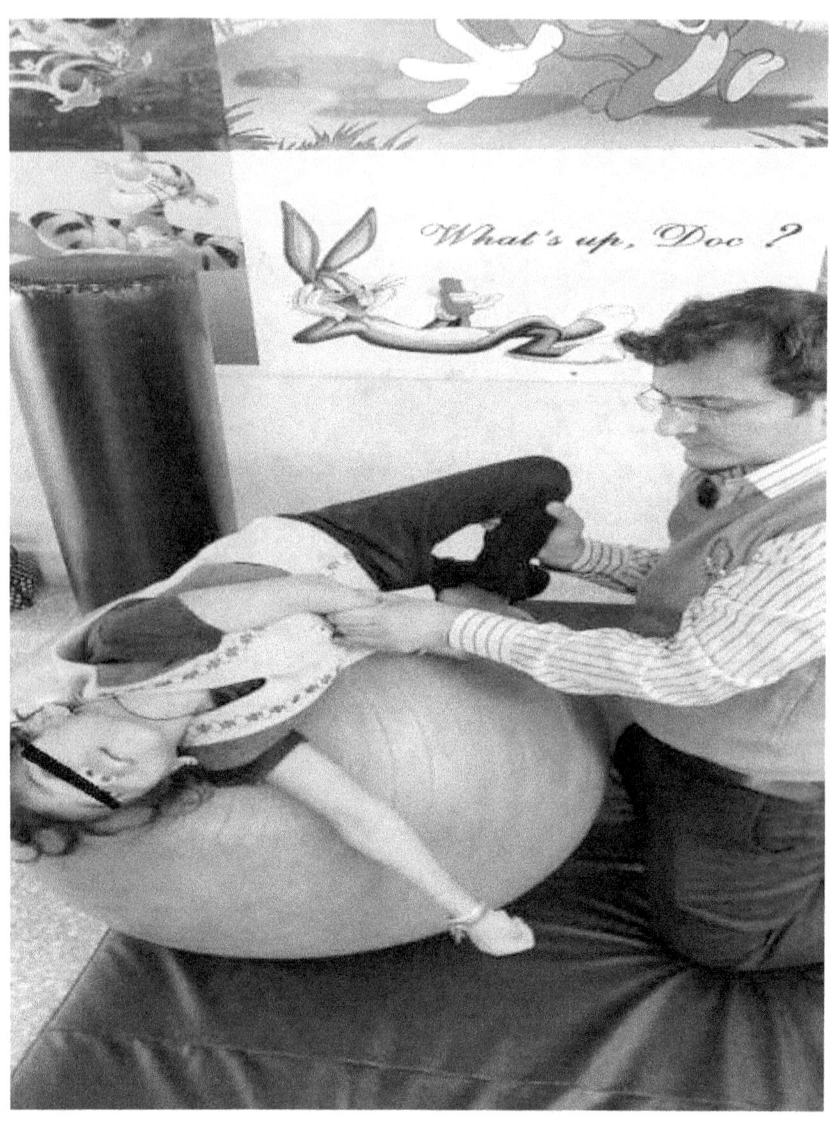

Head and trunk control on vestibular ball

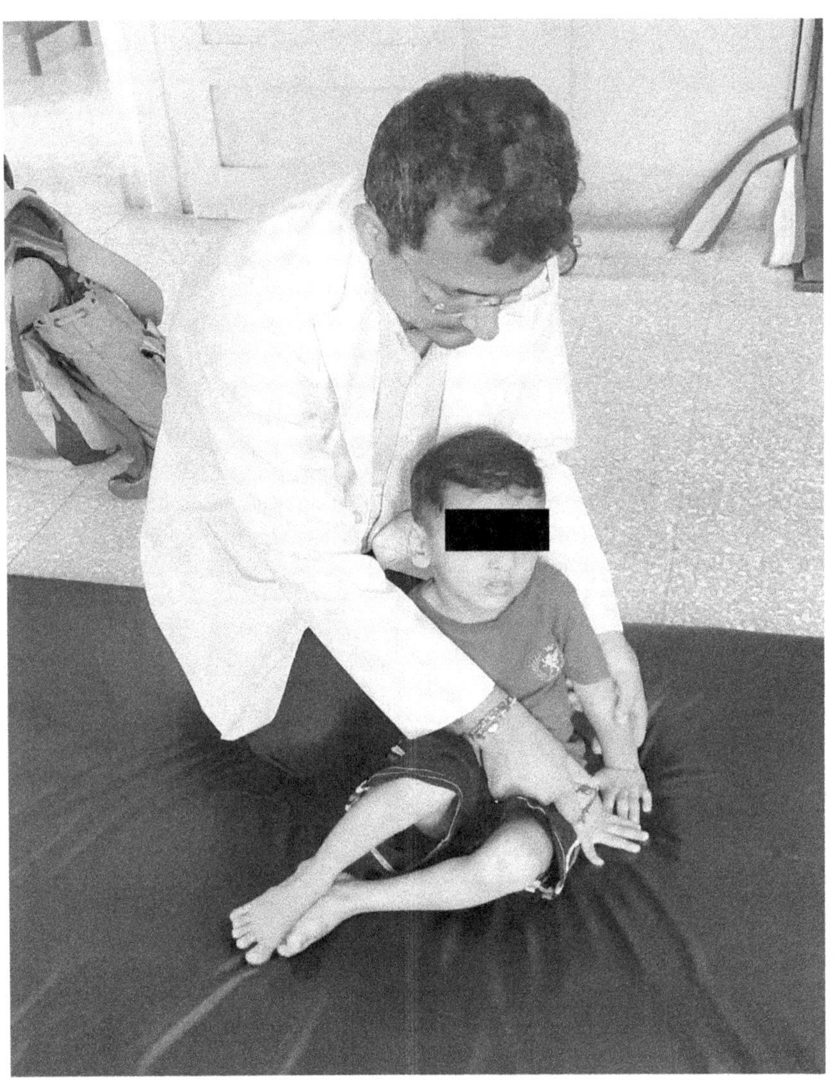

Side sitting with weight bearing on left side

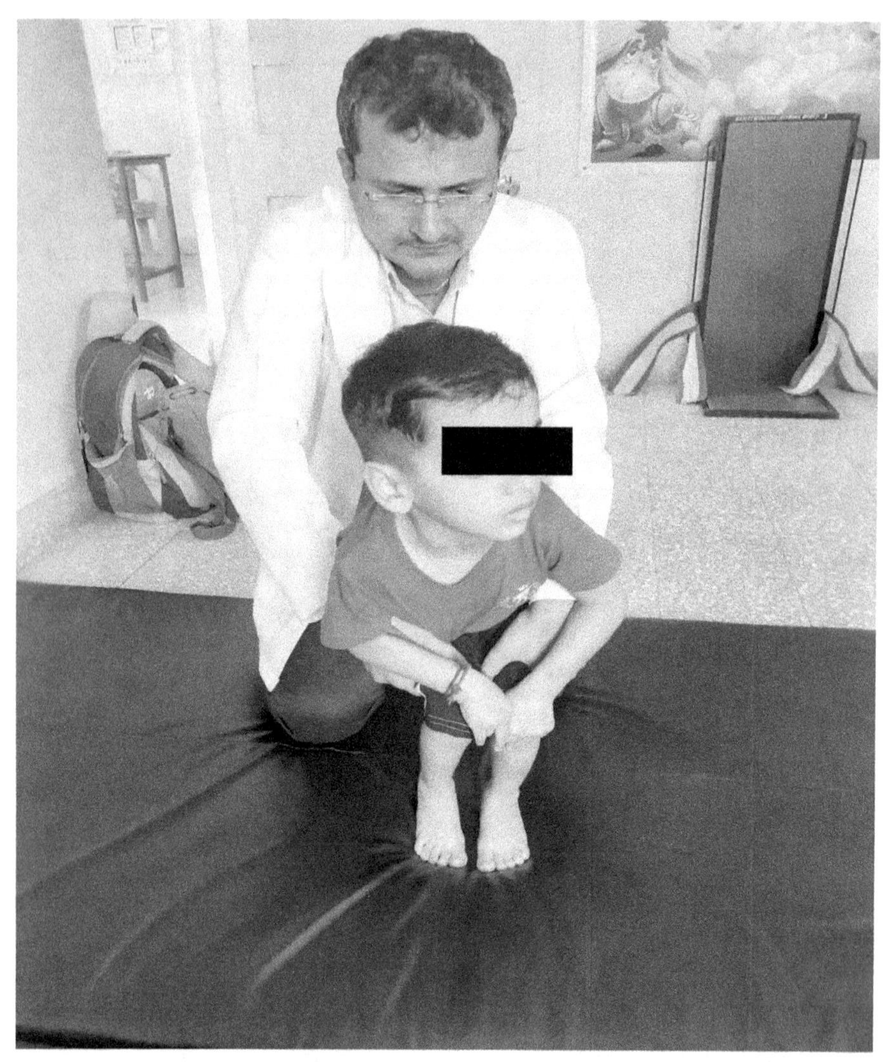

Squatting to improve trunk control

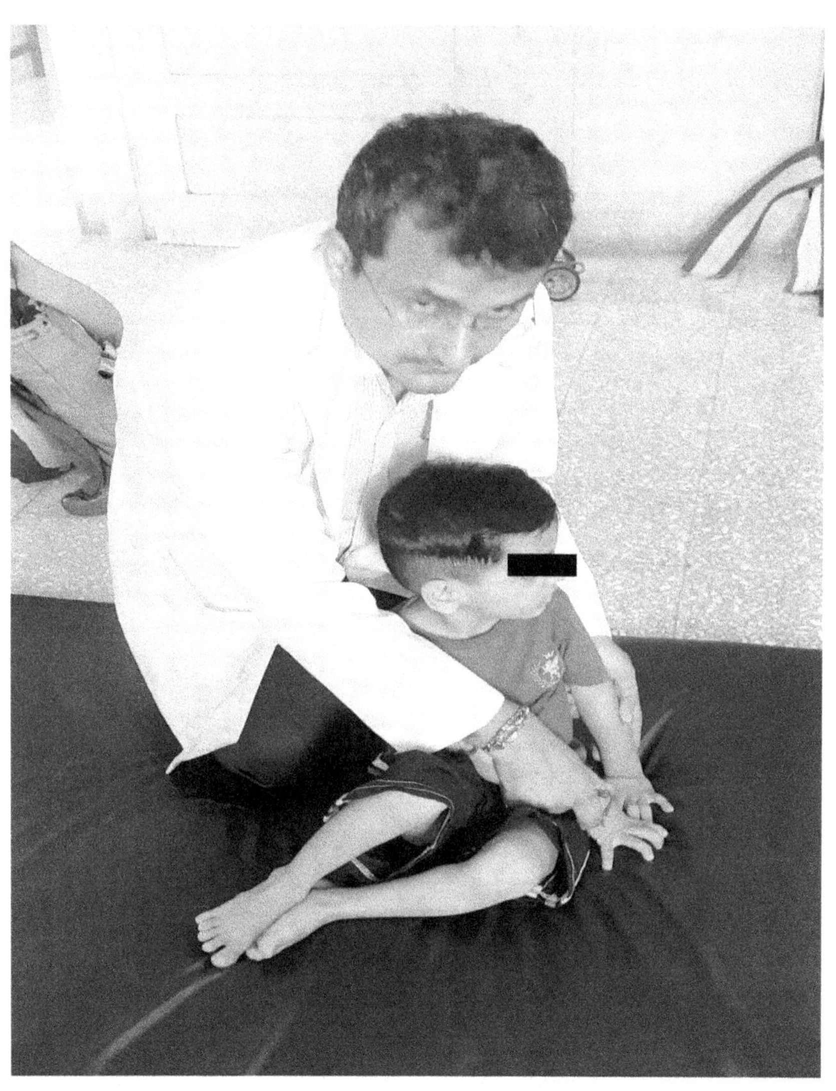

Side sitting with weight bearing to improve trunk control

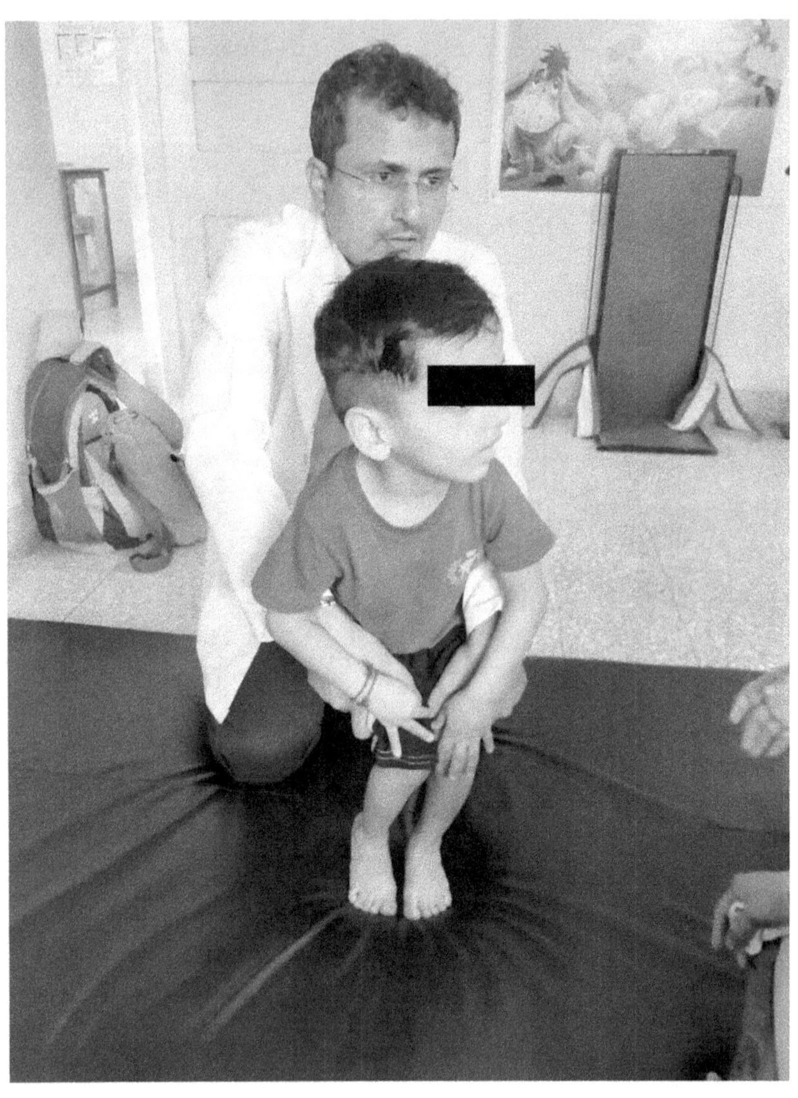

Squatting

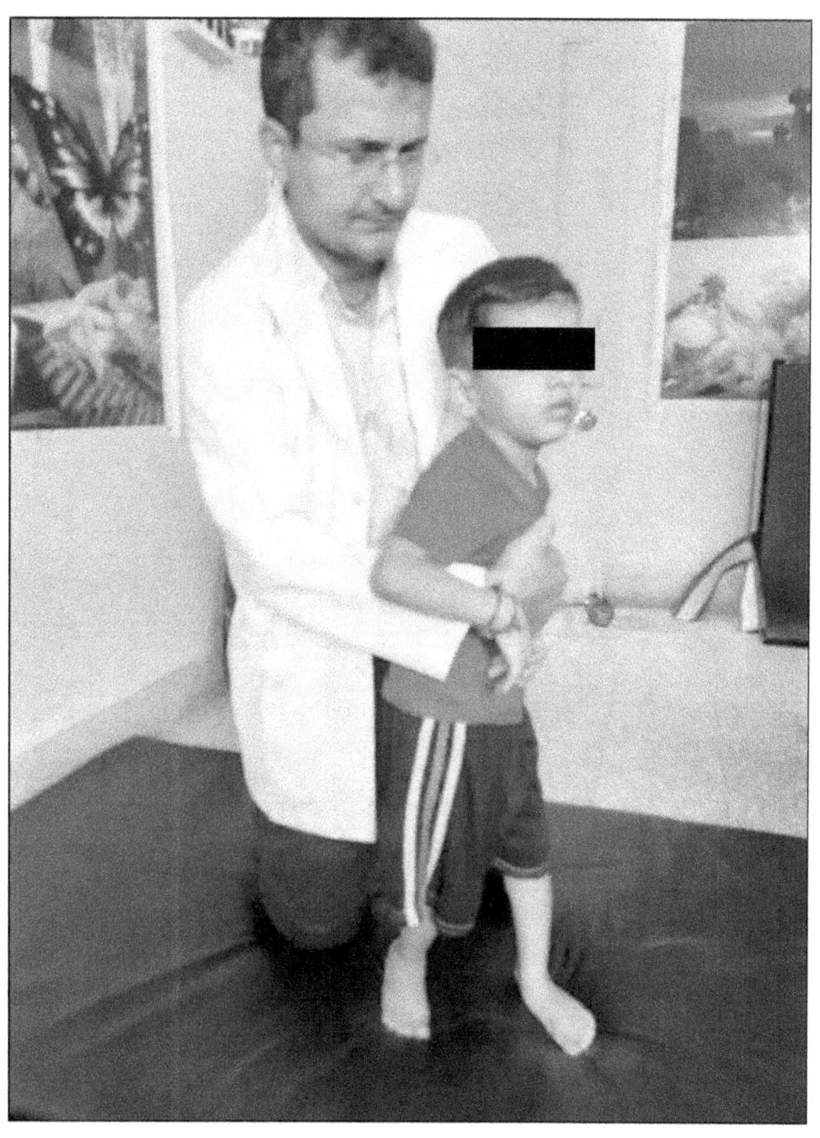

SIDE TRUNK FACILITATION

WEIGHT SHIFTING ON RIGHT LEG

SQUATTING

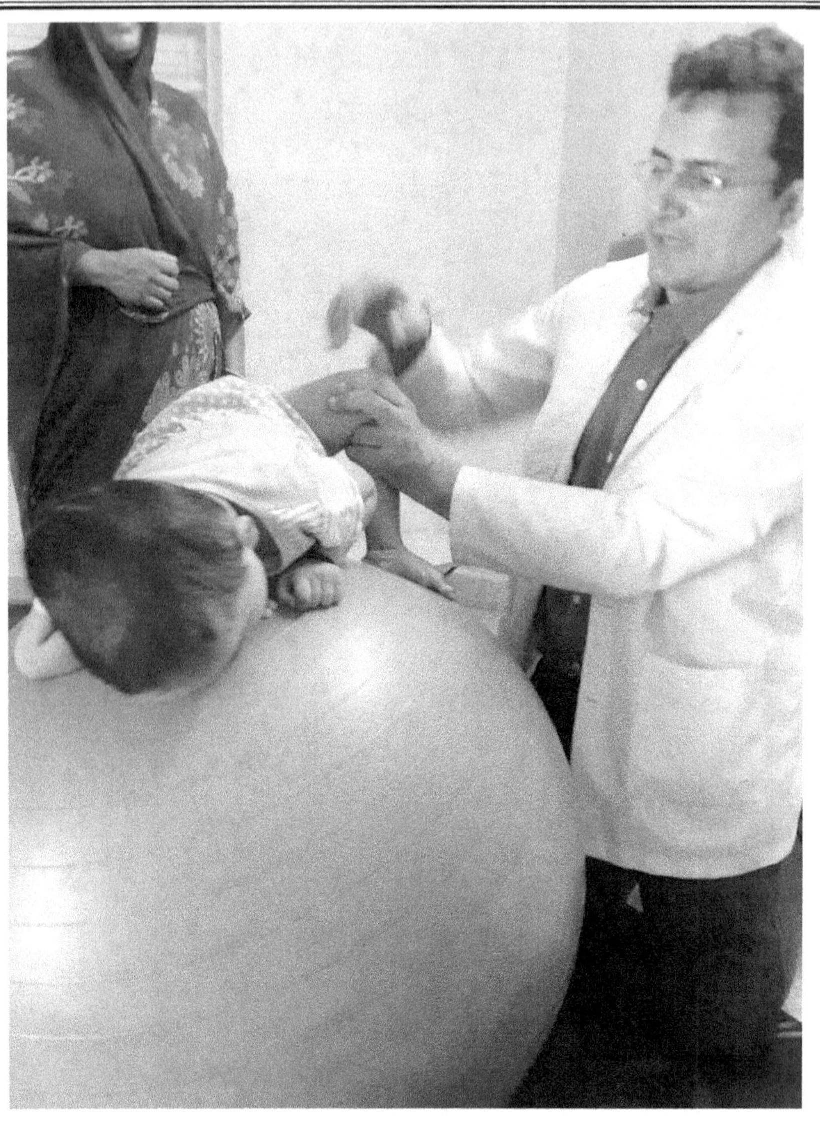

TRUNK FACILITATION ON PHYSIO BALL

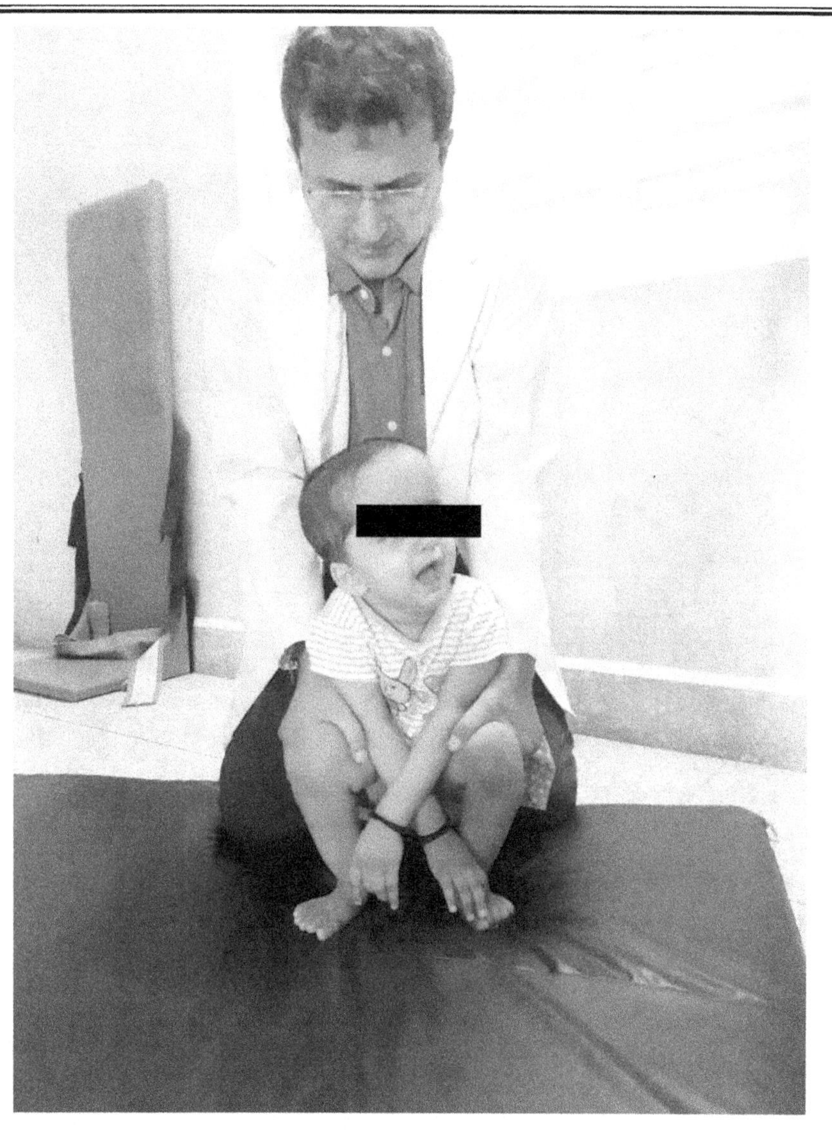

SQUATTING

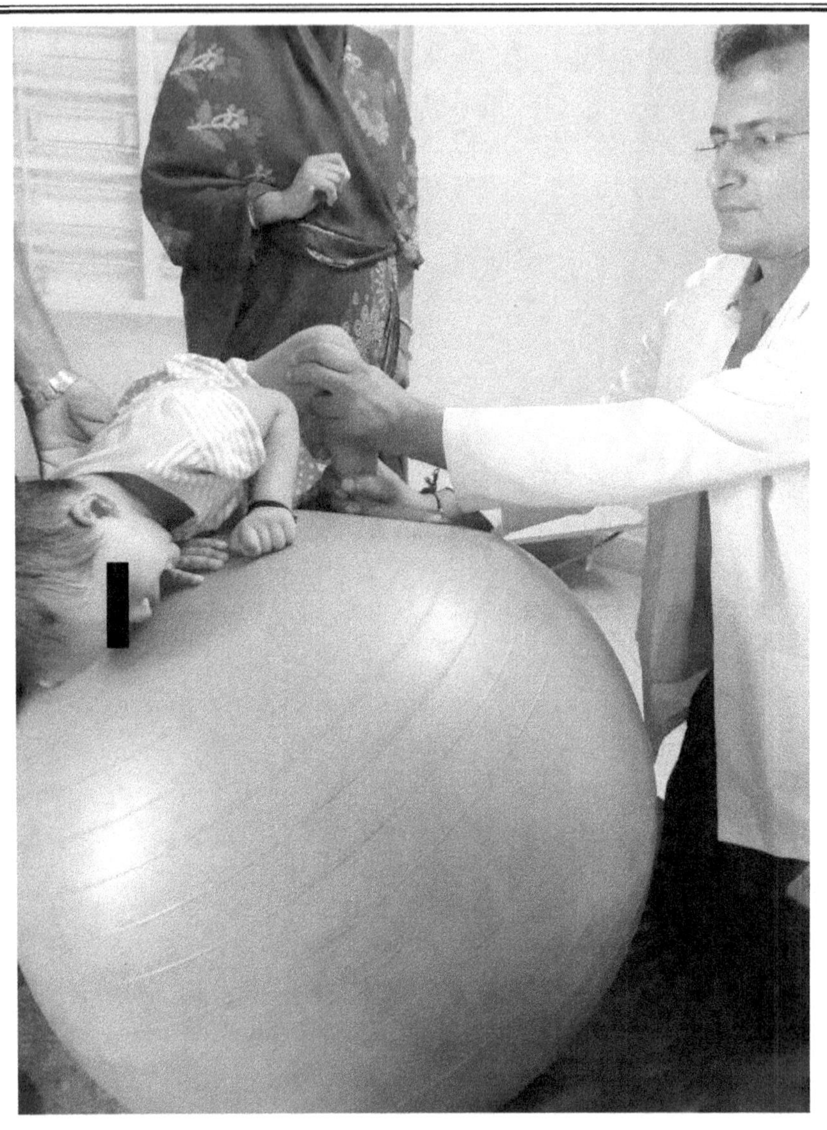

TRUNK FACILITATION ON ALONG WITH HEAD CONTROL

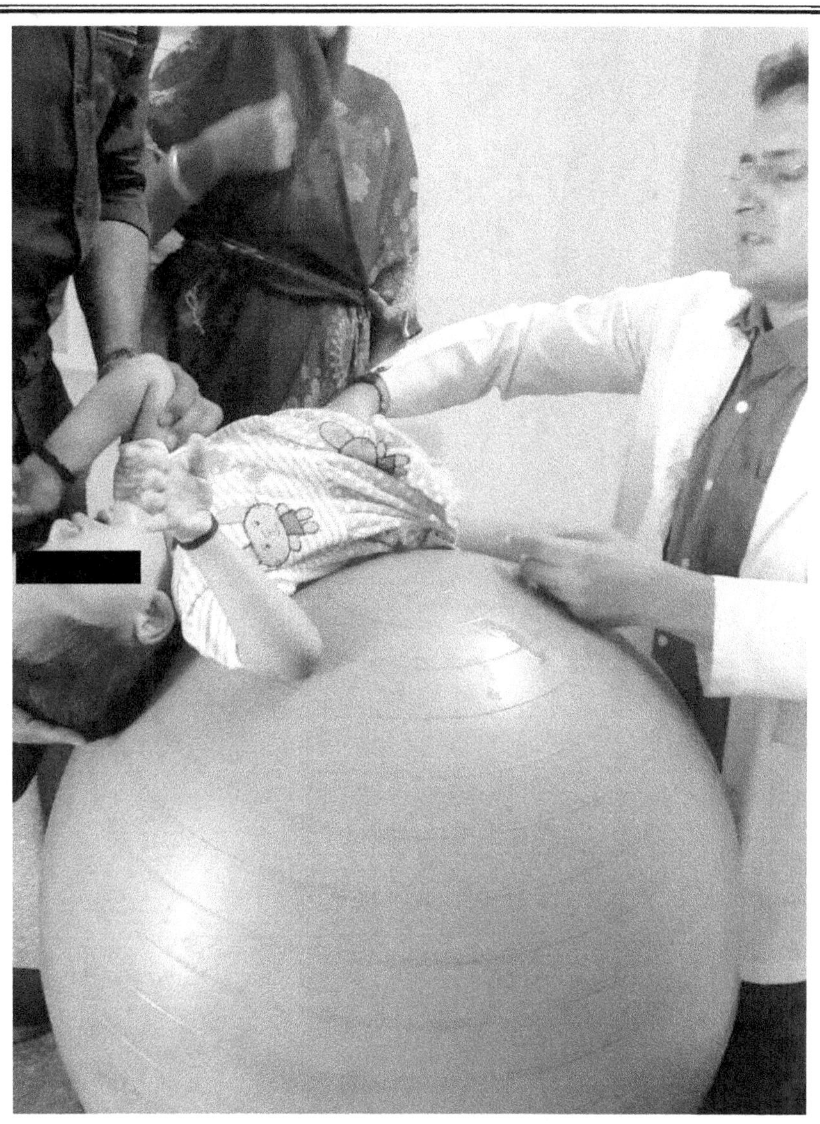

TRUNK FACILITATION ON PHYSIO BALL

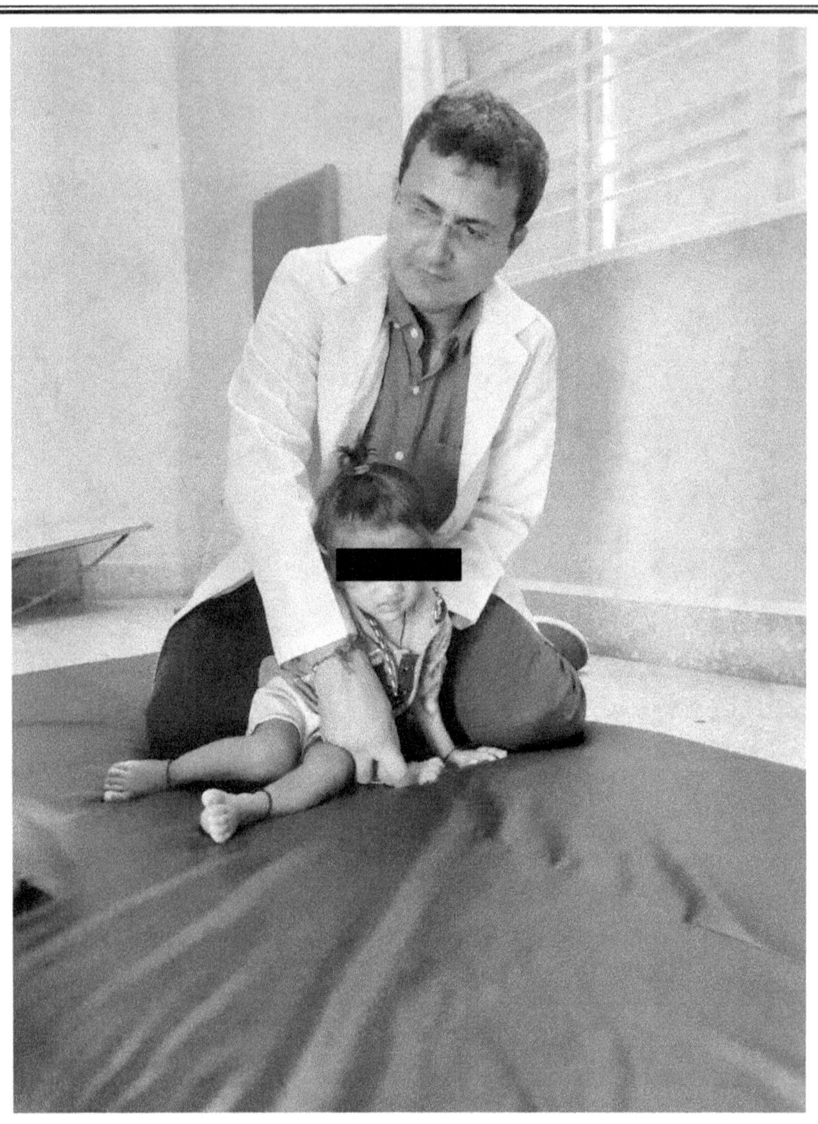

SIDE SITTING WITH TRUNK FACILITATION

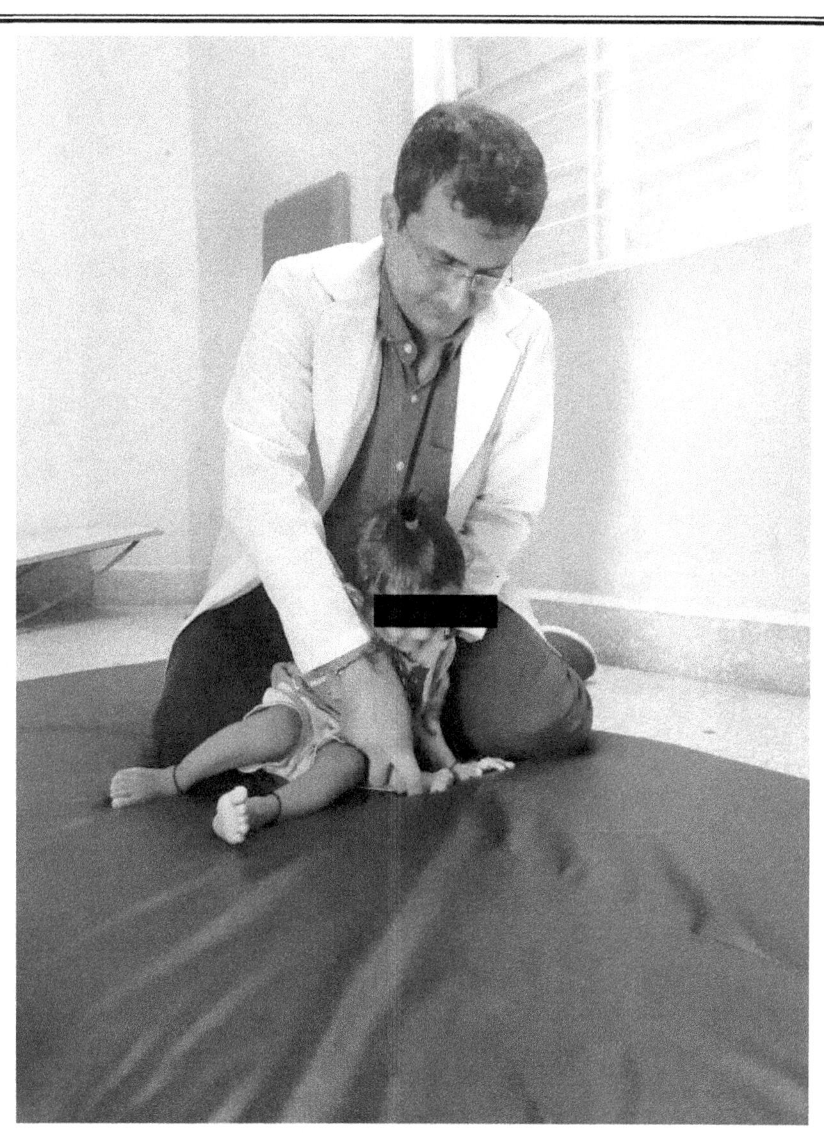

TRUNK FACILITATION TECHNIQUE

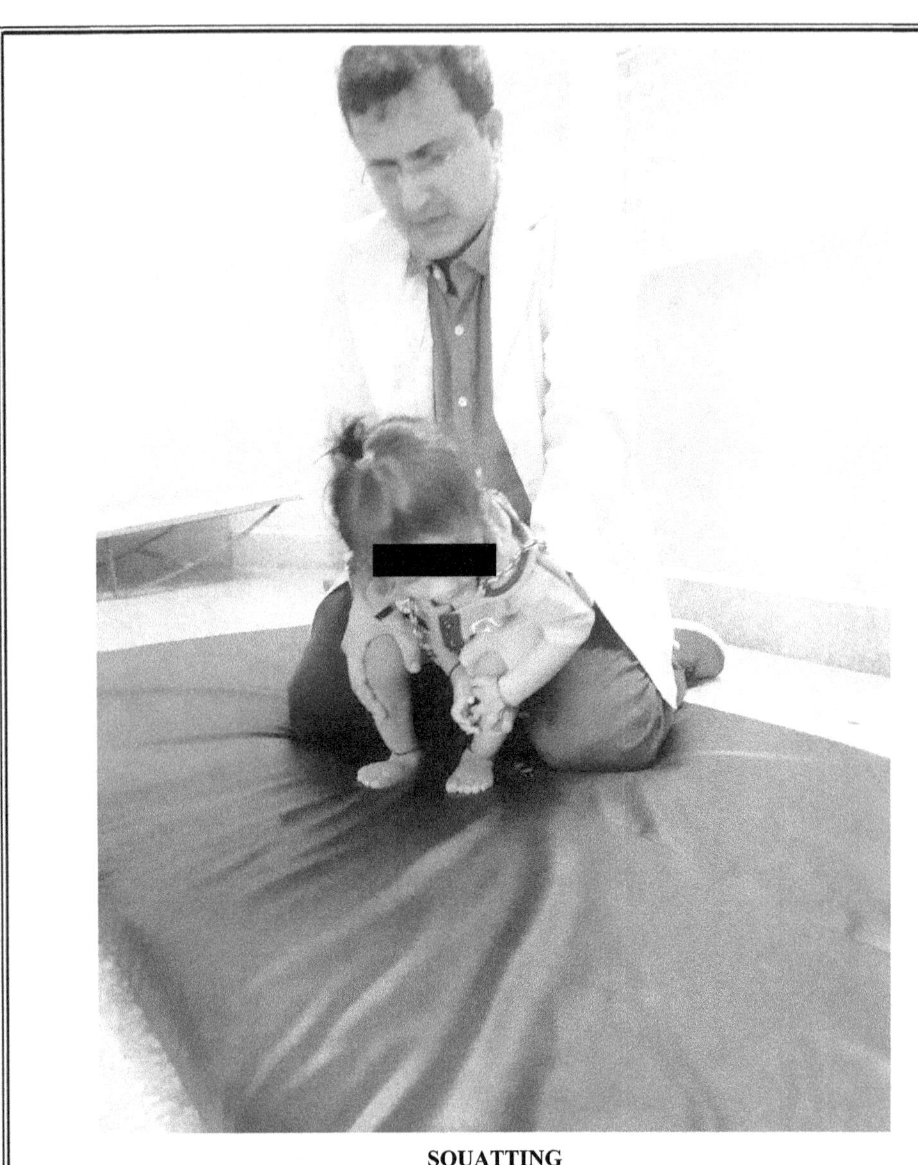

SQUATTING

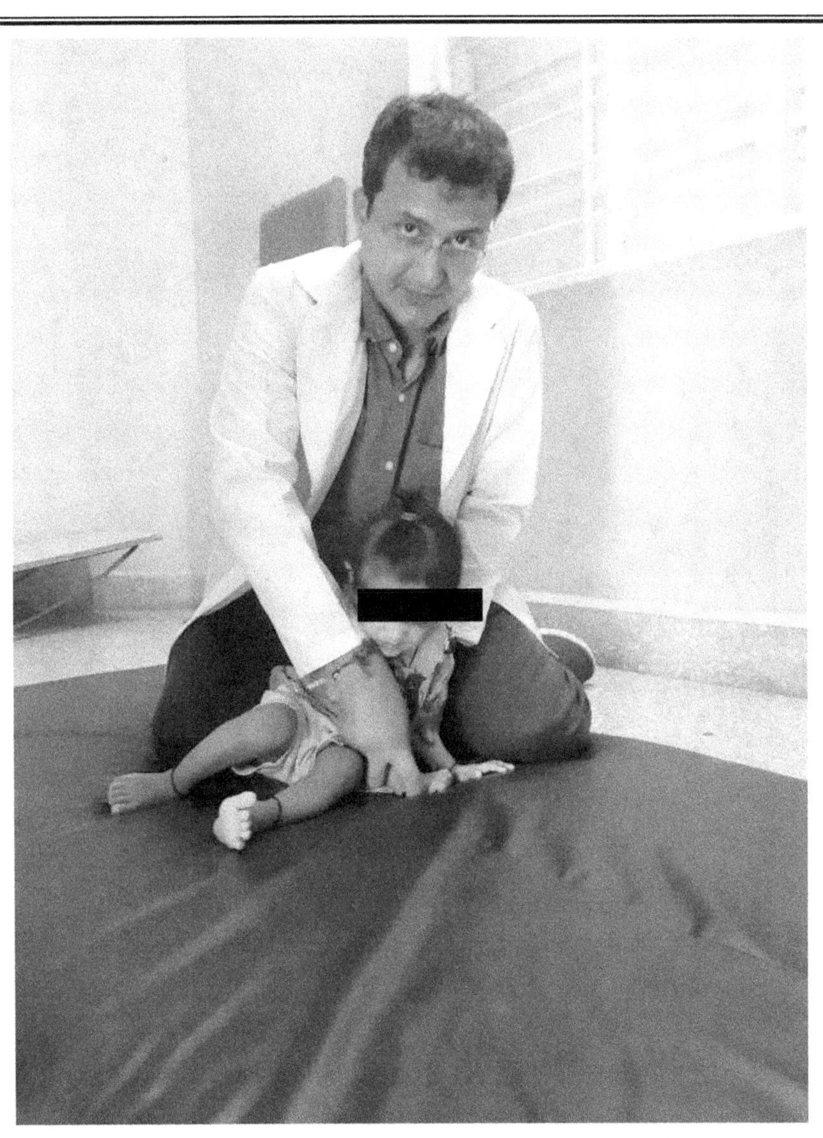

SIDE SITTING WITH WEIGHT BEARING ON LEFT SIDE

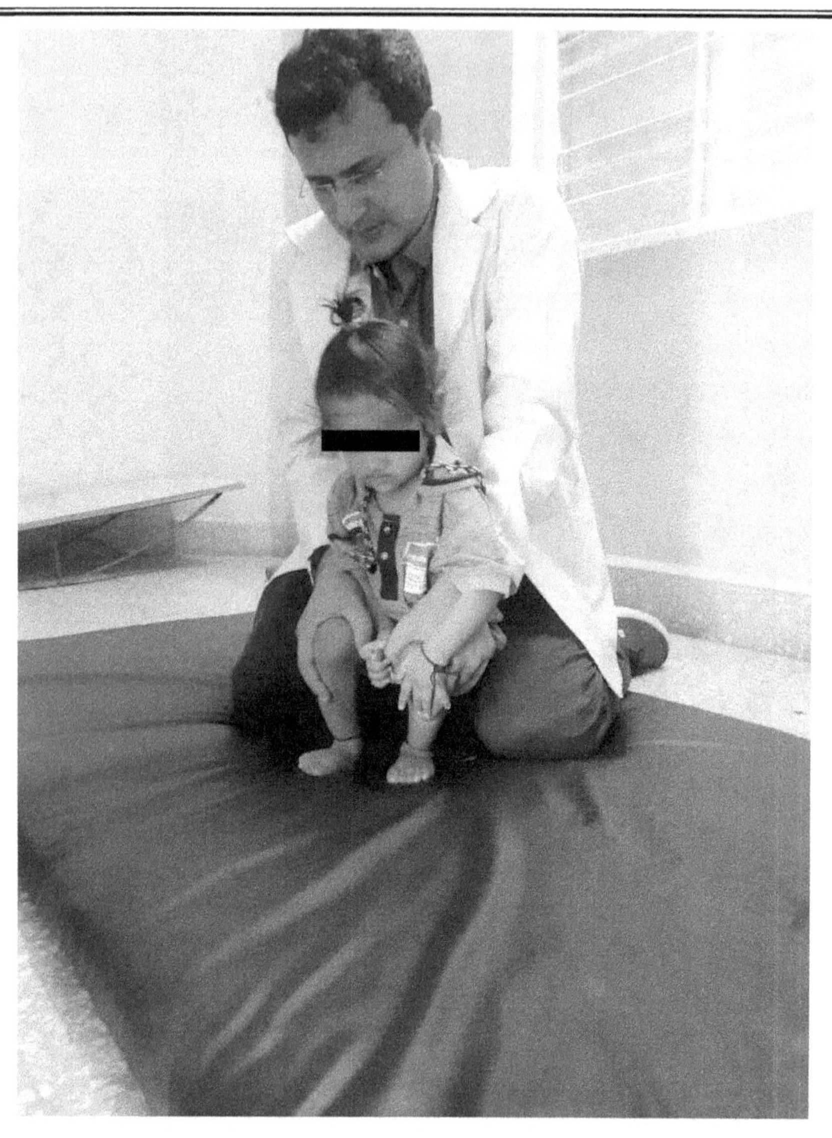

HEAD AND TRUNK CONTROL ON VESTIBULAR BALL

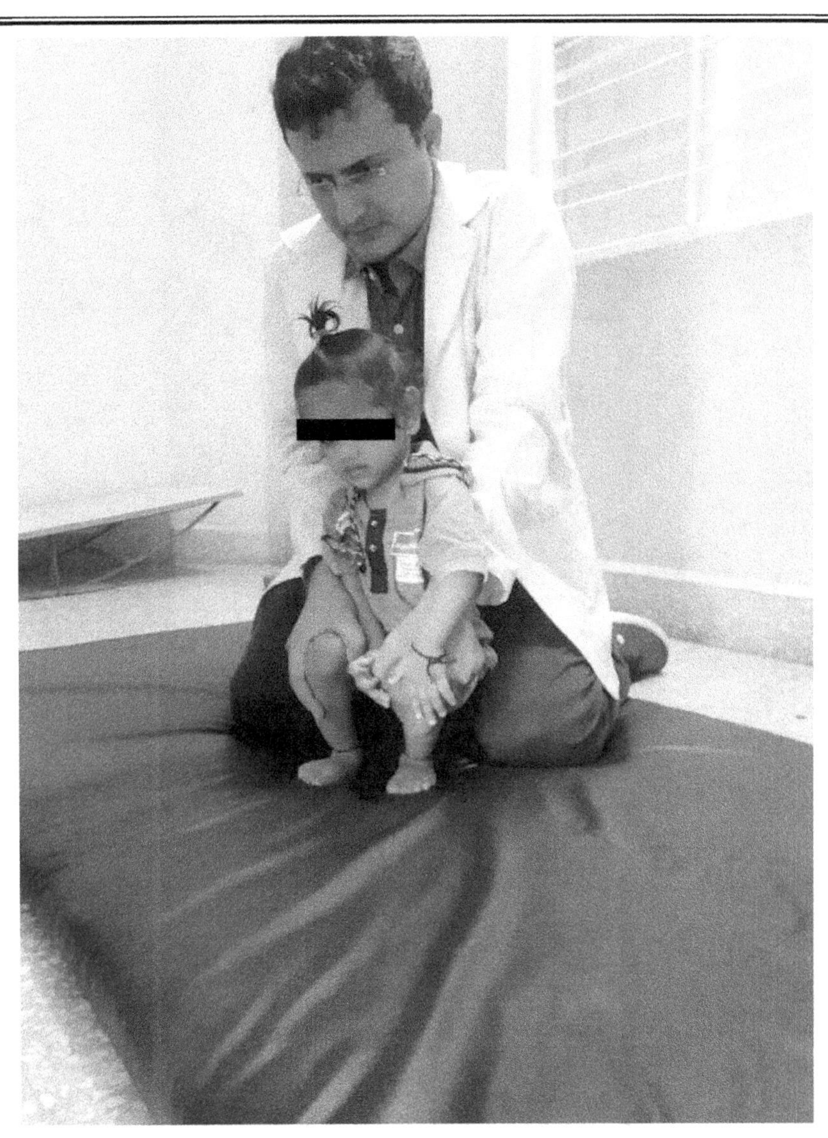

SQUATTING WITH HEAD CONTROL TRAINING

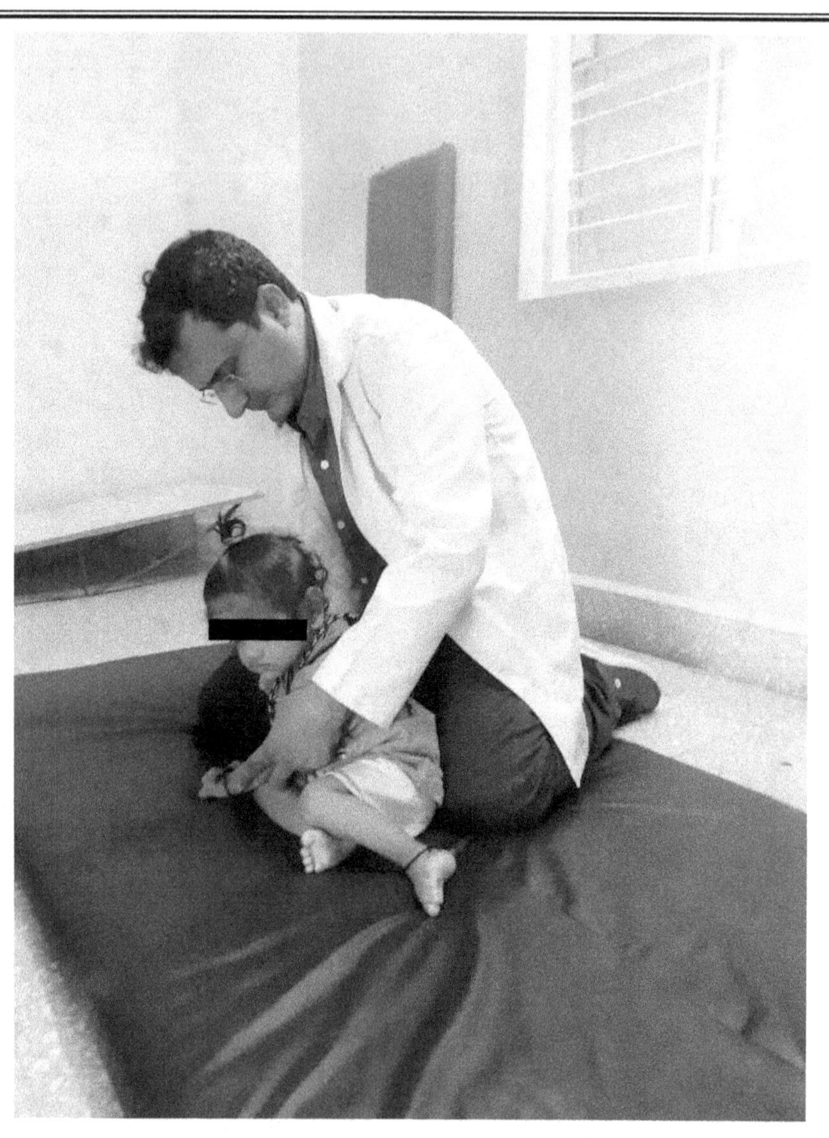

SIDE SITTING WITH WEIGHT BEARING

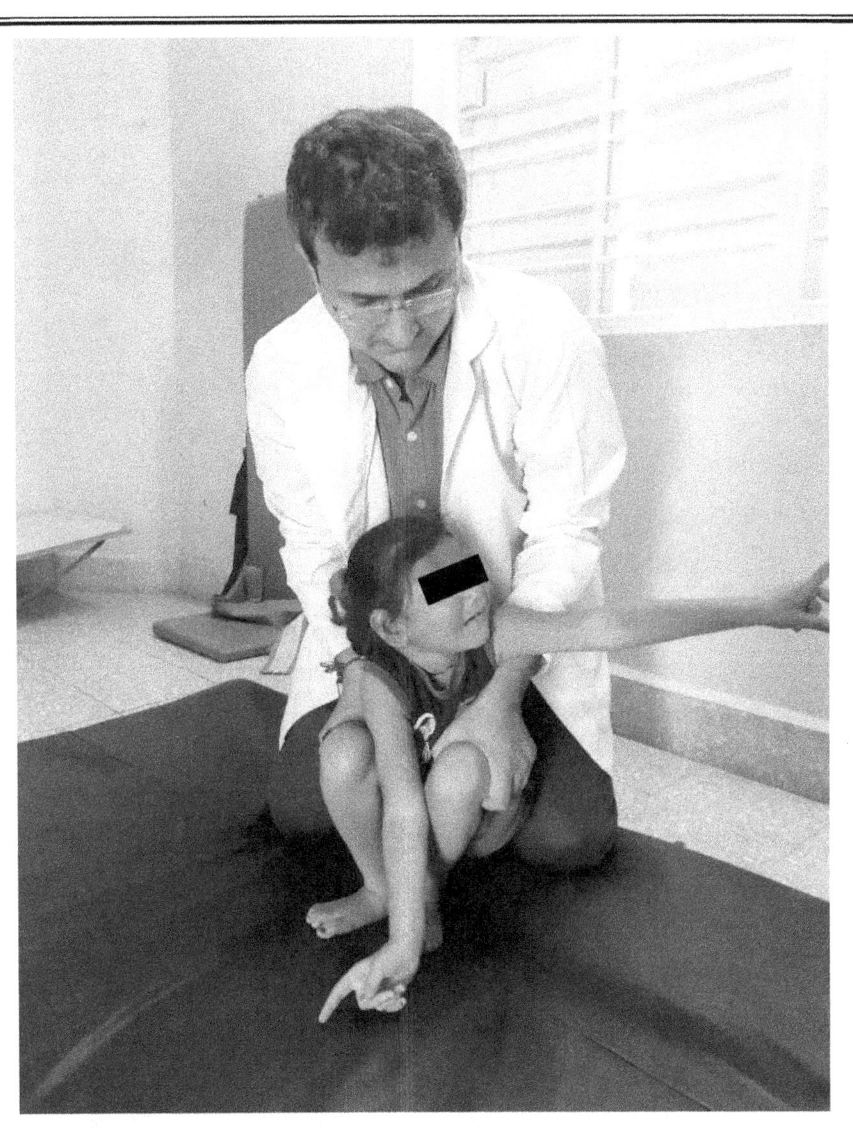

SQUATTING WITH TRUNK CONTROL

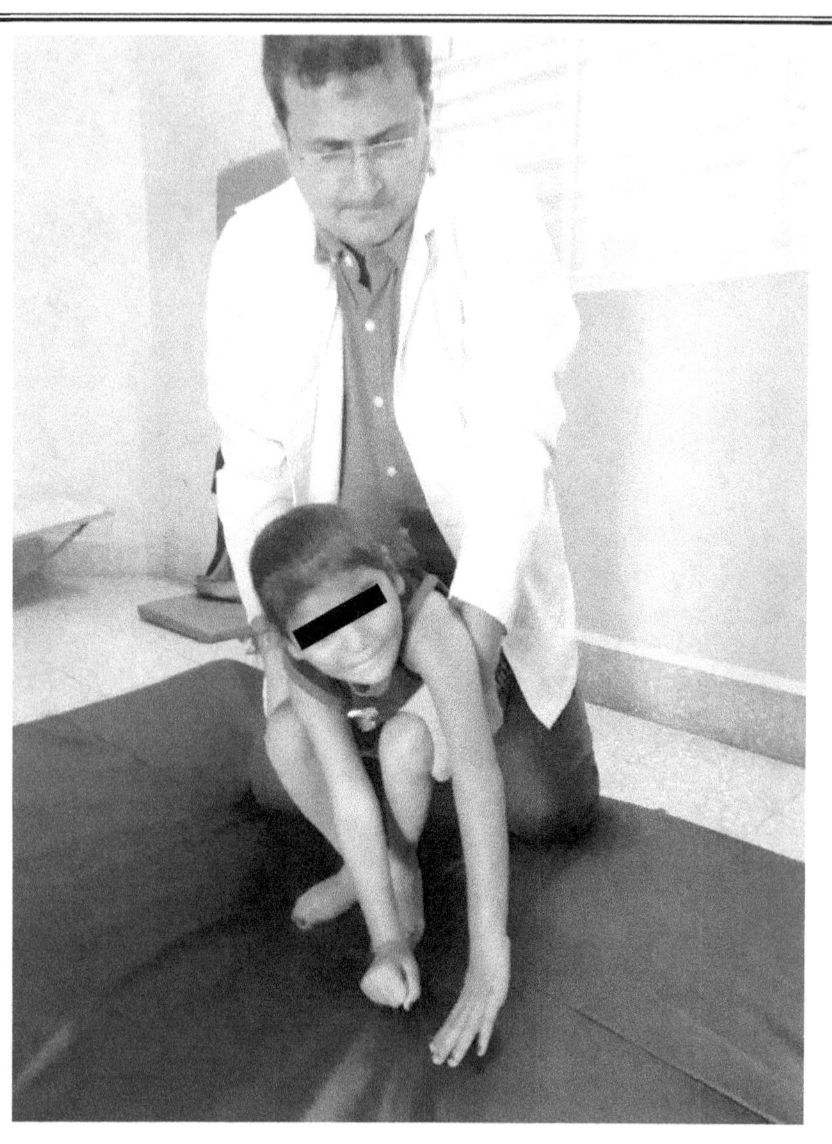

SQUATTING

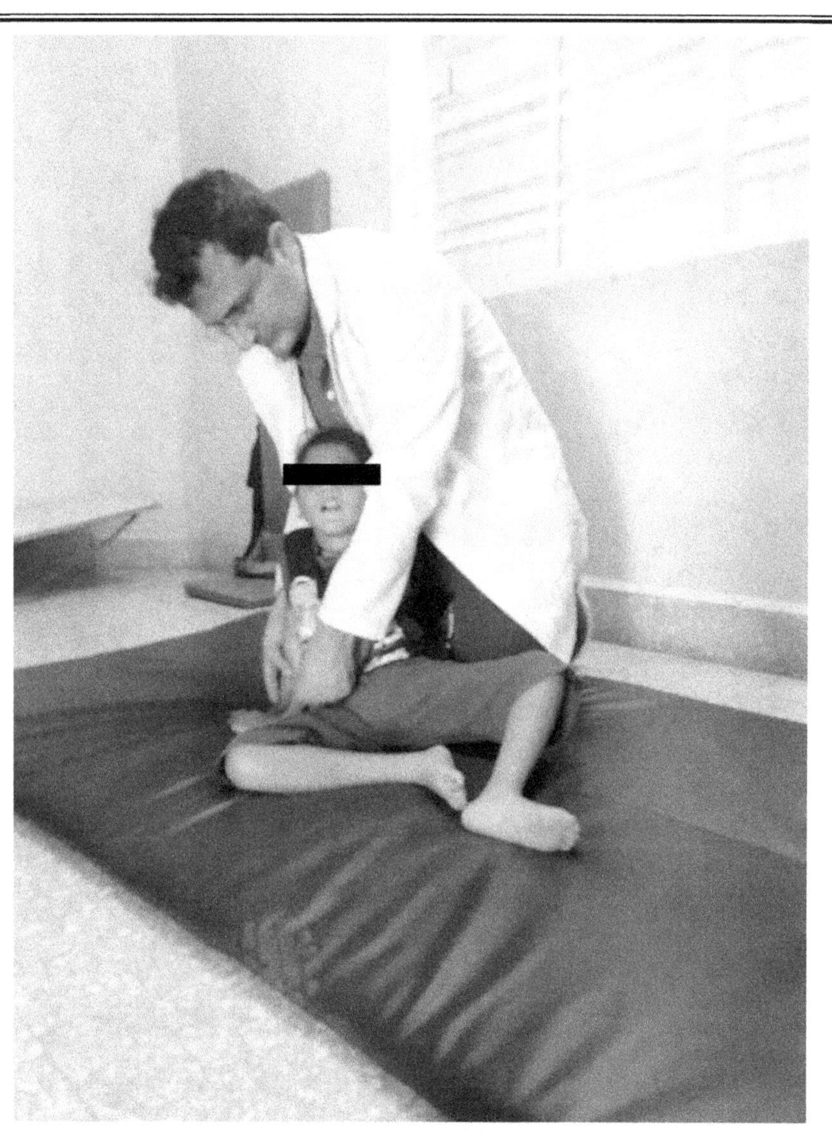

WEIGHT SHIFTING WITH TRUNK FACILITATION TRAINING

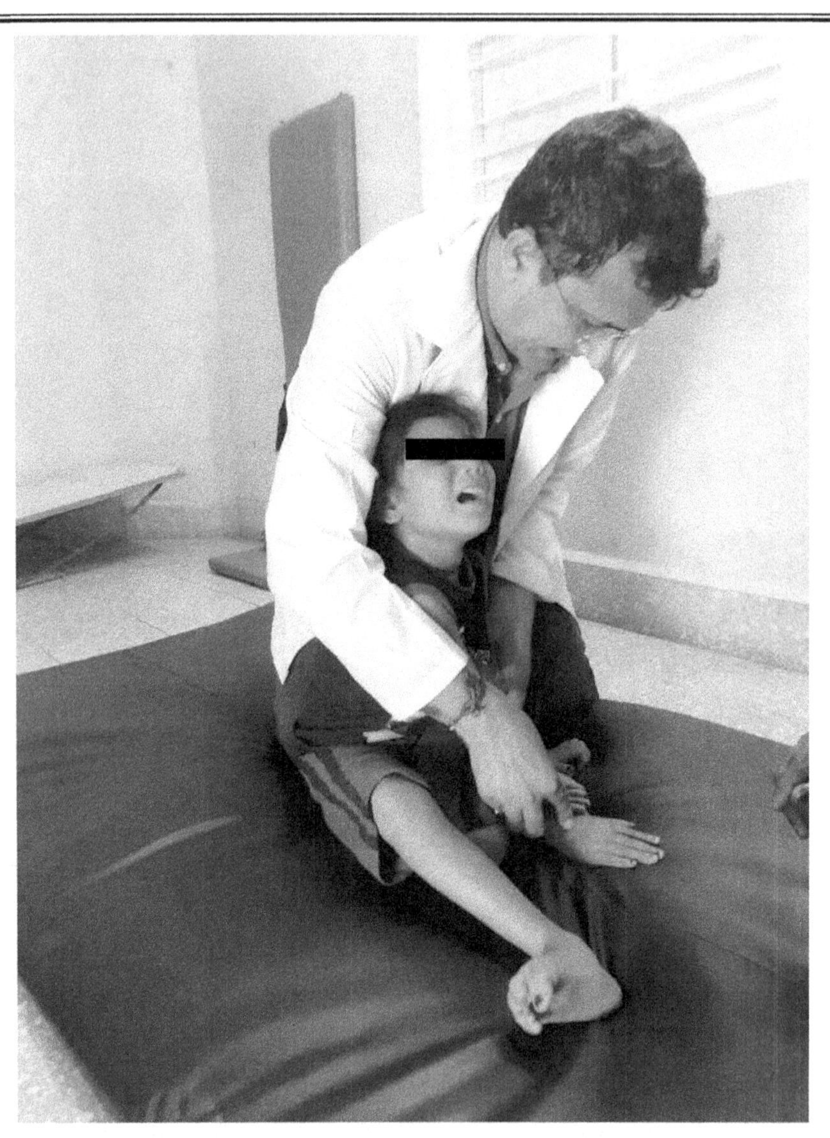

WEIGHT SHIFTING WITH HEAD AND TRUNK CONTROL

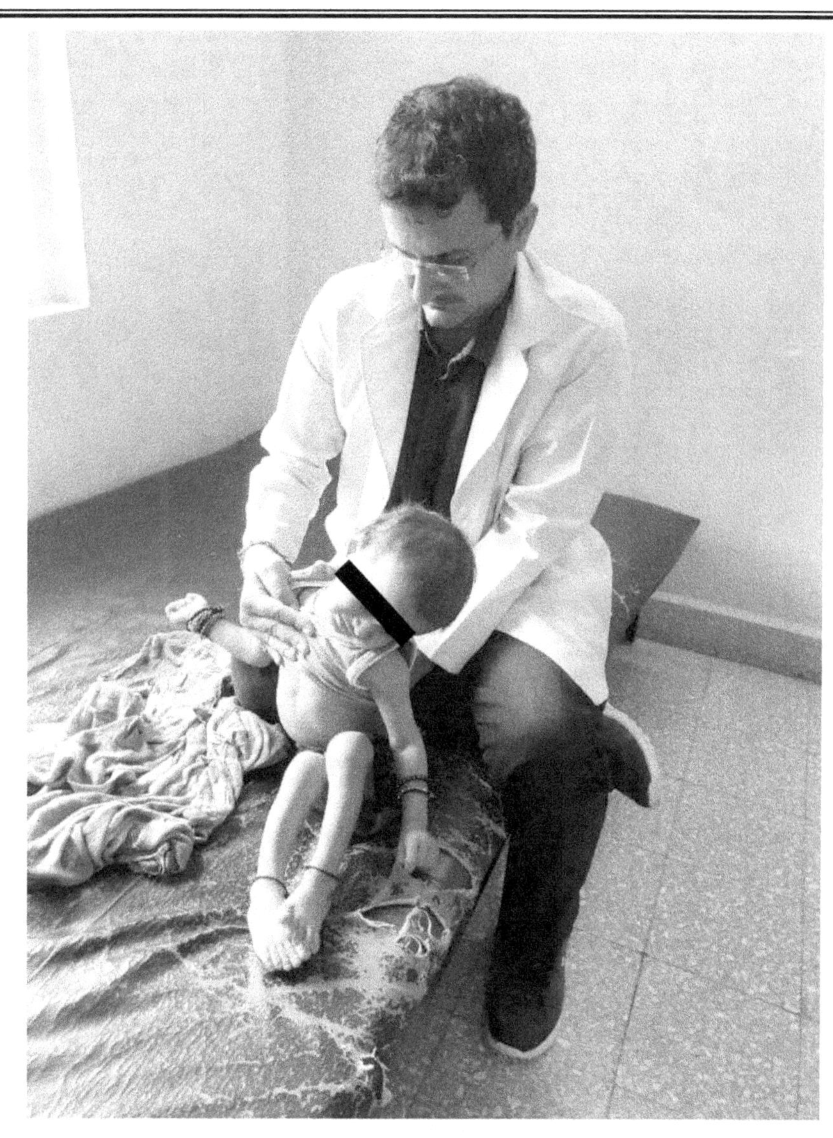

TRUNK CONTROL TRAINING

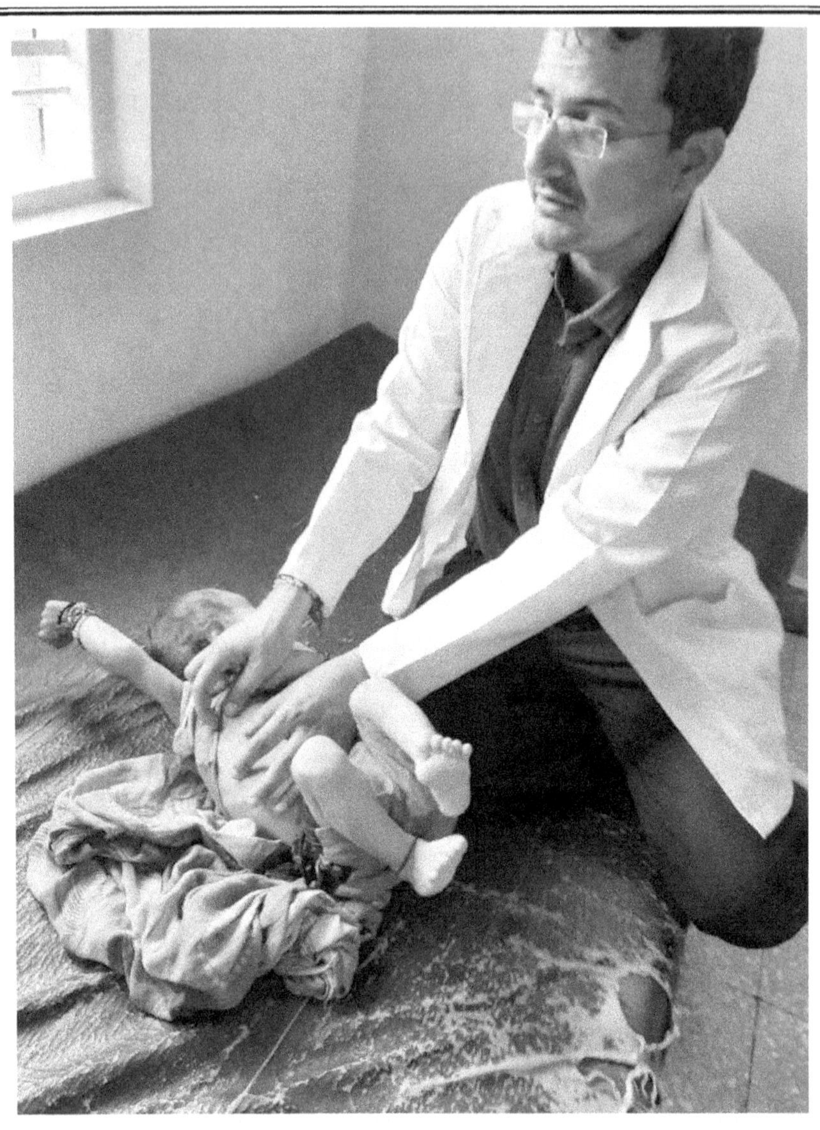

TRUNK SEGMENTAL TRAINING

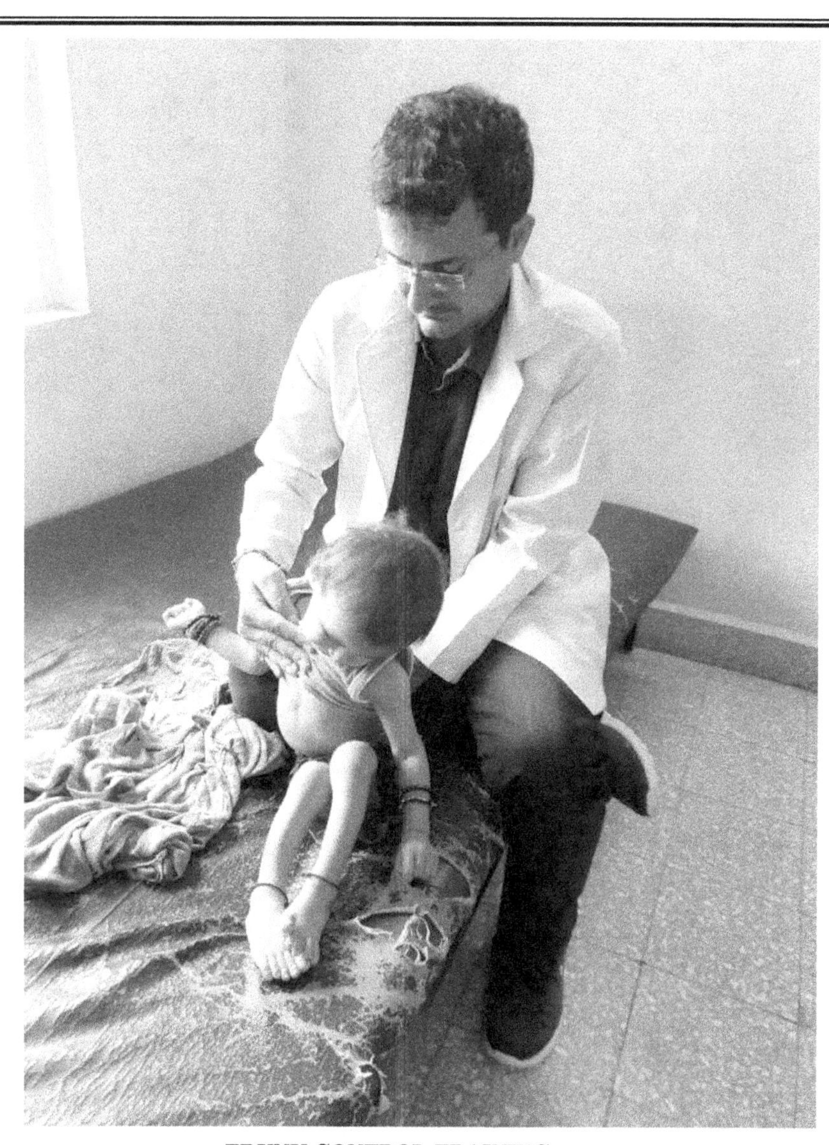

TRUNK CONTROL TRAINING

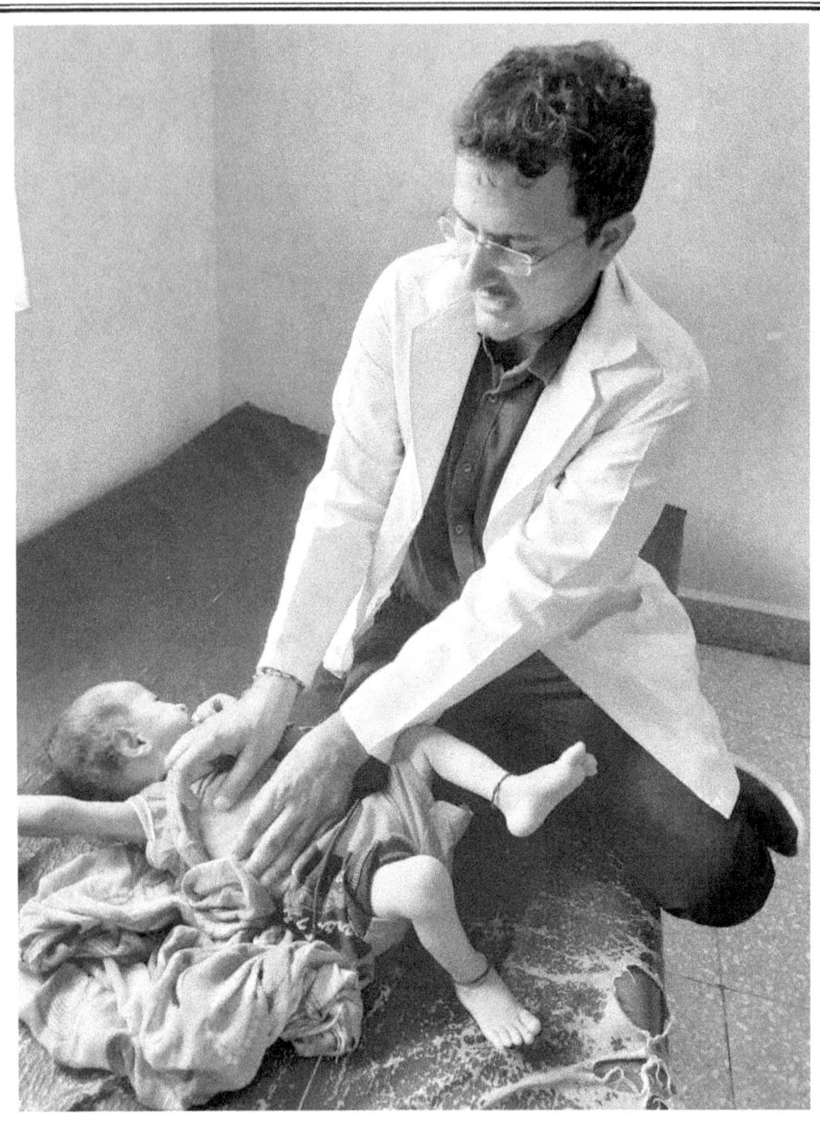

TRUNK SEGMENTAL TRAINING

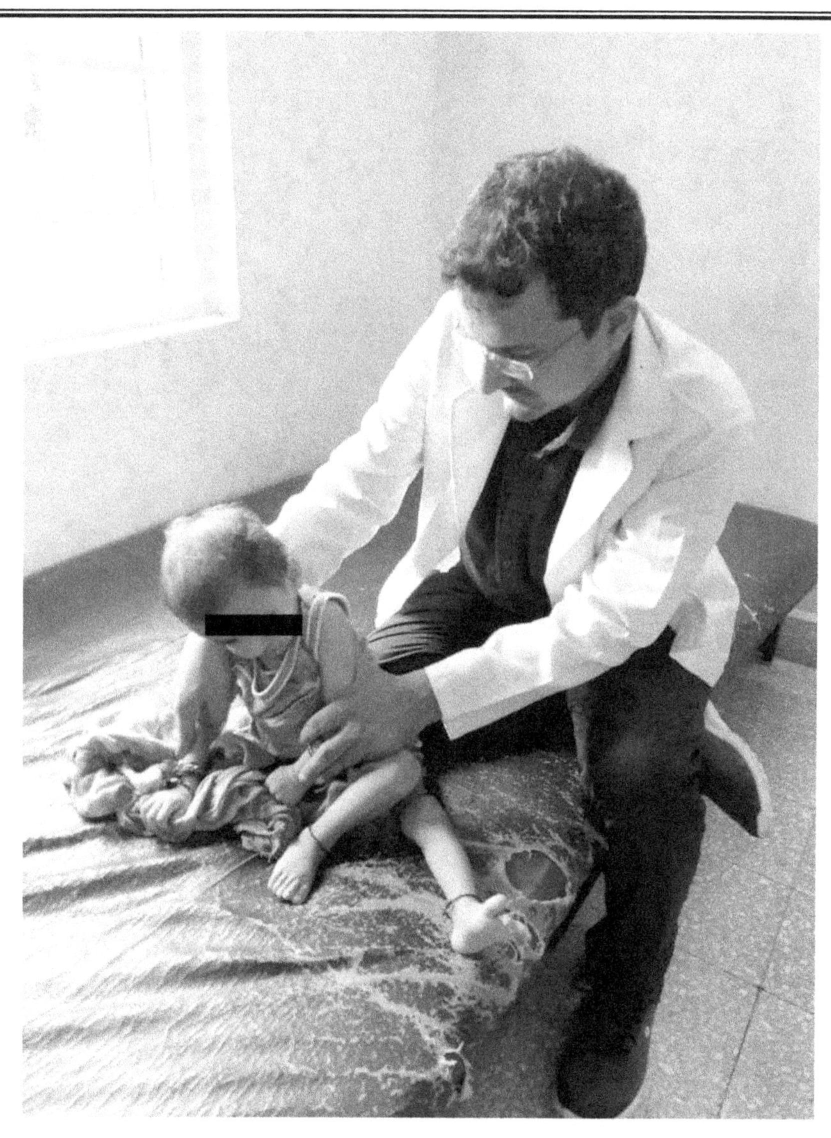

TRUNK CONTROL WITH WEIGHT SHIFTING ON RIGHT SIDE

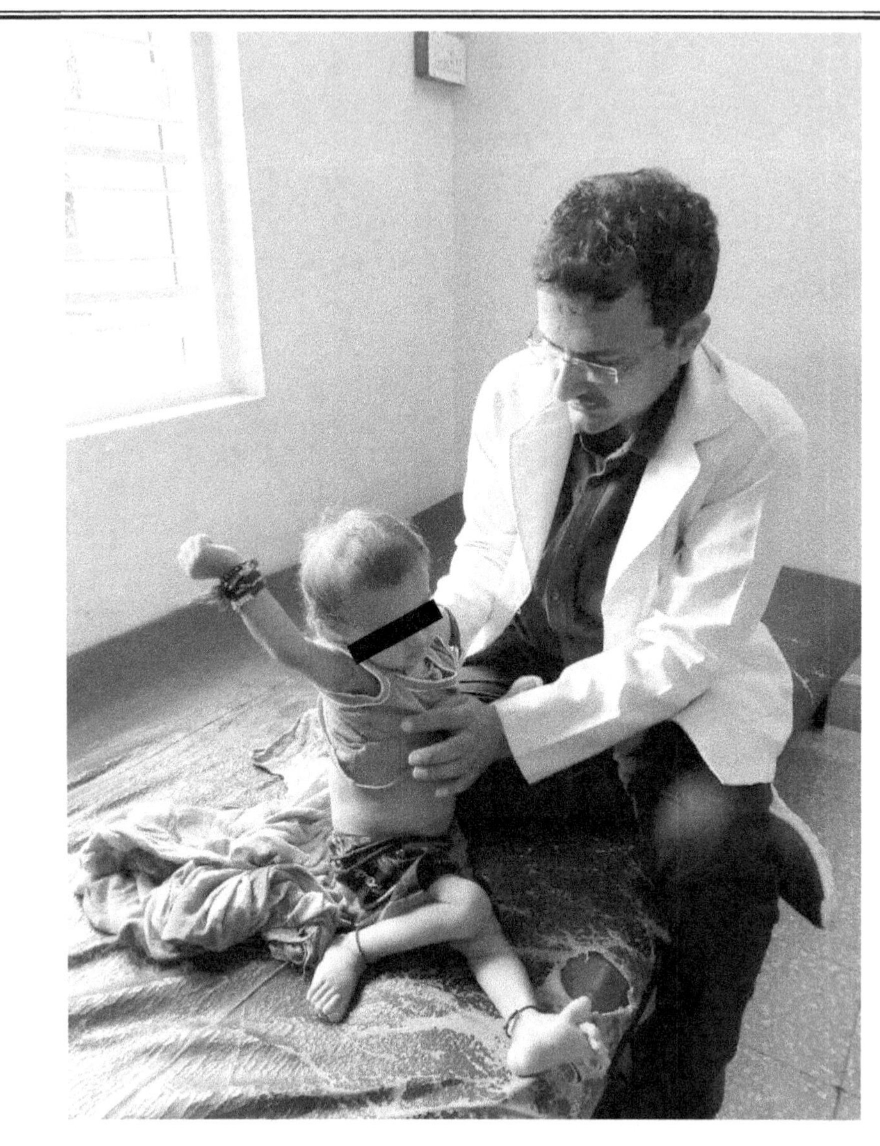

TRUNK AND HEAD CONTROL FACILITATION

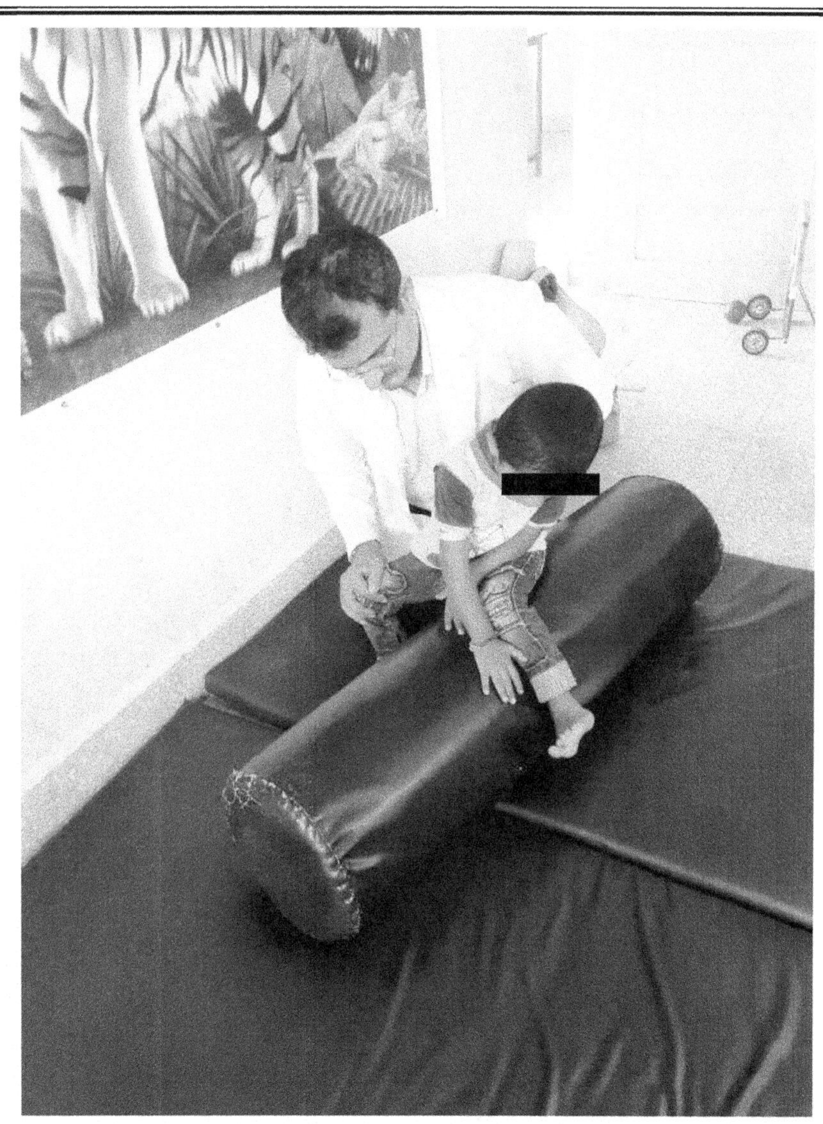

TRUNK FACILITATION WITH WEIGHT SHIFTING ON LEFT SIDE

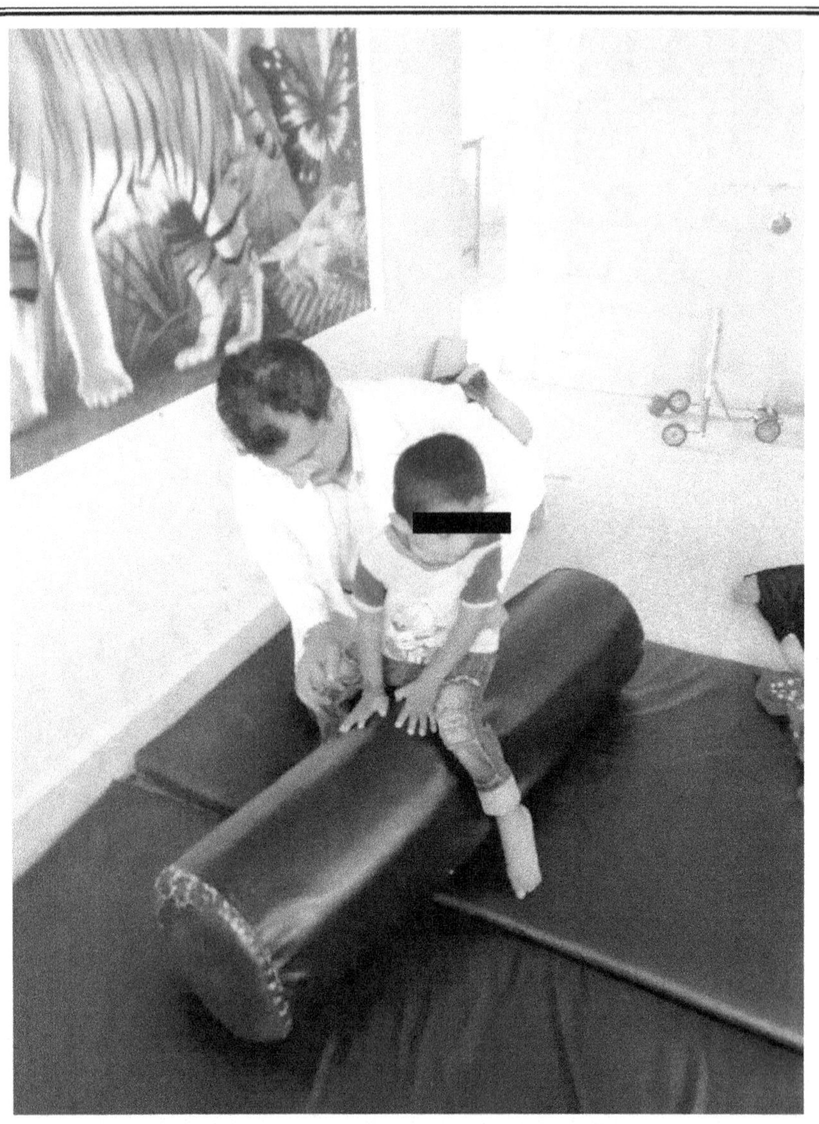

TRUNK FACILITATION ON BALLSTER

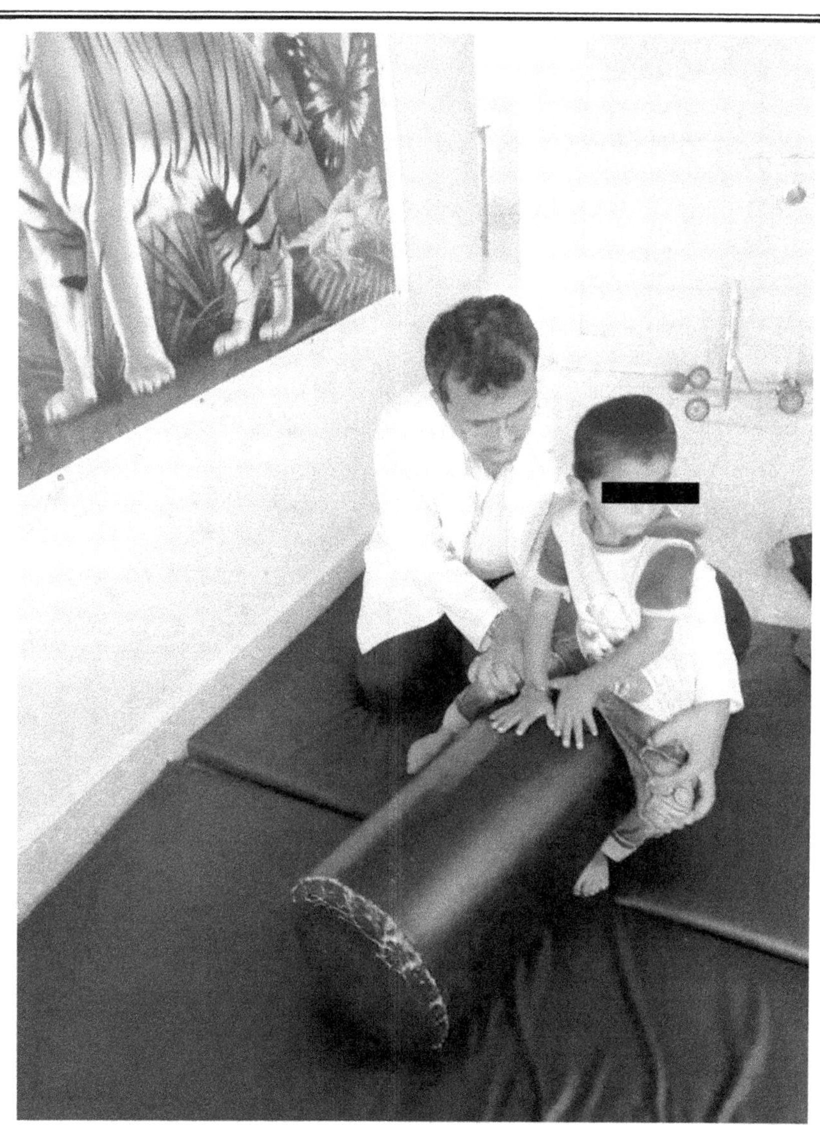

WEIGHT SHIFTING ON RIGHT SIDE

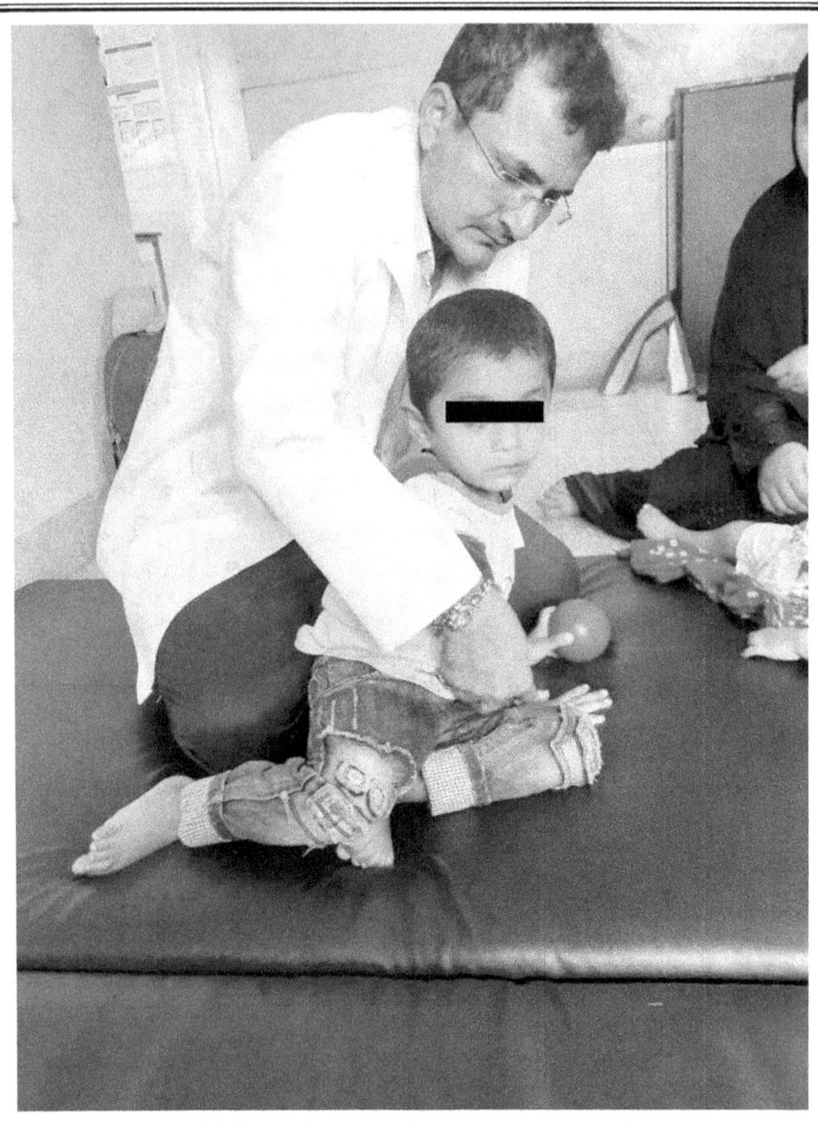

TRUNK FACILITATION WITH SIDE SITTING

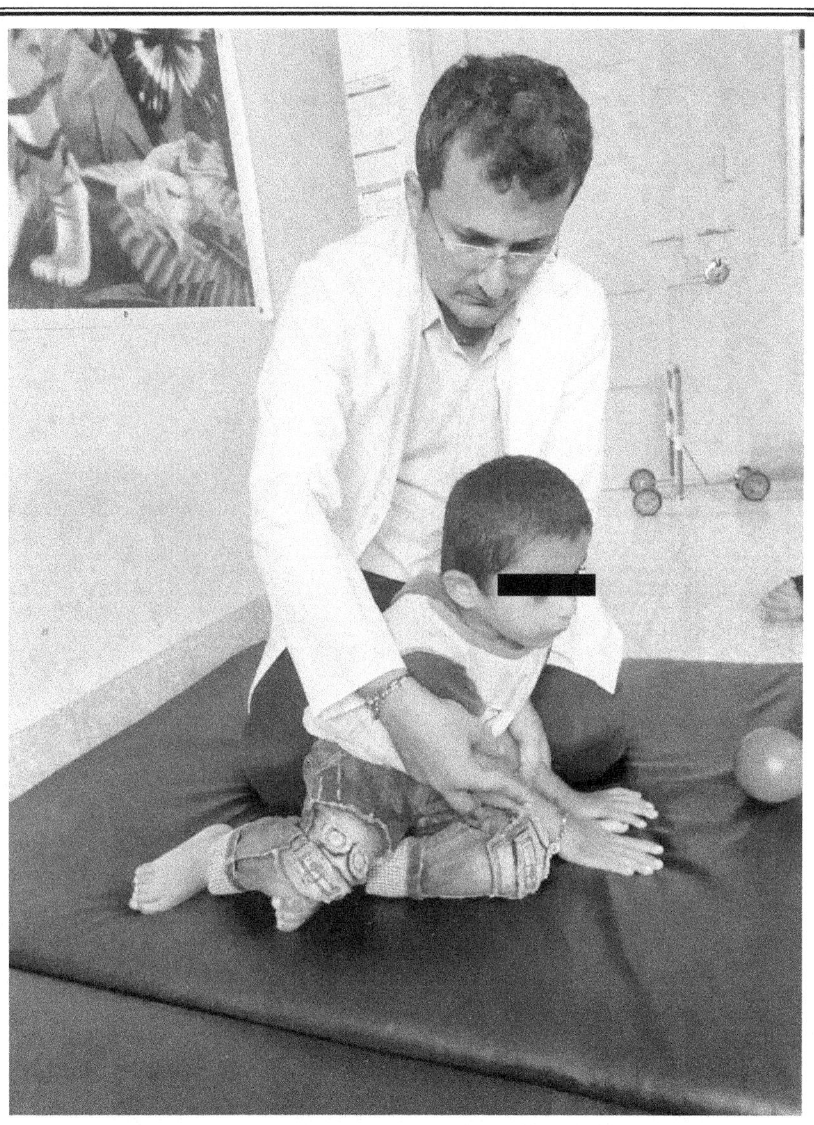

SIDE SITTING ALONG WITH TRUNK FACILITATION

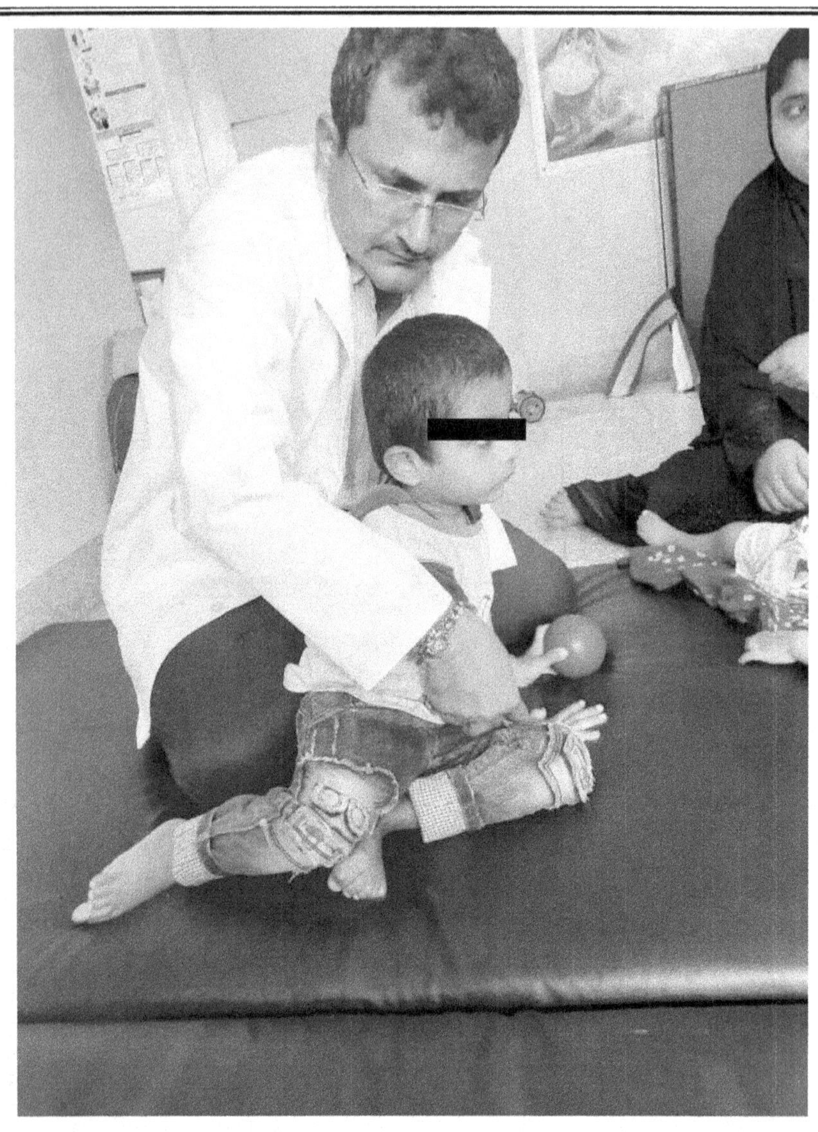

SIDE SITTING WITH WEIGHT BEARING ON RIGHT SIDE

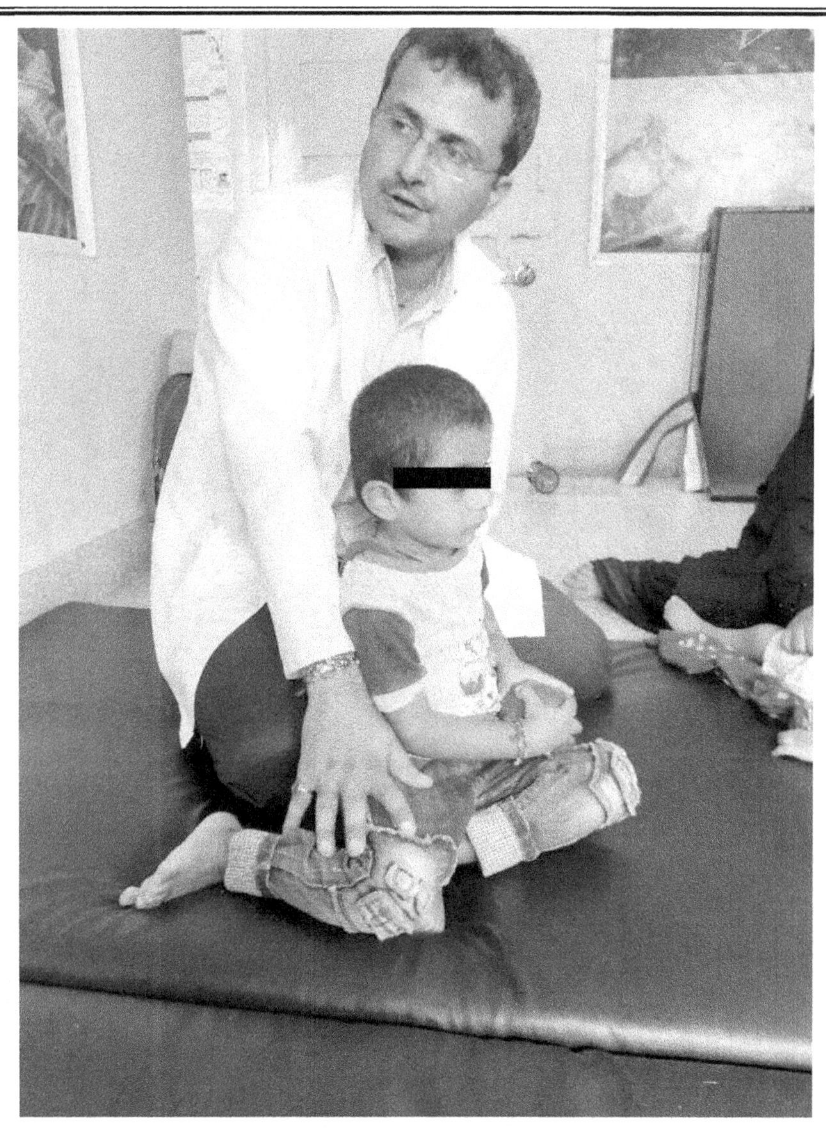

TRUNK FACILITATION TECHNIQUE

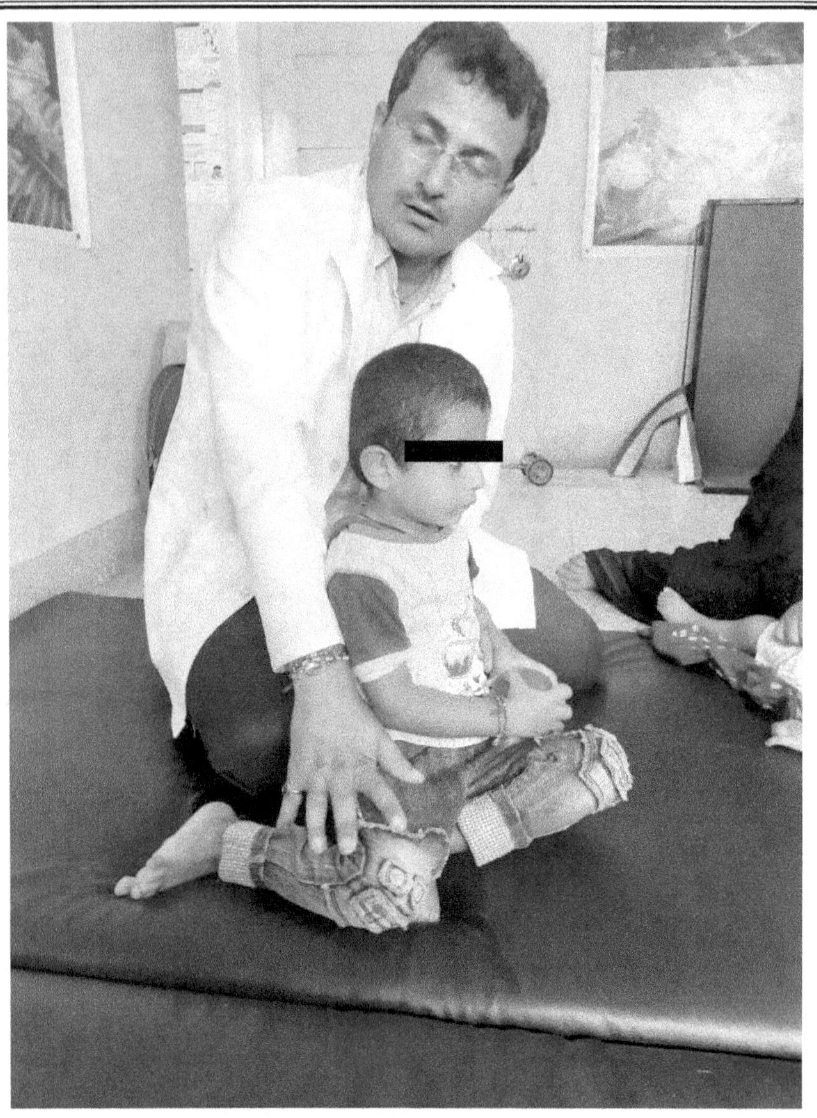

TRUNK FACILITATION TECHNIQUE

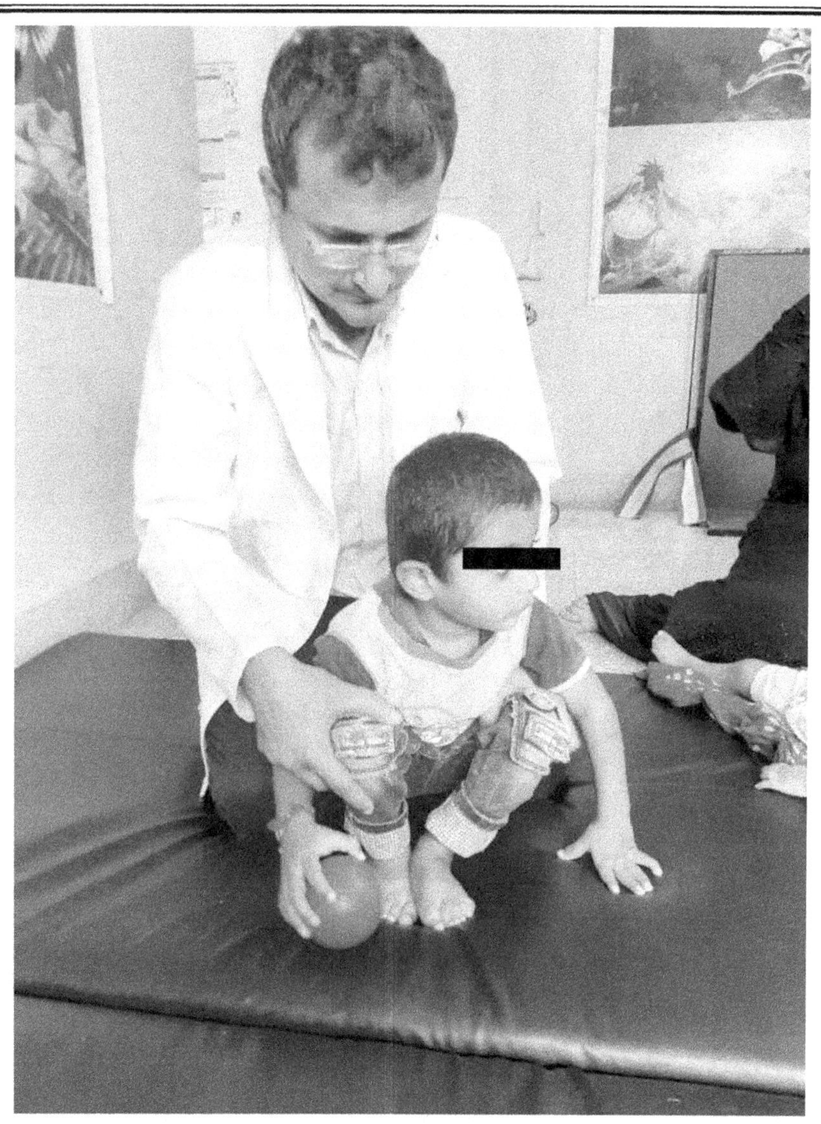

SQUATTING FOR TRUNK FACILITATION

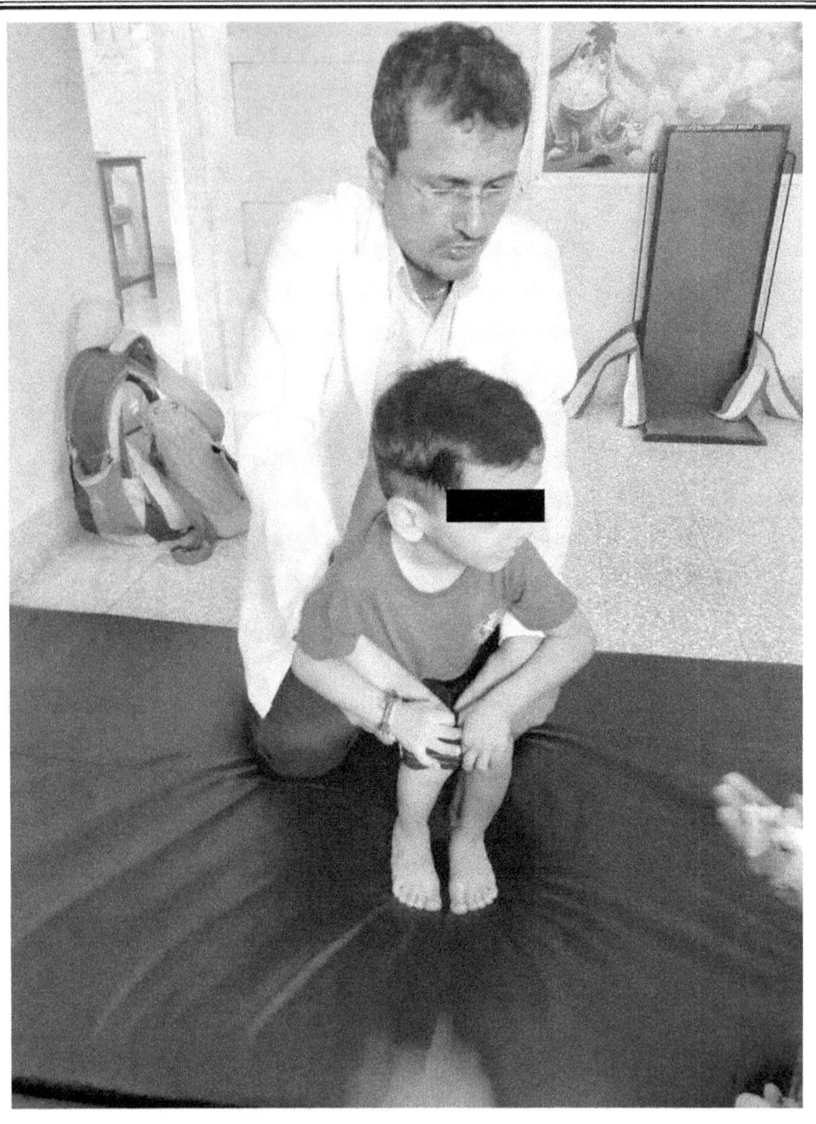

Squatting for trunk facilitation

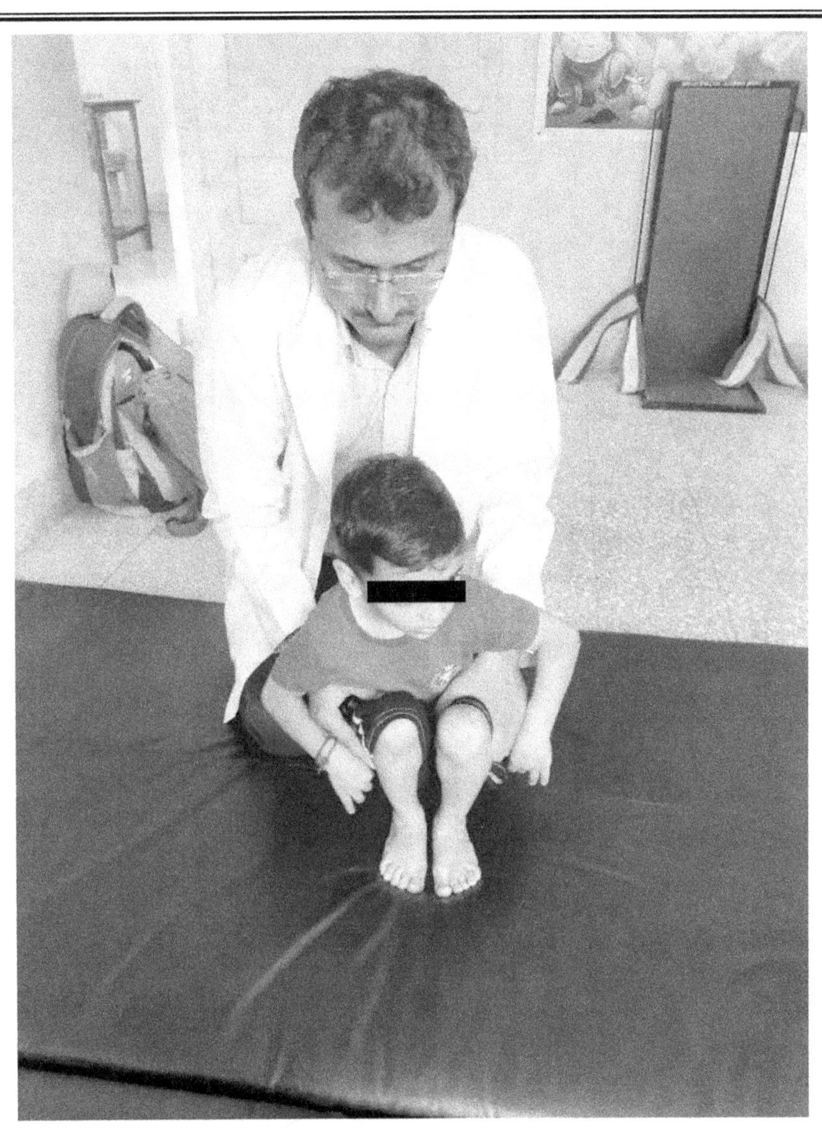

SQUATTING

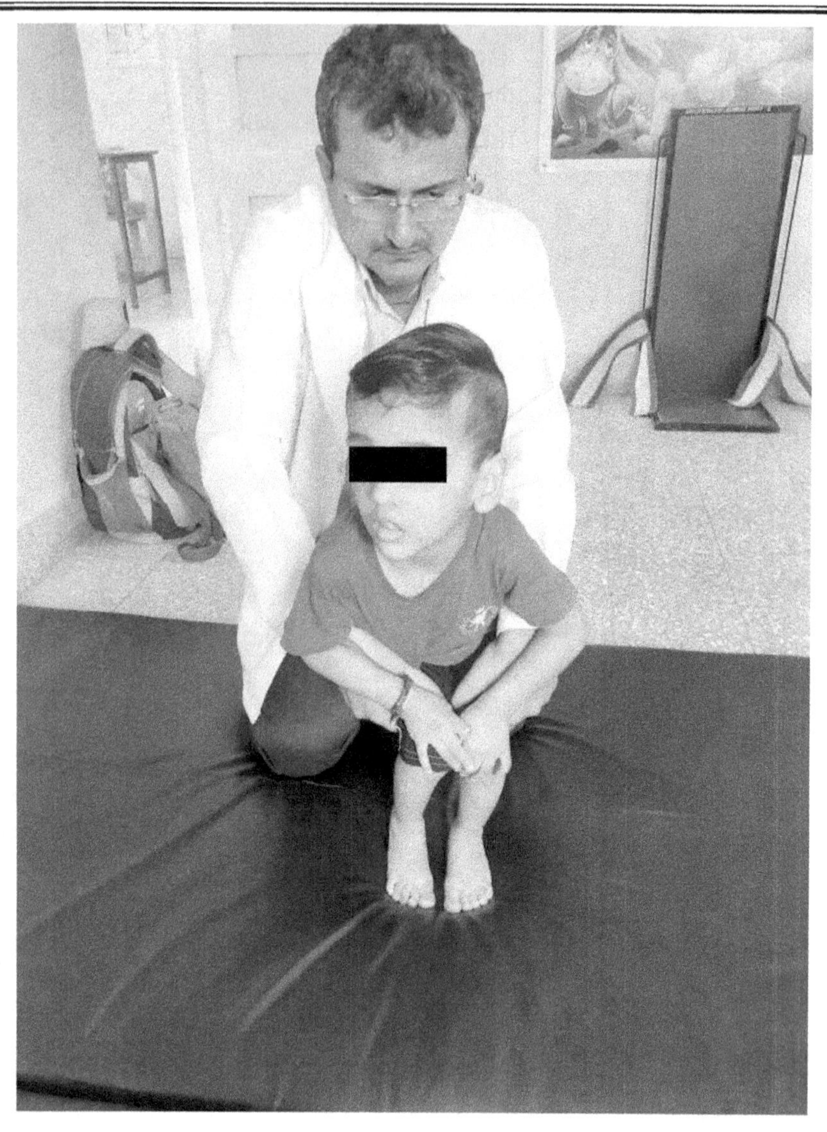

SQUATTING

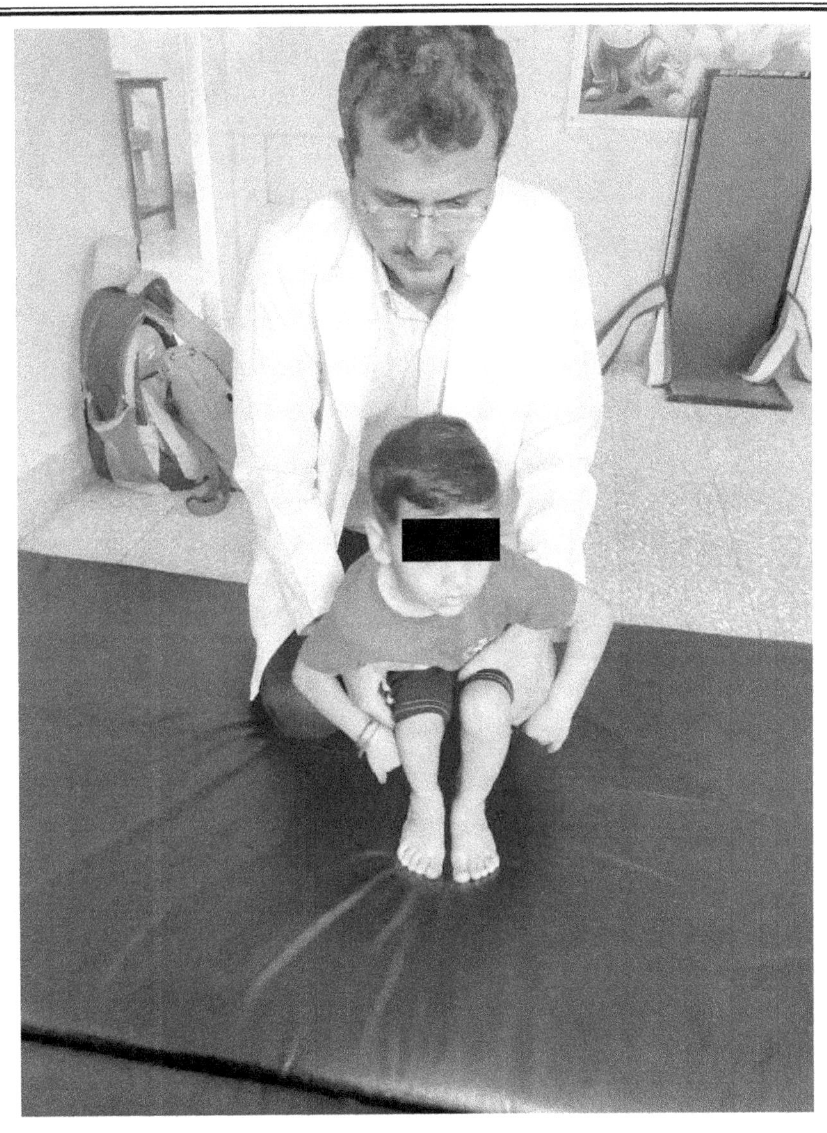

SQUATTING

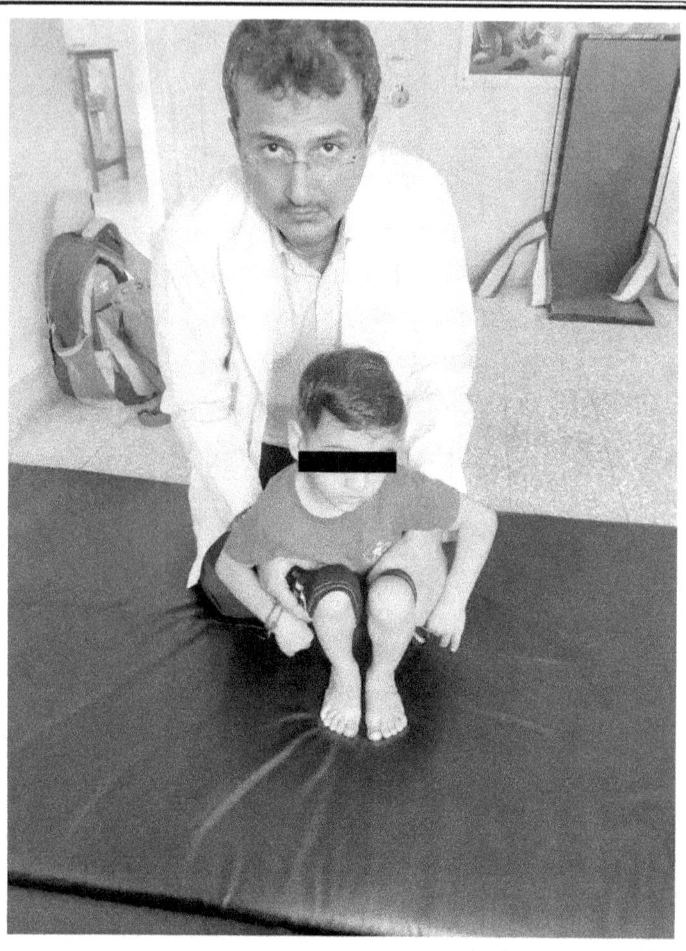

SQUATTING

As an account for dropouts was considered in the sample size calculation, the dropouts were not considered for statistical analysis and intention to treat analysis will not be done. The children's those who inform before getting dropped out were counselled for continuing with the program and if they fail to agree with the counselling the children were considered as dropouts. A consent form was taken from the evaluator for maintaining the confidentiality of the outcome values well before the commencement of the study. This phase of the study was completed within 1 year and six-month duration.

Individualized Functional Outcomes	Patient: Life role, supports systems, home environment, patient's goals ICF: Pathologies, abilities, limitations
Motor Control and movement Optimize	Using systems (sensory, musculoskeletal) and available movement patterns/synergies
Target the Involved Side or limb	Progressive, increased demand and functional use Motor Learning Closed vs. open environment, simple vs. complex, part vs. whole, practice and feedback/knowledge of results
Motor Learning	Closed vs. open environment, simple vs. complex, part vs. whole, practice and feedback/knowledge of results
Team-Approach	Coordination with rehab team, parents/caregivers, and support staff to allow for continual practice and consistent use of facilitation strategies

Table 4.1 . The basic principle adopted for NDT intervention of group B

The therapists must be able to observe and distinguish normal from abnormal alignment and movement patterns.
Therapists must be able to make the functional retraining activities meaningful to the patient; task specific
Therapists must be able to select the optimal practice method, feedback, and environment for maximum function and independence
Therapists must have stable footwear, good flexibility in lumbar spine and lower extremities for optimal body mechanics during mat activities.

Table 4.2 Essentials for Treatment Effectiveness

Alignment	Cannot impose normal movement on misaligned joints
Handling	Inhibition, Facilitation, Key points
Placing	Assisting patients in achieving the appropriate

Table 4.3 Key elements to Applying NDT

Starting Posture	Missing Components	Manual Cues
Begin and assess the most efficient posture from which to move (typically upright)	Observe starting posture and make comparisons to normal	Use hands on key points of control to facilitate normal posture/movement and inhibit abnormal posture/movement
Reorient to midline (head/trunk)		
Neutral alignment of body segments	May includes manual stretching if PT has determined ROM/muscle length interferes with function	May includes manual stretching if PT has determined ROM/muscle length interferes with function

	Child's starting position	Activities Activities initiated by child	Activities Activities imposed by therapist	Key points of control	inhibition or facilitation	Environmental adaptation or equipment used
Preparation activities	Standingpushing Bilateral hands into large ball	Body weight shift forward and UE pushing	L wrist alignment and elongation	L ulnar border andL thumb web space	-	Large orange therapy ball, AFOs on with external rotator straps
ABCs: ABCs: alignment, base of support, center of mass	Prone and sitting	Reaching for Gertie ball (Therapro)	"Superman"- thoracic extension Unyoke UEs Elongation L biceps	B elbows And gluteals	+	Large orange ball, Gertie ball
Core muscle activation	Sitting-pelvis in alignment: extension with rotation	Throwing ball and reaching to ball	UEweight bearing and trunk rotation	L hand thenar and web space, lower thor acic spine	+	Large orange ball, Gertie ball, hula hoop target
Elongation/ Activation	Sitting	R hand graspmg	L hand grasp, sustained grasp and release	L hand ulnar border and web	-	Bench, Play-Doh
Practice time (including repetition and simulation of goal)	Sitting R hand grasp / release		L hand grasp and toy placement	L hand ulnar stabilization	+	Bench, stretchy lizard, snake and worms, plastic eggs, pull string on bumble ball
Vestibular play on therapy ball.	Supine lying	leg dissociation, top leg flexed cross body leading change inCOM to one side				large therapy ball

Table 4.4 NDT Intervention Framework used for group B intervention.

<u>**4.10. Autonomy**</u>

All the participants and care givers were explained regarding the study. The information sheets consisting of the information of the study was distributed. These information sheets were provided in Gujarati /Hindi / English or Tamil languages. The participants were ensured about potential risks and benefits, reimbursements and the termination of the participation. They were guaranteed that their participation in the study is completely voluntary and they are free to withdraw at any time despite consenting to take part earlier. Further the participants was assured that they was at no loss of medical care or any other available treatment to which they are otherwise entitled. The contact details of the primary investigator were provided in case of termination of their participation or clarification of doubts.

<u>**4.11. Confidentiality**</u>

Confidentiality of all records including the personal information of the research participants is guaranteed. At the recruitment the participants were informed about the procedures taken to maintain the confidentiality. Participants were strongly assured that none of the data obtained was disclosed for any purpose without their permission. Information was stored in secure conditions. Only the primary researcher will have the access to the information.

Psychological and interest can be identified risks. If the child feels discomfort while performing the exercise, exercise was discontinued immediately and child was given rest and was referred for further medical care in pediatric unit at a nearby hospital. Participants were advised and are free to contact the primary researcher at any time if they experience any discomfort. Participants can withdraw from the study at anytime. There were no anticipated adverse effects as the children's are treated with regular exercise and NDT exercise protocol.

CHAPTERS

Results

This study which was performed on children with CP intended to find an effective protocol for improving segmental stability of trunk. This study was performed in two phases. In the first phase of the study a randomized control trail was done to analyze the efficacy of newly designed treatment protocol which was framed for the study using elements of **NDT** along with evidence-based approach. This Study was performed at department of Physiotherapy, in Sanjeevani hospital, Rajkot, Gujarat. The data were collected from 21.01.2017 till 10.09.2018.

5.1 Data management:

The data collected by the blinded evaluators were submitted to the principal investigator which was then entered in a Microsoft excel sheet. The principal investigator collected the data from the evaluator as soon as the evaluation is done either through email or in person. The principal investigator first described the demographic, baseline, and post intervention evaluation data of each group using means and standard deviation for all variables. Homogeneity of variances of the data at baseline and significant differences of post intervention data for all the two groups were analyse. An overall significance level was maintained at $p < 0.05$. Out of the 80 subjects 7 patients did not complete the study due to various reasons and they were considered as drop outs. The analysis of data was done only for the subjects who successfully completed the 4 weeks of intervention. The drop outs were not considered for statistical analysis.

5.2. Analysis of demographic data:

Statistical analysis for the study was done using Sigma Plot 12.0 (Systat software, USA). There were four outcome measures that were used for the study. Non-parametric analysis was done for all the 4 outcome measures. The median and percentile values (central tendency) at 25% and 75% of the pre-test and post-test 1 (post-test taken on the end of the 2nd week of intervention), post-test 2 (post-test taken on the end of the 4th week of intervention), values of TCMS, GMFM, SATCO and Cerebral palsy quality of life questionnaire version 2 were used for within group analysis and between group analysis.

At the base line the homogeneity of the group was tested using the demographic data of the participants of both the group. Age was a factor that was proved to show significant influence on the improvement following any intervention in cerebral palsy children. Hence the age between the two groups were analyzed using a chi square analysis. (Bertoncelli CM et al, 2019) The mean and standard deviation of age group of group A and group **B** was 7.5(3.3) and 8.3 (4.1) respectively. This shows that age group of group B was marginally high with more variation than in group A To know whether this had an effect on the results a chi square analysis of the age difference between both the groups was done. The subjects were categories according to two age groups of 3-8years and 9-14 years. The analysis showed that there was no significant difference between the two groups, with a p-value of 0.512129. This meant groups were similar at the time of recruitment and the results were not influenced by the age criteria. The chi-square statistic with Yates correction was found out to be 0.1672 with a p-value of 0.682643. The analysis is represented in the table 5.1 and figure 5.1.

In any intervention gender plays a very important role in determining the improvement gained with the intervention. It is true in the case of cerebral palsy where there are studies which show that there is difference among different genders prognosis following NDT as well as other treatment interventions. The influence of the gender on the intervention results was analysed and whether it influenced the results as an confounding variable was tested. In group A there were 19 male and 17 female in group be there were 21 mail and 16 female. Analysis was done there was no significant difference between the two groups with the P value 0.732 and Chi squared value of 0.116. The results are shown in table 5.2 and figure 5.2.

Type of cerebral palsy is an vital factor that determines both long term and short term outcome of intervention following CP management. There are athetoid types and quadriplegic types which cannot prognose as better as hemiplegic and diplegic types. This is why we preferred only hemiplegic and diplegic types of CP. In spite of similar prognosis rate in both types of spastic CP (hemiplegic and diplegic) the researcher wanted to know whether there was any difference which might act as an confounding variable between the dependent and independent variable. Chi square analysis was done to know the difference between two groups which showed that there was no significant difference among the two groups as far as the number of hemiplegic and diplegic patients are concerned with a p value of 0.491 and a chi square value of 0.483086. The results are shown in table 5.3 and figure 5.3.

GMFCS score was analysed for the difference among both the groups as it may influence the results. Chi square analysis was done to know the difference between two groups which showed that there was no significant difference among the two groups as far as the GMFCS scores are concerned with a p value of 0.250 and a chi square value of 1.3199. The results are shown in table 5.4 and figure 5.4 .

	Age 3-8 (SD) [P value]	Age 9-14 (SD) [P value]	*Totals*
Group A	11 (12.33) [0.14]	25 (23.67) [0.07]	36
Group B	14 (12.67) [0.14]	23 (24.33) [0.07]	37
Totals	25	48	73 (Total)

The chi-square statistic is 0.4297. The p-value = 0.512129.
The chi-square statistic with Yates correction is 0.1672.
The p-value is 0.682643.

Table 5.1 Chi square analysis of the age distribution among group A and group B

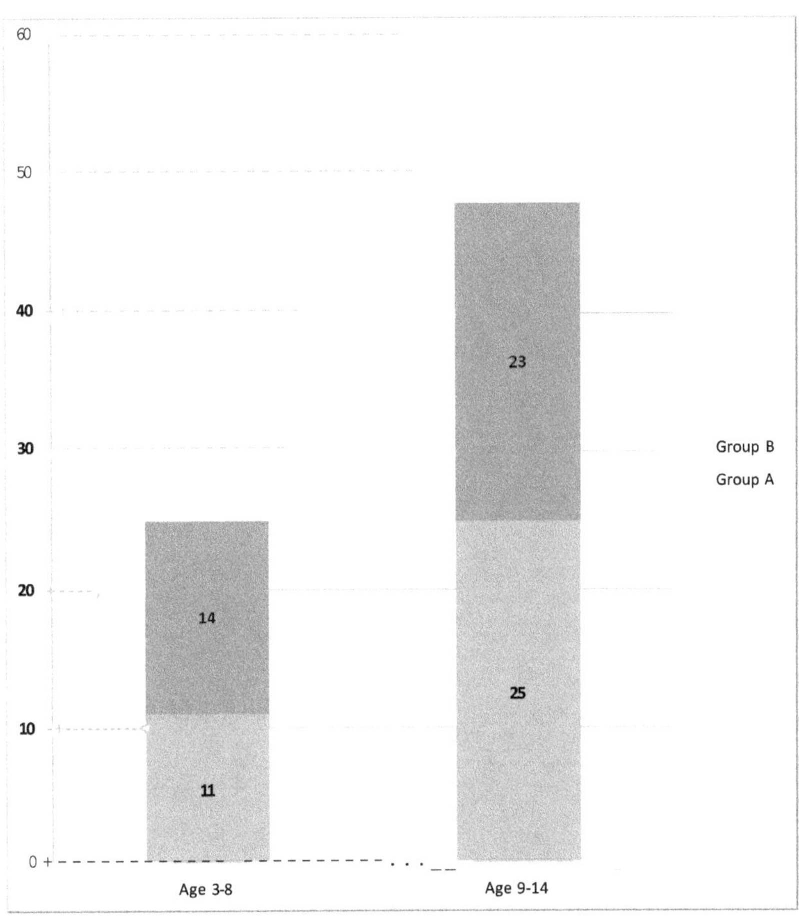

Fig 5.1. Age distribution among groups.

	GMFCS 3 (SD) [Pvalue]	GMFCS 4 (SD) [P value]	*Totals*
Group A	26 (23.67) [0.23]	10 (12.33) [0.44]	36
GroupB	22 (24.33) [0.22]	15 (12.67) [0.43]	37
Total	48	25	73

The chi-square statistic is 1.3199. The p-value is 0.250613.

No statistical significance at p < .05.

The chi-square statistic with Yates correction is 0. 814. The p-value is 0. 366954.

	MALE (SD) [P value]	FEMALE(SD) [P value]	*Totals*
Group A	19 (19.73) [0.03]	17 (16.27) [0.03]	36
Group B	21 (20.27) [0.03]	16 (16.73) [0.03]	37
Totals	40	33	73 (Total)

The chi-square statistic is 0.1166. The p-value is 0 .732723.

The values are not significantly different at p < .05.

The chi-square statistic with Yates correction is 0.0113. p-value = 0.91533.

Table 5.2. Chi square analysis of the gender distribution among group A and group B

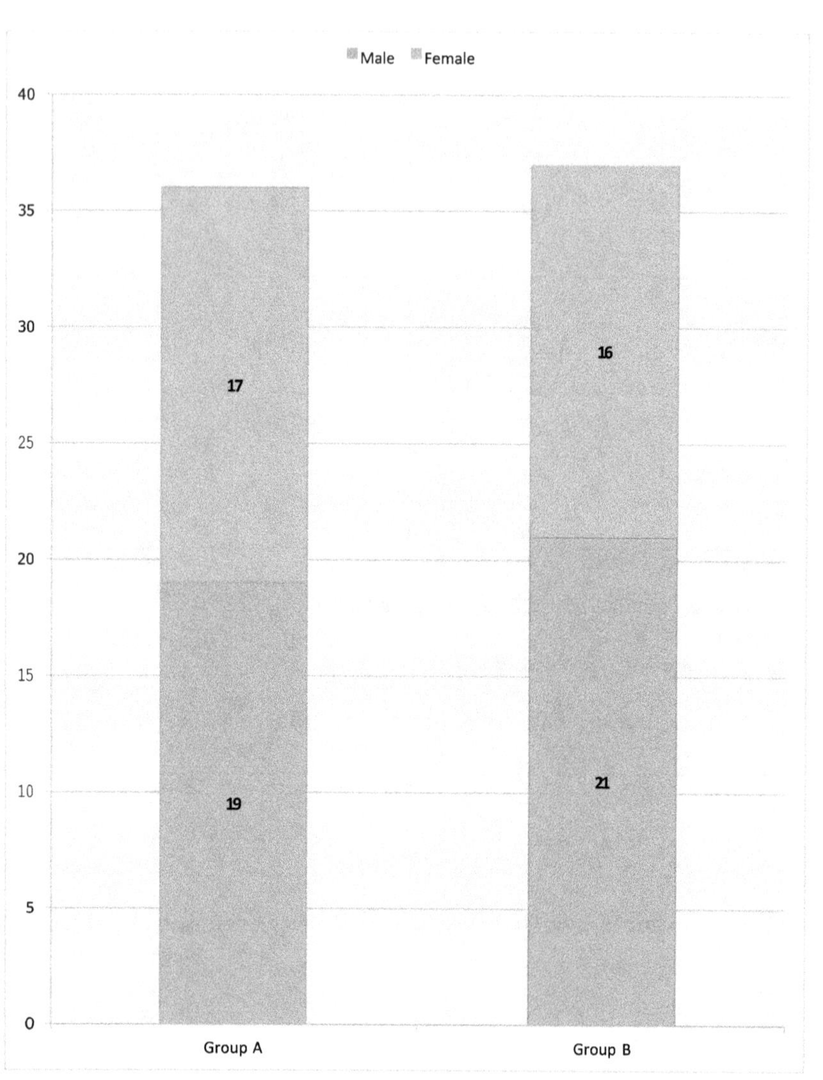

Fig 5.2. Gender distribution among groups

	Hemiplegic (SD) [P value]	**Diplegic** (SD) [P value]	*Totals*
Group A	9 (10.36) [0.18]	27 (25.64) [0.07]	36
Group B	12 (10.64) [0.17]	25 (26.36) [0.07]	37
	21	52	73 (Total)

The chi-square statistic is 0.4919. The p-value is 0.483086.

This result is not significant at p < .05.

The chi-square statistic with Yates correction is 0.196. The p-value is .657932.

Table 5.3 Chi square analysis of the CP type distribution among group A and group B

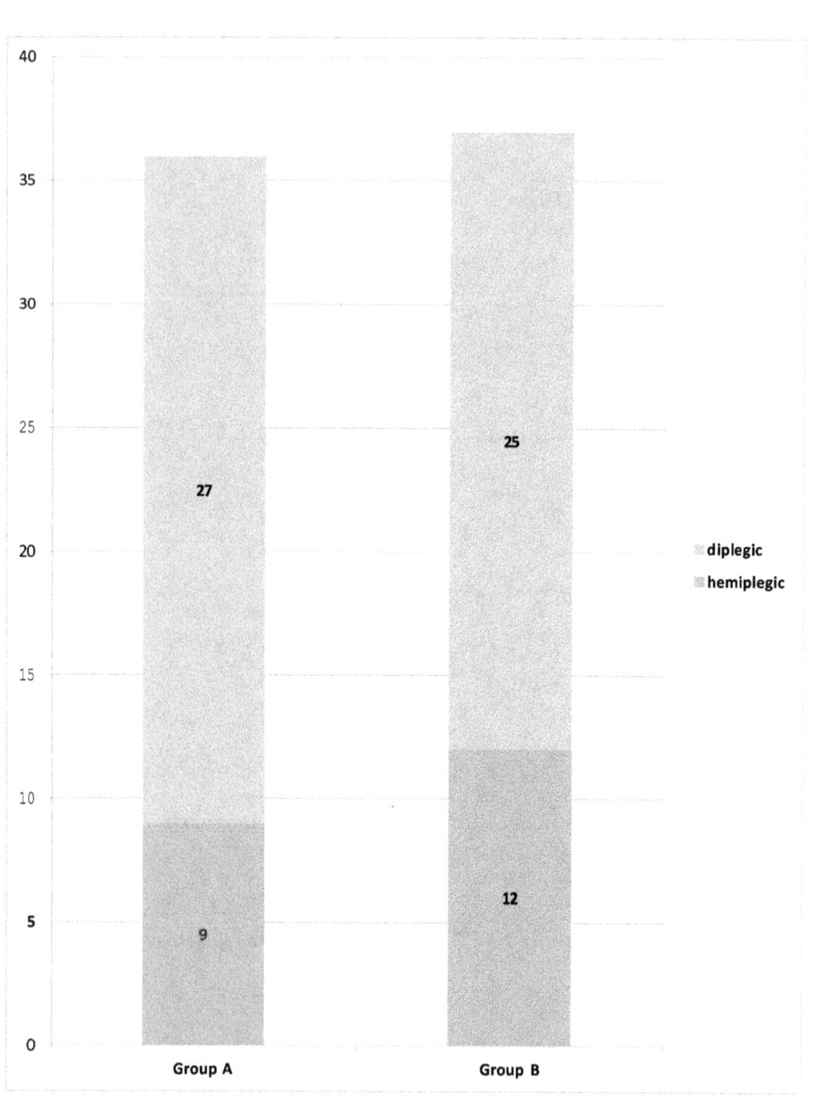

Fig 5.3 Distribution of type of CP among groups

	GMFCS 3 (SD) [P value]	GMFCS 4 (SD) [P value]	*Totals*
Group A	26 (23.67) [0.23]	10 (12.33) [0.44]	36
GroupB	22 (24.33) [0.22]	15 (12.67) [0.43]	37
Total	48	25	73

The chi-square statistic is 1.3199. The p-value is 0.250613.

No statistical significance at p < .05.

The chi-square statistic with Yates correction is 0.814. The p-value is 0.366954.

Table 5.4 Chi square analysis of the GMFCS score distribution among group A and group B

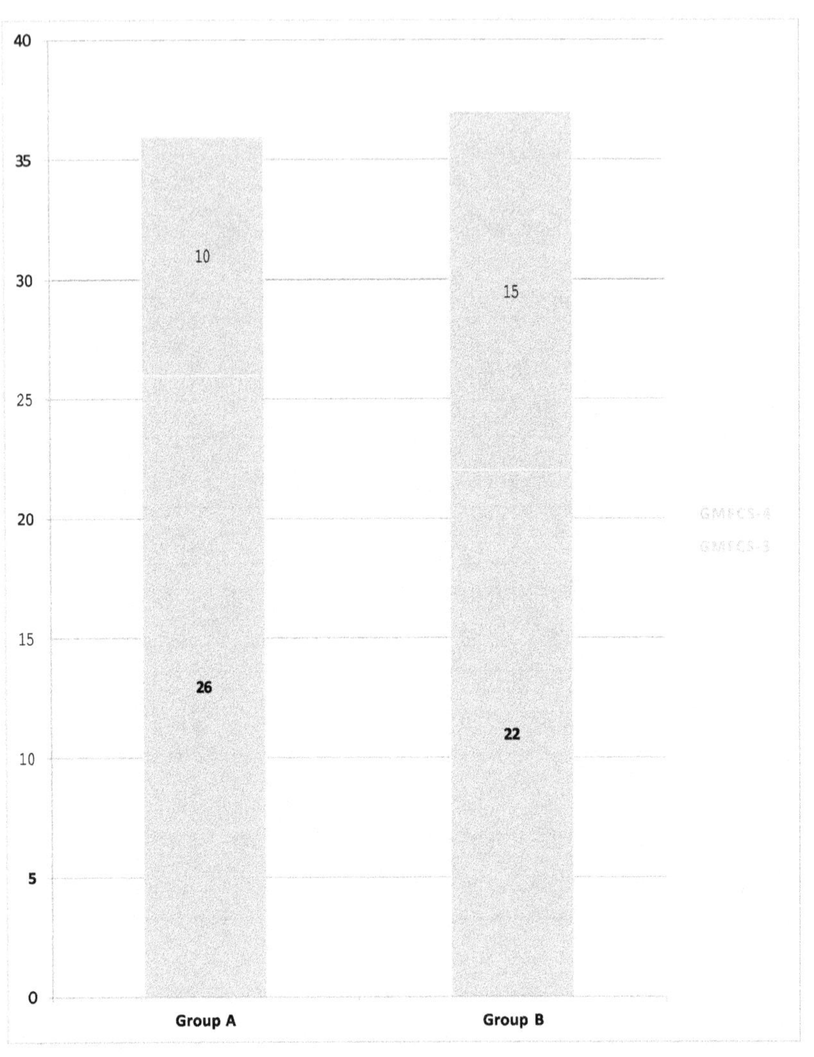

Fig 5.4. Distribution of type of GMFCS score among groups

5.3. Analysis of the outcome measures

5.3.1. GMFM

Between groups analysis was performed using Mann-Whitney U Test as the data were non-parametric values. In the between group analysis of pre-test values of group A and group B showed that the z-score was 0.3549 and the p-value was 0.36317 and hence the there is no significant difference among the groups at $p < .05$. In the between group analysis of post-test 1 values of group A and group B showed that the z-score was 1.26186 and the p-value was 0.10383 and hence the there is no significant difference among the groups at $p < .05$. The between group analysis of post-test 2 values of group A and group B showed that the z-score was 11.74633 and the p-value was 0.04006 and hence the there is a significant difference among the groups at $p < .05$.

Within group analysis of the pre-test values and the two post-test values was done using Friedman Repeated measures analysis of variance on rank. The analysis of the group A showed the differences in the median values are greater than would be expected by chance with $x2 = 174.38$ with 2 degrees of freedom and $p < 0.001$. A multiple comparison using Dunn's method showed that there was no significant difference between pre-test vs post-test 1, ($p = 0.523$) but there was a significant difference in pre-test vs post-test 2 ($p = 0.026$). The analysis of group B showed the differences in the median values among the control group are greater than would be expected by chance with $x2 = 183.60$ with 4 degrees of freedom and $p < 0.001$. A multiple comparison using Dunn's method showed that there was a significant difference between pre-test values and the two post-test values with a p value of 0.036 and 0.001 respectively.

5.3.2. SATCO

Between groups analysis was performed using Mann-Whitney U Test as the data were non-parametric values. In the between group analysis of pre-test values of group A and group B showed that the z-score was 0.409 and the p-value was 0.2627 and hence the there is no significant difference among the groups at $p < .05$. In the between group analysis of post-test 1 values of group A and group B showed that the z-score was 9.726 and the p-value was 0.0383 and hence the there is a significant difference among the groups at $p < .05$. In the between group analysis of post-test 2 values of group A and group B showed that the z-score was 12.74633 and the p-value was 0.0226 and hence the there is a significant difference among the groups at $p < .05$.

Within group analysis of the pre-test values and the two post-test values was done using Friedman Repeated measures analysis of variance on rank. The analysis of the group A showed the differences in the median values are greater than would be expected by chance with $x2 = 177.68$ with 2 degrees of freedom and $p < 0.001$. A multiple comparison using Dunn's method showed that there was no significant difference between pre-test vs post-test 1, but there was a significant difference in pre-test vs post-test 2 with p value of 0.125 and 0.034 respectively. The analysis of group B showed the differences in the median values among the control group are greater than would be expected by chance with $x2 = 199.60$ with 2 degrees of freedom and $p < 0.001$. A multiple comparison using Dunn's method showed that there was a significant difference between pre-test values and the two post-test values with p value of 0.002 and 0.001 respectively.

5.3.3. TCMS

Between groups analysis was performed using Mann-Whitney U Test as the data were non-parametric values. In the between group analysis of pre-test values of group A and group B showed that the z-score was 0.332 and the p-value was 0.317 and hence the there is no significant difference among the groups at $p < .05$. In the between group analysis of post-test 1 values of group A and group B showed that the z-score was 2.26 and the p-value was 0.283 and hence the there is no significant difference among the groups at $p < .05$. In the between group analysis of post-test 2 values of group A and group B showed that the z-score was 12.23 and the p-value was 0.021 and hence the there is a significant difference among the groups at $p < .05$.

Within group analysis of the pre-test values and the two post-test values was done using Friedman Repeated measures analysis of variance on rank. The analysis of the group A showed the differences in the median values are greater than would be expected by chance with $x2 = 187.38$ with 2 degrees of freedom and $p < 0.001$. A multiple comparison using Dunn's method showed that there was no significant difference between pre-test vs post-test 1, but there was a significant difference in pre-test vs post-test 2 with a p value of 0.063 and 0.027 respectively. The analysis of group B showed the differences in the median values among the control group are greater than would be expected by chance with $x2 = 197.60$ with 2 degrees of freedom and $p < 0.001$. A multiple comparison using Dunn's method showed that there was a significant difference between pre-test values and the two post-test values with a p value of less than 0.001 for both analyses.

5.3.4. CP-QOL

Between groups analysis was performed using Mann-Whitney U Test as the data were non-parametric values. In the between group analysis of pre-test values of group A and group B showed that the z-score was 0.3634 and the p-value was 0.302 and hence the there is no significant difference among the groups at $p < .05$. In the between group analysis of post-test 1 values of group A and group B showed that the z-score was 1.274 and the p-value was 0.108 and hence the there is no significant difference among the groups at $p < .05$. In the between group analysis of post-test 2 values of group A and group B showed that the z-score was 2.74633 and the p-value was 0.1006 and hence the there is a no significant difference among the groups at $p < .05$.

Within group analysis of the pre-test values and the two post-test values was done using Friedman Repeated measures analysis of variance on rank. The analysis of the group A showed the differences in the median values are greater than would be expected by chance with $x2 = 184.38$ with 2 degrees of freedom and $p < 0.001$. A multiple comparison using Dunn's method showed that there was no significant difference between pre-test vs post-test 1, but there was a significant difference in pre-test vs post-test 2 with a p value of 0.298 and 0.032 respectively. The analysis of group B showed the differences in the median values among the control group are greater than would be expected by chance with $x2 = 190.86$ with 2 degrees of freedom and $p < 0.001$. A multiple comparison using Dunn's method showed that there was a no significant difference between pre-test values and post-test 1 but there was a significant difference in pre-test and post-test 2 values with a p value of 0.211 and 0.001 respectively.

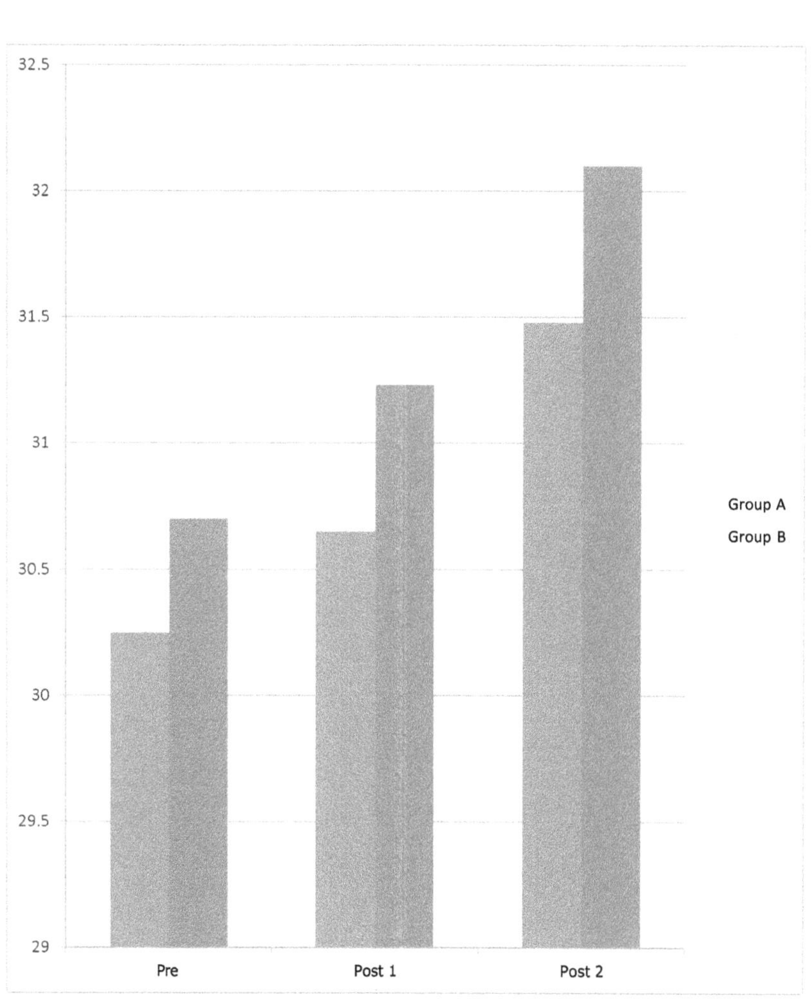

Fig. 5.5 GMFM scores of group A and group B

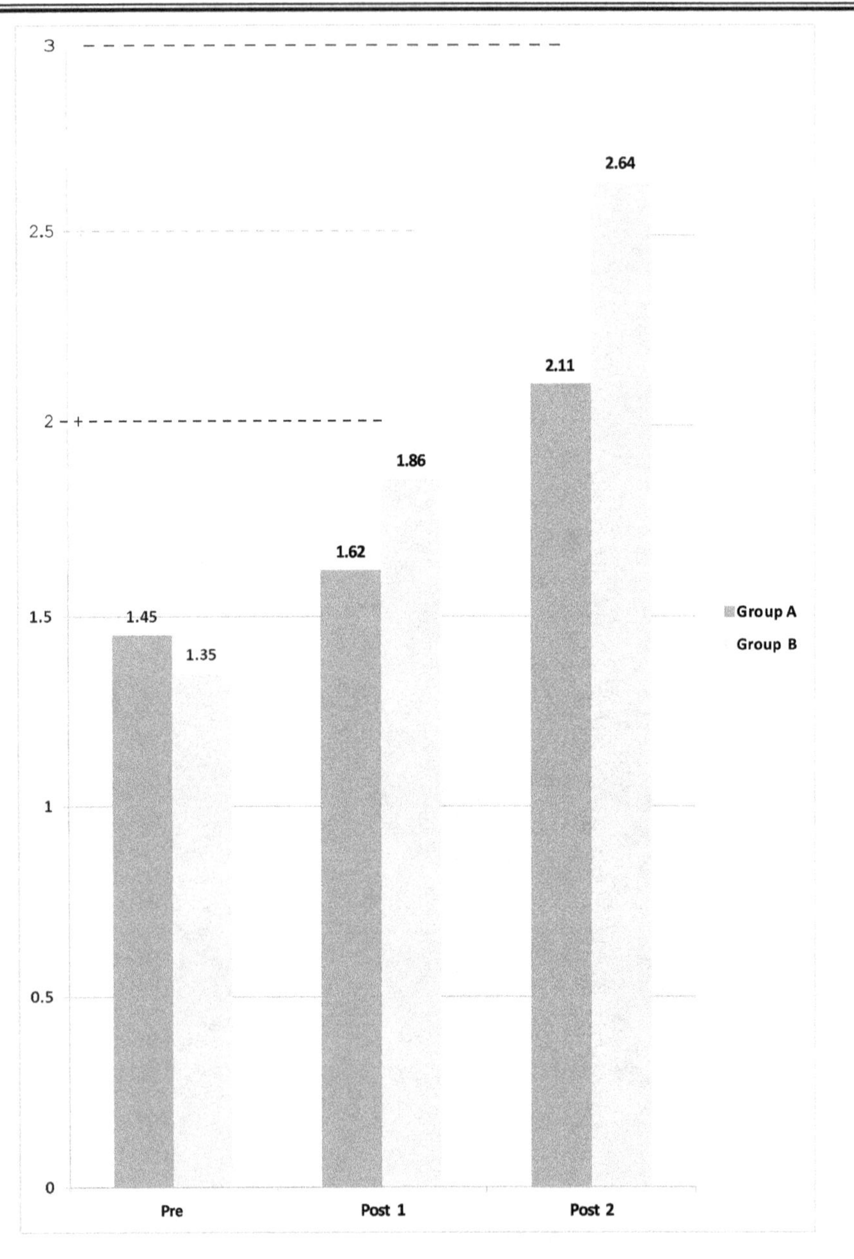

Fig . 5.6. SATCO scores of group A and group B

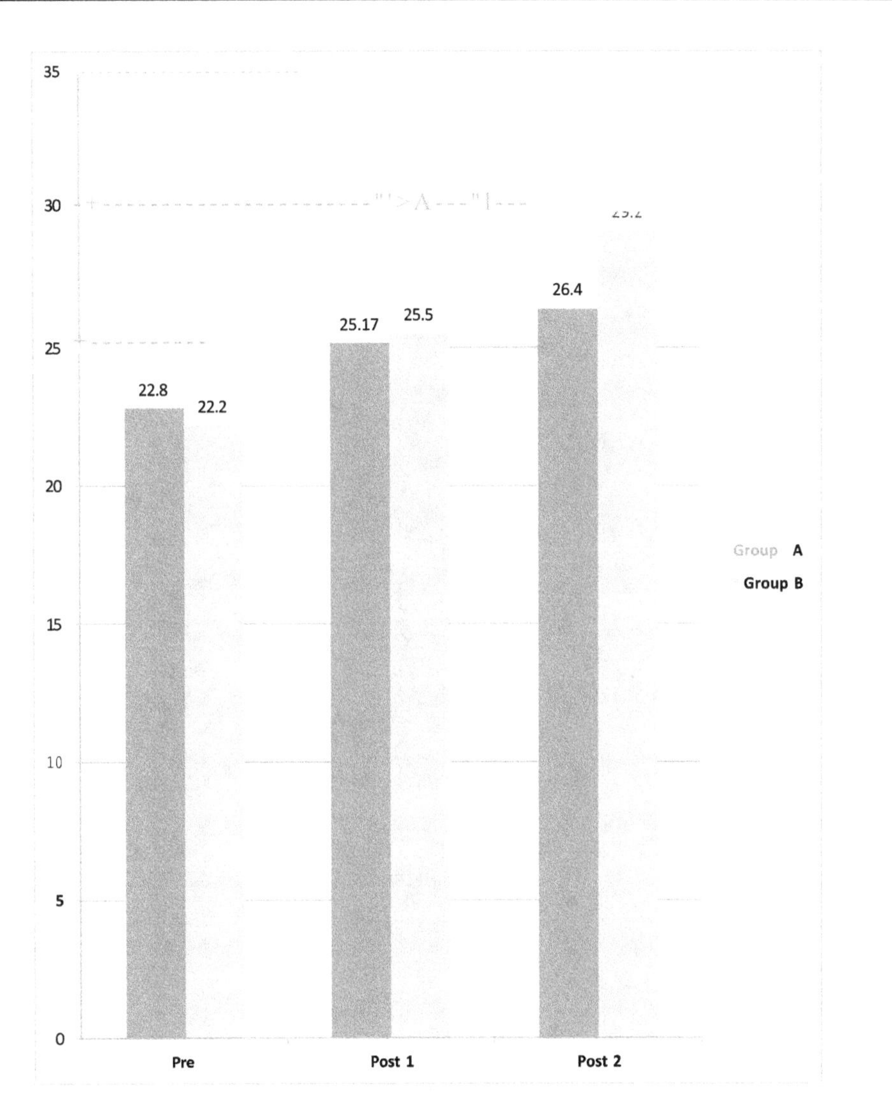

Fig. 5.7. TCMS scores of group A and group B

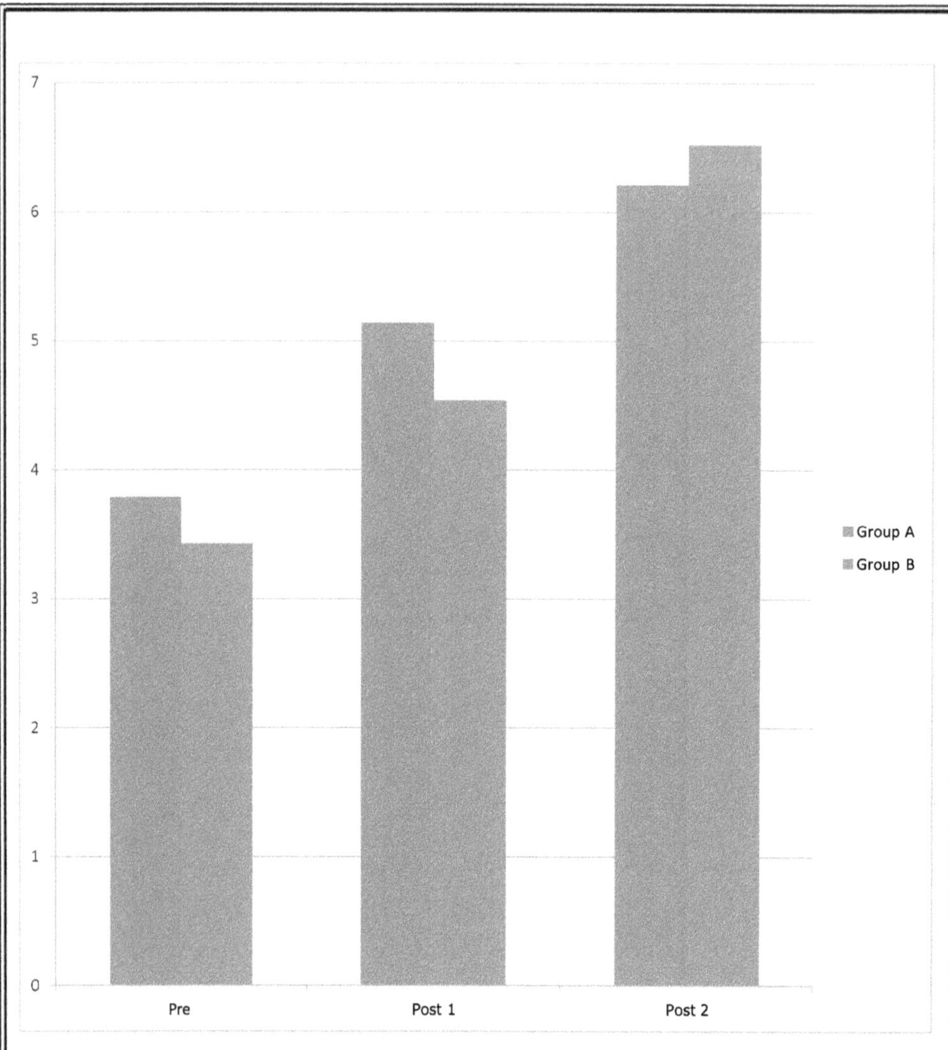

Fig. 5.7. CP-QOL scores of group A and group B

CHAPTER6

Discussion

Though there are different exercise regimes for CP children to improve postural control among CP children has progressed significantly in the recent decade, there is no clear exercise protocol. There is need for more studies in this regard to be performed to explore the connection between impairments in postural control, interventions for postural control impairments and their outcome measures. Hence this study was designed to find out an intervention regime using NDT segmental trunk control training to improve postural control in CP children with low cost, that engages the child.

The interpretation of the present study was that segmental training showed improvement in CP children when compared to conventional physiotherapy. At the end of 1 month of segmental trunk control training a positive prognosis was found in the postural control among CP children with GMFCS level III and IV. This study does greatly influence the existing knowledge of importance of trunk control in determining the motor function of CP children. this study also precisely explains the relationship between gross motor function after the intervention and individual trunk segments in CP children with level III and IV GMFCS. The Segmental Assessment of Trunk Control (SATCo) is a tool that measures and quantifies the control of segmental trunk level of CP children that allows more precise measurements. Also, this study showed that an increase in SATCo score was proportional to significant increase in GMFM score. This analysis would additionally recommend that there's a trunk postural control threshold for the transition between the different GMFM dimensions, which a rise in trunk control might be one among the principal factors separating one GMFCS level from succeeding.

It might appear potential from this study that increasing the segmental level of trunk control through training or bracing the area of the trunk wherever control is weak may turn out clinically vital improvements in gross motor performance and quality. This is true for all aspects of trunk postural control, static, active, and reactive, because it would seem from this study that these 3 aspects of segmental postural control are strongly related to gross motor perform and quality. This study indicates that segmental trunk control ought to be one among the principal focus areas within the testing and intervention in this population.

Though different exercise regimes for CP children to improve postural control among CP children has improved significantly in the recent decade, there is no clear exercise protocol. This study found the intervention regime using NDT segmental trunk control training improved postural control in CP children with low cost. A systematic review that was done recently showed 45 studies recommending 13 exercise regimes aimed to enhance postural control in CP children. Only 4 studies out of 45 studies included CP children based upon GMFCS levels IV and V. This study recommended intervention such as hippotherapy, hippotherapy stimulator and NDT, out of which hippotherapy stimulator showed improvement in postural control among CP children of GMFCS Level II (Dewar R et al, 2015).

There were few factors that affected the expected motor outcome of CP children such as afebrile seizures, poor respiratory condition, nutritional deficiencies, increased bed ridden days and difficulty in performing activities of daily living (ADL). Hence the outcome measures used in this study also focused on finding the effectiveness of the segmental trunk control training in ADLs. The intervention either influences other factors such as afebrile seizures, poor respiratory condition, nutritional deficiencies, increased bed ridden days and difficulty in performing activities of daily living or vice versa.

Shumway Cook et al in 2003 described that reactive balance training control in CP children showed less Centre Of Pressure (COP) displacement and lesser time for balance recovery. Improvements were found in directional specificity of responses and temporal organisation and spatial organisation. In 2010, A study by Anastasia Kyvelidu et al, reported that linear and non-linear interpretation of COP data was a reliable method to assess sitting trunk control in CP children with Intra Class Correlation (ICC) values as 0.19 to 0.75.

A research in 1984 by Seeger and Mc Clenghan in 1992 showed that CP children improved in manipulator skills postural control in sitting or standing was trained. In 2001, Eva Brogren, Hans Forssberg ,MijnaHadders- Algra studied that gross dysfunction for precise postural adjustments tuning to task specific treatment among children with CP had basic level of control. In 2005, a study done by Doreen Bartlett observed that Alignment of spine and Range of Motion Measure for trunk control had ICC values above 0.80 and validity 0.44.P Butler in 2010, in a study showed that SATco is a reliable and valid clinical tool to measure trunk control in typically developing infants and neuromotor disabled children. This study also showed an overall score for reliability was more than 0.80 with validity p value< 0.01.

In 2001, Lesley Wiart, Johanna Darrah performed a systematic review of four test of gross motor development that resulted in PDMS having r value 0.96(item by item) and r = 0.99(total score). Test retest ICC = 0.95. in 2004, Kathleen Washington et al observed that muscles were activated in spatial and temporal organization in response to perturbation given in forward sitting in high risk infants, found that directionally appropriate phasic muscle frequency were significantly lowered in high risk infants. In 1994, Hadders - Algra et al found that infants who lacked directionally inappropriate phasic muscles response had less chances of attaining independent sitting balance. The same author in 1999 found that the ability to initiate and manipulate postural responses varied in preterm children when compared to term children.

In 1996, Brogren et al showed that in response to perturbation in sitting, spastic diplegic children showed a caudal to cephalic pattern of activation along with increased antagonistic neck and hip muscles co-activation. In 1968, Cbrriereye et al, performed Neuro-developmental approach to the treat Cerebral palsy children. His study concluded that 'facilitation' techniques in NDT encouraged automatic postural reactions and further emphasized that these automatic postural reaction patterns are more easily elicited in the very young even before hypertonicity or dystonia has become well established. In 1997, Carolyn Ann et al,(1997) in his study with a series of single-subject performed in school of rehabilitation therapy found that NDT improved gross motor function in CP children.

In 2015, Heba M Youssr El-Basatiny et al, tried to find out the Effectiveness of Trunk Exercises on Trunk control, Balance and Mobility Function in spastic Hemiparetic Cerebral Palsy Children. His study showed that trunk exercises to did improve trunk control, balance and mobility function in spastic hemiparetic cerebral palsychildren.

In 2005, Susan R. Harris et al, performed a study to find the Efficacy and Effectiveness of physical therapy intervention in Enhancing Postural Control in CP Children. in his study he concluded that interventions to postural control must focus on functional motor performances which will lead into meaningful ADLs for Neuromotor disabled children. Julie Chung, et al in 2008in her study effectiveness of adaptive Seating on Sitting Posture and Postural Control in Children with Cerebral showed that there was no independent treatment approach proved to be effective in improving sitting posture and postural control in comparison to combined therapy. There are limited studies that observed improving postural control leading to improvement in functional activities.

In 2015, Shamsoddini A et al proved that neuro developmental approach did improve four dimensions (lying and rolling, sitting, crawling and kneeling, and standing) of gross motor function in cerebral palsy children that showed a statistically significant difference.

This segmental training to trunk control and its significance in regard to functional ability has been addressed inthree recent studies. The primary study by Saavedraet al in 201 0evaluated postural control at a simplified task level by measurement head stability throughout quiet sitting whereas systematically manipulating the extent of trunk support and vision in fifteen youngsters with CP (6-16y), twenty-six youngsters with typical development (4-14y), and eleven adults. Another study by Saavedra et al in 2009 used an analogous analytical approach using kinematics, visual tracking, and a trunk support tool to examine the purposeful coupling of the eye, head, and hand, and also the extent to that it had been forced by trunk postural control in ten youngsters with CP (6-16y).

Bernstein, who also participated in the development of motor program theories, looked at the nervous system and the body in a new way, and contributed to the development of system theory. He recognized that one cannot understand the neural control of movement without an understanding of characteristics of the system in which one is moving and external and internal forces acting on the body. System theory takes into account not only the nervous system's contribution to action, but also the contribution of the muscular and skeletal systems, as well as forces of gravity. Movement emerges from the interaction of three factors: the individual, the task, and the environment. Movements are organized around both task and environmental demands.

Postural control requirements thus vary with the task and environment. Bernstein was the first to realize that the central problem of motor control, including postural control and trunk control, was organizing the redundant sets of elements, muscles and joints in task-specific ways. He suggested that the motor problem posed by excessive degrees of freedom might be solved by organizing the elements into synergies. Synergies have been defined as neural organizations of sets of elements with the purpose of stabilizing a particular feature of performance.

Forsberg and Hirchfeld developed a functional model of the organization of postural control, during externally trigged perturbations studies in sitting adults. This model, called the CPG model, may be useful for discussing development of postural control. The CPG refers to neural networks coordinating the activity of many muscles, described in motor program theory. The activity level in the networks is controlled by reticulospinal neurons, and afferent input results in a modulation of the output pattern. Essential to the CPG model for postural adjustments is its organization of two functional levels of control.

These levels can be of interest when investigating trunk control in children with CP. The first level consists of a network which coordinates the basic structure of postural synergies. At this level, direction-specific synergies are performed. This means that a forward sway induces activity in the muscles on the dorsal side of the body, while backward sway induces activity in the muscles in the ventral muscles, and a similar synergy is present in the frontal plane. It has been hypothesized that the basic structure of postural synergies is generated by the above-mentioned spinal networks. To counteract a perturbation in a specific direction, there is a repertoire of direction-specific adjustments patterns which are activated in terms of muscle recruitment.26

The second level of control is involved in the fine tuning of the basic pattern of adjustment on the basis of multisensory afferent input from somatosensory, visual, and vestibular systems. Modulation can occur by means of: 1) the selection of the best-fitting muscle activation pattern out of the repertoire of direction specific-patterns; 2) the recruitment of antagonist 12 muscles; 3) the recruitment order of the direction specific muscles; and 4) the degree of contraction of the direction-specific muscles.

In 2013, a study by Rachwani et al investigated the impact of various levels of postural support on the success of reaching postural stability and reaching mechanics whereas infants reached for a toy in seventeen infants with typical development between four months and six months older. These studies demonstrated an apparently close relationship between segmental trunk control and head stability and eye-hand coordination, however failed to measure the impact of segmental trunk control on a world-wide measure of gross motor perform or purposeful mobility.

An earlier study by butler et al in 2010 demonstrated a correlation between the SATCo test and Gross Motor function measure (GMFM66) Dimension B (sitting) (R= 0.731- 0.833) for 24 youngsters with neuromotor disability (21 with CP). From this study it'd seem that there is also a relationship between the segmental level of trunk management and gross motor performance in sitting for neuro motor disabled children. According to the same study a correlation between SATCo and the paediatric evaluation of disability Inventory (PEDI) quality Domain child (R= 0.695- 0.803) showing an apparent relationship between functional mobility and segmental trunk control.

In order to enhance the efficacy of segmental training, it is must to attain that interactive computer play (ICP) as described in the study by Barton et al in 2013, that might be used as a supplement throughout the segmental training sessions. This could give further motivation for training participation for CP children. A recent review Fehlings D et al in 2013 revealed that the literature evaluating ICP to improve gross motor performance in CP children showed probable effectiveness evidence. This review further was known to include studies that included CP children with GMFCS IV and V. A study by Gordon C in 2013 showed a rise in the total GMFM-88 score when intervention was recommended for once in 2 days per week for six weeks in an exceedingly a group of CP children who were either capable of unsupported sitting or standing. Another study by Wade W et al in 2012 involved CP children from GMFCS IV and V who had achieved either unsupported sitting or prop-sitting.

This study used a seat platform sensitive to movements in COP coupled to a laptop with games controlled by outer platform. The study reported no modification within the support level of sitting, but significantly there was an increase in an exceedingly range of overall scores when compared to children with inability to perform sitting. A study by Derek John Curtis in 2017 revealed that sitting activities wherever the focus is on self-guided play might be helpful in improving sitting ability. The support provided by the segmental training equipment might permit a lot of severely affected CP children to train through computer play in an exceedingly similar way of their healthy peers whereas training specific postural control skills.

Steady-state sway has been used as an alternate measure of postural control in an exceeding amount of studies that found out sitting postural control in CP children. A study by curtis et al in 2015 showed as significant and powerful relationship between head and trunk postural control and gross motor function measured using GMFM and purposeful abilities using the PEDI test self-care and mobility domains, variety of studies have conjointly connected decreased sway with increased motor function in CP children.

The analysis of the demographic data of the study participants revealed that there was no significant difference among them as far as age, gender and GMFCS scores are concerned, which says the groups were similar at the time of randomisation. Any changes that had happened in completely attributed to the intervention provided. There were 7 drop outs from the study, 3 in group A and 4 drop outs in group B. As drop outs were accounted during sample size calculation an intention to treat analysis was done. GMFCS 3 and 4 was selected for the study because trunk impairment was major issue among these subjects and an intervention tool proved effective for this category is assumed to be effective for GMFCS score 1 and 2 also.

A wide range of age was used for this study because the researcher wanted to standardise the treatment protocol for a wide range of age group of people suffering with cerebral palsy. The GMFCS score was adopted to bring about a homogeneity among the population because cerebral palsy manifest with different ranges of motor deficits. The researcher was particular that, the influence of chronicity or disability variations of the cerebral palsy should not influence the treatment outcome and the intervention should not be termed ineffective for other confounding reasons.

There are four outcome measures used in the study which addresses different aspects of rehabilitation following cerebral palsy. The gross motor function scale (GMFM) was used to analyse the gross motor functions of the child like lying and rolling, sitting, crawling, kneeling, standing, walking, running and jumping which are very vital in the developmental stages of a kid. Though the study did not analyse the fine motor function which is beyond the scope of this intervention it did assess the gross motor function to the maximum. In the baseline analysis of GM FM scale, it is very obvious that the groups were similar at the time of recruitment as there was no significant difference between values of both groups. In the analysis of subsequent post-test- I there was no significant difference between the groups but there was a significant difference between the two groups at the end of the intervention in post-test 2, which clearly signifies that though there was no improvement in the early stages of the intervention there was a slow and steady improvement in favour of our intervention tool.

In the within group analysis of group A there was no difference between the pre-test and post-test- I value but there was a significant difference between the pre-test and post-test two values which clearly says that the conventional treatment takes its own time for showing a significant result. But in the group B analysis there was a significant difference between the pre-test I and the post-test 2 which signifies that there was a steady improvement following the group B intervention.

The second outcome measure used for the study was segmental assessment of trunk control (SATCO). When it comes to segmental control, the vital coordinated movement of neck and head, neck and thorax, thorax and pelvis and finally the pelvis and the lower limb are emphasised. The Scale measures the various anatomical locations of the body and its position. The major anatomical landmarks which were discussed in the scale are shoulder girdle, axial, scapula, ribs, pelvis and thigh. The analysis of the study also reveal the same pattern for the pre-test evaluation like that of the previous scale with baseline equality but in analysis of the post-test values show that there was a significant difference between both the groups for post-test I and post-test 2.

This clearly sends a message that this intervention is very effective in bringing about a quick change in the segmental alignment of trunk in cerebral palsy children. This might be explained by the fact that the intervention is attesting the inter segmental coordinated moment of axial skeleton and appendicular skeleton in a neuro developmental sequence. Within the group A analysis shows that there is no significant difference between the pre-test and the post-test I values but there was a marginal difference in the pre-test and the post-test 2 value. The analysis of group B showed that there was a highly significant difference between the pre-test values and the two post-test values, which signifies that the group B intervention brings about a quick improvement and a sustained improvement in gross motor functions of the cerebral palsy children.

The third scale used for the study was trunk control measures scale. The scale was included to analyse the static and dynamic balance of cerebral palsy children, which is a very important component of day to day activity. The previous scales did assess the static component of balance but did not assess the dynamic component of balance. It was assumed that if dynamic component of the balance if when included, it will add value in demonstrating the improvements gained following NDT intervention from various dimensions. The between group analysis showed that there was no difference at the base line and at the end of first phase of the intervention in post-test 1. In the analysis of the post-test 2 values there was a significant difference between the both groups in favour of group B. This clearly demonstrates that balance could not be improved within a short span but with continuous intervention there is a a significantly better improvement with NDT than the conventional intervention.

Within group analysis showed that in group A there was no significant difference between the pre-test and the post-test 1 value but there was a significant difference between the pre-test and the post-test 2 values but in group B analysis there was a significant difference between the pre-test value and both the post-test 1 and 2 values. Though the within group and between group analysis contradict each other marginally, it is obvious that group B intervention proved to be superior to the convention intervention.

The quality of life was perceived to be a very important aspect and outcome of any intervention particularly in neurological deficits and paediatric conditions. Hence cerebral palsy quality of life scale was used for this study. Analysis of the outcome measures show that there was a no significant difference between group A and group B at any stages of the intervention. Within group analysis of both group A and group B showed that there was no significant difference between the pre-test values and the post-test 1 values but there was a significant difference between the pre-test and the post-test 2 values which clearly signify that the quality of life did not change within a short span of time but it took some time in both the intervention groups.

Thus, from the analysis of the outcome measures it is quite obvious that the group-B intervention (NDT) are far superior to group A intervention in terms of bringing about a significant improvement in the gross motor function, the segmental stability of the trunk and dynamic and static balance. As far as the quality of life is concerned as both are exercise intervention and the difference between them is beyond the comprehension of the patience, there was no superior efficacy of the new intervention tool in comparison to the conventional tool.

Further scopes for the study

Gross motor function was only analysed in the study. In future interventions can be framed for improving the fine motor functions of cerebral palsy children using GMFCS classification.

Future studies can also concentrate on finding various other improvements gained using NDT with a segmental approach as a tool like Gait, cognitive function and so on.

Future studies can concentrate on developing new equipment for improving segmental trunk control like trunk dissociation Re trainer which was used for stroke subjects.

A long-term outcome analysis of the sustainability of the effects the intervention can be studied.

Studies with long term analysis of quality of life following NDT can be performed.

CHAPTER 7

Conclusion

This study tried analyze the effect of NDT on improving the segmental trunk control of cerebral palsy children falling under GMCS score 3 and 4. 80 subjects were recruited into the study and were randomly allotted into two groups namely group A (conventional group) and group B (experimental group treated using NDT). Four outcome measures were used namely GMFM, SATCO, TCMS and CP-QOL. The intervention was provided for a period of 4 weeks.

(1) From the analysis of the results of the study it is clearly understood that both conventional physiotherapy and NDT have brought about significant improvement in all the outcome measures.

(2) The NDT intervention used with a segmental approach in group B have brought about a superior improvement than the conventional intervention.

(3) Further except the quality of life all other parameters have shown a faster and sustained improvement following the NDT intervention compared to the conventional physiotherapy.

(4) Thus, it is concluded from this study that NDT with a segmental approach is a better intervention tool in bringing about improvement in gross motor function, segmental trunk control, static and dynamic balance in cerebral palsy children with GMFCS scale 3 and 4.

CHAPTER-8

BIBLIOGRAPHY

Adolph KE, Berger DE. Motor development. In: Kuhn D, Siegler RS, eds. Cognition, Perception, and Language. 6th ed. New York, NY: John Wiley and Sons; 2006:61-213. Handbook of Child Psychology, Vol 2

Adolph KE, Berger SE, Leo AJ. Developmental continuity? Crawling, cruising, and walking. Dev Sci 2011 ;14(2):306-318

Adolph KE. Learning to Move. Curr Dir Psychol Sci 2008;17(3): 213-218

Advisory Committee (1999) Joint position statement on evidencebased practice in occupational therapy. Canadian Journal of Occupational Therapy, 66, 267-69.

Alexander R, Boehme R, Cupps B. Normal Development of Functional Motor Skills: The First Year of Life. San Antonio, TX: Therapy Skill Builders; 1993

Alsop A (1997) Evidence-based practice and continuing professional development. British Journal of Occupational Therapy, 60, 503-508. Bannigan K (1997) Clinical effectiveness: systematic reviews and evidencebased practice in occupational therapy. British Journal of Occupational Therapy, 60, 479-83.

Anttila H, Suoranta J, Malmivaara A, Makela M, Autti-Ramo I. Effectiveness of physiotherapy and conductive education interventions in children with cerebral palsy: a focused review. Am J Phys Med Rehabil 2008; 87: 478-501.

Arndt SW, Chandler LS, Sweeney JK, Sharkey MA, McElroy JJ. Effects of a neurodevelopmental treatment-based trunk protocol for infants with posture and movement dysfunction. Pediatr Phys Ther 2008;20(1): 11-22

Ashwal S, Russman BS, Blasco PA, et al, and the Quality Standards Subcommittee of the American Academy of Neurology, and the Practice Committee of the Child Neurology Society. Practice parameter: diagnostic assessment of the child with cerebral palsy: report of the Quality Standards Subcommittee of the American Academy of Neurology and the Practice Committee of the Child Neurology Society. Neurology 2004; 62: 851-63.

Assaiante C, Mallau S, Viel S, Jover M, Schmitz C. Development of postural control in healthy children: a functional approach. Neural Plast 2005;12(2-3): 109-118, discussion 263-272
Bahtiyar MO, Dulay AT, Weeks BP, Friedman AH, Copel JA. Prevalence of congenital heart defects in monochorionic/diamniotic twin gestations: a systematic literature review. J Ultrasound Med 2007; 26: 1491-98.

Bannigan K, Droogan J, Entwistle V (1997) Systematic reviews: what do they involve? Nursing Times, 93(18), 52-53.

Bartlett D, Purdie B. Testing of the Spinal Alignment and Range of Motion Measure: a discriminative measure of posture and flexibility for children with cerebral palsy. Dev Med Child Neurol. 2005;47:739-743

Bax M, Goldstein M, Rosenbaum P, et al. Proposed definition and classification of cerebral palsy, April 2005. Dev Med Child Neurol. 2005;47:571-576

Bax, Martin C.O. Terminoligy and Classification of Cerebral Palsy. Developmental Medicine & Child Neurology. June, 1964, Vol. 6, 3, pp. 295-297 DOI: 10.1111/j.1469-8749.1964.tbl0791.x.

Bayley, Nancy. Bayley Scale of Infant and Toddler Development, 3rd edition. San Antonio, Texas : Hardcourt Assessment Inc, 2005.

Beckung E, Hagberg G. Correlation between ICIDH handicap code and Gross Motor Function Classification System in children with cerebral palsy. Dev Med Child Neurol. 2000;42:669-673.

Bennet L, Tan S, Van den Heuij L, et al. Cell therapy for neonatal hypoxia-ischaemia and cerebral palsy. Ann Neurol 2012; 7: 586-600.

Benson, Janette B. and Haith, Marshall M. Diseases and Disorders in Infancy and Early Childhood. Oxford: Elsevier inc, 2009. 9780123750686.

Benson, Janette B. and Haith, Marshall M. Diseases and Disorders in Infancy and Early Childhood. Oxford: Elsevier inc, 2009.

Bertenthal B, Von Hofsten C. Eye, head and trunk control: the foundation for manual development. NeurosciBiobehav Rev 1998;22(4):515-520

Bertoncelli CM, Altamura P, Identifying Factors Associated With Severe Intellectual Disabilities in Teenagers With Cerebral Palsy Using a Predictive Leaming Model, J Child Neurol. 2019 Jan 22: 883073818822358.

Bertoti DB (1986) Effect of short leg casting on ambulation of children with cerebral palsy. Physical Therapy, 66, 1522-29.

Bigongiari A, de Andrade e Souza F, Franciulli PM, et al. Anticipatory and compensatory postural adjustments in sitting in children with cerebral palsy. Human Movement Science. 2011;30(3):648-57.

Bjornson KF, Belza B, Kartin D, Logsdon RG, McLaughlin J. Self-reported health status and quality of life in youth with cerebral palsy and typically developing youth. Arch Phys Med Rehabil 2008;89, 121-27.

Blair E, Stanley FJ. Issues in the classifi cation and epidemiology of cerebral palsy. Ment Retard Dev Disabil Res Rev 1997; 3: 184-93.

Blair E, Watson L, Badawi N, Stanley FJ. Life expectancy among people with cerebral palsy in Western Australia. Dev Med Child Neurol 2001; 43: 508-15.

Blair E, Watson L. Epidemiology of cerebral palsy. Semin Fetal Neonatal Med 2006; 11: 117-25.

Blanche EI, Halloway M (1998) Historical perspective: neurodevelopmental treatment in occupational therapy [Special issue]. Developmental Disabilities, 21(3), 1-3.

Bly L (1991) A historical and current view of the basis of NDT. Pediatric Physical Therapy, 3, 131-36.

Bly L. Components of Typical and Atypical Motor Development. Laguna Beach, CA: NDTA; 2011

Bly L. Motor Skills Acquisition in the First Year: An Illustrated Guide to Normal Development. Tucson, AZ: Therapy Skill Builders; 1994

Bobath K. (1980) Neurophysiological basis for the treatment of cerebral palsy. London:William Heinemann Medical.

Bobath K. Bobath B (1984) The neurodevelopmental treatment. In: D Scrutton, ed. Management of the motor disorders of children with cerebral palsy. Philadelphia: JB Lippincott, 6-18.

Bobath K. Bobath B. The neurodevelopmental treatment. In: Scrutton D, ed. Management of the Motor Disorders of Children with Cerebral Palsy. Philadelphia, PA: JB Lippincott; 1984:155-166
Bodkin, Amy Winter MS, PT, PCS; Robinson, Cordelia PhD; Perales, Frida P. MA Reliability and Validity of the Gross Motor Function Classification System for Cerebral Palsy Pediatric Physical Therapy, 2003,15(4); 247-252.

Brogren Carlberg E, Hadders-Algra M. Postural control in sitting children with cerebral palsy. In: Hadders-Algra M, Brogren Carlberg E. eds. Postural Control: A Key Issue in Developmental Disorders. London, UK: MacKeith Press; 2008:74-96. Clinics in Developmental Medicine, No.

Brogren E, Forssberg H, Hadders-Algra M. Influence of two different sitting positions on postural adjustments in children with spastic diplegia. Dev Med Child Neurol. 2001 Aug;43(8):53446.
Brogren E, Hadders-Algra M, Forssberg H. Postural control in children with spastic diplegia: muscle activity during perturbations in sitting. Dev Med Child Neurol. 1996 May;38(5):379-88.
Brogren E, Hadders-Algra M, Forssberg H. Postural control in sitting children with cerebral palsy. Neurosci Biobehav Rev. 1998 Jul;22(4):591-6.

Brunton L K Bartlett DJ. Validity and reliability of two abbreviated versions of the Gross Motor Function Measure. PhysicalTherapy Journal 2011;91:577-588.

Buckon CE, Thomas SS, Piatt JH Jr, Aiona MD, Sussman MD. Selective dorsal rhizotomy versus orthopedic surgery a multidimensional assessment of outcome efficiency. Arch Phys Med Rehabil 2004; 85: 457-65.

Burguet A, Monnet E, Pauchard JY, et al. Some risk factors for cerebral palsy in very premature infants: importance of premature rupture of membranes and monochorionic twin placentation. Biol Neonate 1999; 75: 177-86.

Burton, Allen William and Miller, Daryl E. Movement Skill Assessment. Leeds, UK : Human Kinetics, 1998. 0873229754.

Butler PB, Saavedra S, Sofranac M, Jarvis SE, Woollacott MH. Refinement, reliability and validity of the Segmental Assessment of Trunk Control. Pediatr Phys Tuer 2010: 22:1-13.

Butterworth G, Hicks L. Visual proprioception and postural stability in infancy. A developmental study. Perception 1977;6(3):255-262

Campbell P. The child's development of functional movement. In: Campbell S K Palisano RJ, Orlin MN, eds. Physical Therapy for Children. 3rd ed. St. Louis, MO: Elsevier Saunders; 2006:37

Canadian Association of Occupational Therapists, Association of Canadian Occupational Therapy University Programmes, Association of Canadian Occupational Therapy Regulatory Organisations, The Presidents'

Carlberg EB, Hadders-Algra M. Postural dysfunction in children with cerebral palsy: some implications for therapeutic guidance. Neural Plas. 2005;12(2-3):221-8.

Carlsen PN (1975) Comparison of two occupational therapy approaches for treating the young cerebral-palsied child. American Journal of Occupational Therapy, 29, 267-72.

Carol K. and Rider, Elizabeth A Life-Span Human Development. Belmont, CA : Wadsworth Cengage Learning, 2012. 1111342733.
Carranza-de! Rio J, Clegg NJ, Moore A, Delgado MR Use of trihexyphenidyl in children with cerebral palsy. PediatrNeurol 2011; 44: 202-06.

Chandra RK, Kumari S. Nutrition and immunity: an overview. J Nutr 1994; 124 (suppl): S1433-35. 107 Dutton G, Bax M, eds. Visual impairment in children due to damage to the brain. Clinics in developmental medicine no. 186. London: Mac Keith Press, Wiley-Blackwell, 2010.

Cignetti F, Kyvelidou A, Harboume RT, Stergiou N. Anterior-posterior and medial-lateral control of sway in infants during sitting acquisition does not become adult-like. Gait Posture 2011;33(1):88-92

Cioni G, Duchini F, Milianti B, et al. Differences and variations in the patterns of early independent walking. Early Hum Dev 1993;35(3): 193-205

Cloud LJ, Jinnah HA Treatment strategies for dystonia. Expert Opin Pharmacother 2010; 11: 5-15.

Clover, Allan. Classification of cerebral palsy: Padiatric perspective. Developmental Medicine & Child Neurology. February, 2007, Vol. 49, Supplement s2, pp. 15 DOI: 10.1111/j.1469-8749.2007.00201.

Colver AF, Sethumadhavan T. The term diplegia should be abandoned. Arch Dis Child 2003; 88: 286-90.

Cook DB, Sackett DL, Spitzer WO (1995) Methodologic guidelines for systematic reviews of randomised controlled trials in health care from the Potsdam consultation on meta-analysis. Journal of Clinical Epidemiology, 48, 167-71.

Cook DJ, Guyatt GH, Laupacis A, Sackett DL, Goldberg RJ (1995) Clinical recommendations using levels of evidence for antithrombotic agents. Chest, 108 (4, Suppl), 227S-230S.

Cook DJ, Guyatt GH, Ryan G, Clifton J, Buckingham L, Willan A, Mcilroy A, Oxman A (1993) Should unpublished data be included in metaanalyses? Current convictions and controversies. Journal of the American Medical Association, 269(21), 2749-53.

Corbetta D, Snapp-Childs W. Seeing and touching: the role of sensory-motor experience on the development of infant reaching. Infant Behav Dev 2009;32(1):44-58

Creasy, Robert K., Resnik, Robert and Iams, Jay D. Maternal-Fetal Medicine. Philadelphia, Pennsylvania : Saunders, 2004. 0721600042.

Croen LA, Grether JK Curry CJ, Nelson KB. Congenital abnormalities among children with cerebral palsy: More evidence or prenatal antecedents. J Pediatr 2001; 138: 804-10.

D a Costa CS, Batistao MV, Rocha NA Quality and structure of variability in children during motor development: a systematic review. Res Dev Disabil 2013;34(9):2810-2830

Dan B, Motta F, Vles JS, et al. Consensus on the appropriate use of intrathecal baclofen (1TB) therapy in paediatric spasticity. Eur J Paediatr Neurol 2010; 14: 19-28.

David, Ronald B. Child and Adolecent Neurology. Malden, Massachusetts: Blackwell publishing, 2005. 1405117672. 92

De Graaf-Peters VB, Bakker H, van Eykem LA, Otten B, Hadders-Algra M. Postural adjustments and reaching in 4- and 6-month-old infants: an EMG and kinematical study. Exp Brain Res 2007;181(4):647-656

Deffeyes JE, Harboume RT, Kyvelidou A, Stuberg WA, Stergiou N. Nonlinear analysis of sitting postural sway indicates developmental delay in infants. Clin Biomech (Bristol, Avon) 2009;24(7):564-570

Delgardo M, Hirtz D, Aisen M, Ashwal S. Practice parameter: pharmacologic treatment of spasticity in children and adolescents with cerebral palsy (an evidence-based review). Report of the Quality Standards Sub-Committee of the American Academy of Neurology and Practice Committee of the Child Neurology Society. Neurology 2010; 24: 336-43.

Dickinson HO, Parkinson KN, Ravens-Sieberer U, et al. self-reported quality of life of 8-12-year-old children with cerebral palsy: a cross-sectional European study. Lancet 2007; 369: 2171-78.

Dickson R, Entwistle V (1996) Systematic reviews: keeping up with research evidence. Nursing Standard, 10(19), 32.

Dodge, Nancy N. Medical Management of Cerebral Palsy. [book auth.] Dilip R. Patel, et al. Neurodevelopmental Disabilities-Clinical care for children and young adults. New York : Springer Verlag, 2011.

Dolk, Helen, Pattenden, Sam and Johnson, Ann. Cerebral palsy, low birthweight and socio-economic deprivation: inequalities in a major cause of childhood disability. Paediatric and Perinatal Epidemiology. 2001, Vol. 15, pp. 359-363.

Doyle LW, Crowther CA, Middleton P, Marret S, Rouse D. Magnesium sulphate for women at risk of preterm birth for euro protection of the fetus. Cochrane Database Syst Rev 2009; 1: CD004661.

Dumas, Helene. Clinical review of Pediatric Evaluation of Disability Inventory. Pediatric Physical Therapy. Spring, 2001, Vol. 13, 1, pp. 47-48.

Dunn J, Pretell E, Daza C, Viteri F, eds. Towards the eradication of endemic goitre, cretinism and iodine deficiency. Austin, TX, USA: Pan American Health Organization, 1986.

Dusing SC, Harbourne RT. Variability in postural control during infancy: implications for development, assessment, and intervention. Phys Ther 2010;90(12):1838-1849

Dusing SC, Izzo TA, Thacker LR, Galloway JC. Postural complexity differs between infant born full term and preterm during the development of early behaviors. Early Hum Dev 2014;90(3): 149-156

Edelman GM. Bright Air, Brilliant Fire: On the Matter of the Mind. New York, NY: Basic Books; 1992

Edelman GM. Neural Darwinism. The Theory of Neuronal Group Selection. New York, NY: Basic Books; 1987

Edwards AD, Brocklehurst P, Gunn AJ, et al. Neurological outcomes at 18 months of age after moderate hypothermia for perinatal hypoxic ischaemic encephalopathy: synthesis and meta-analysis of trial data. BMJ 2010; 340: c363.

Eishima K. The analysis of sucking behaviour in newborn infants. Early Hum Dev 1991;27(3): 163-173

Elena Mitteregger and Petra Marsico, Translation and construct validity of the Trunk Control Measurement Scale in children and youths with brain lesions, Research in Developmental Disabilities 45-46 (2015) 343-352

Eliasson AC, Krumlinde-Sundholm L, Rosblad B, et al. The Manua Ability Classi fi cation System (MACS) for children with cerebral palsy: scale development and evidence of validity and reliability. Dev Med Child Neurol 2006; 48: 549-54.

Eliasson, Ann-Christin, et al. The Manual Classification System (MACS) for children with cerebral palsy: scale development and evidence of validity and reliability. Developmental Medicine & Child Neurology. July, 2006, Vol. 48, 7, pp. 549-554 DOI:10.1017/S0012162206001162.

Eliasson, Ann-Christin. Manual Ability Classification System for Children with Cerebral Palsy 4-18 years. www.macs.nu. [Online] 2005 (updated 2010). [Cited: 23 March 2012.] http://www.macs.nu/files/MACS_English_2010.pdf.

Evans PM, Alberman E. Certified cause of death in children and young adults with cerebral palsy. Arch Dis Child 1991; 66: 325-29.

Fairhurst C, Cockerill H. Management of drooling in children. Arch Dis Child Pract Ed 2011; 96: 25-30.

Fauconnier J, Dickinson HO, Beckung E, et al. Participation in life situations of 8-12 year old children with cerebral palsy: cross sectional European study. BMJ 2009; 338: b1458.

Fehlings D, Switzer L, Agarwal P, et al. Informing evidence-based clinical practice guidelines for children with cerebral palsy at risk of osteoporosis: a systematic review. Dev Med Child Neurol 2012; 54: 106-16.

Feldman, Amy b., Haley, Stephen M. and Coryell, Jane. Concurrent and Construct Validity of the Pediatric Evaluation of Disability Inventory. Physical Therapy-Journal of the American Physical Therapy Association. October, 1990, Vol. 70, 10, pp. 602-610.

Fetters L. Cerebral palsy: contemporary treatment concepts. In: Lister M, ed. Contemporary Management of Motor Control Problems. Proceedings from II Step Conference. Foundation for Physical Therapy. Alexandria, VA: American Physical Therapy Association; 1991:219-224

Fetters L. Perspective on variability in the development of human action. Phys Ther 2010;90(12): 1860-1867

Field DA, Roxborough LA. Responsiveness of the Seated Postural Control Measure and the Level of Sitting Scale in children with neuromotor disorders. Disabil Rehabil Assist Technol 2011; 6: 473-82.
Fife SE, Roxborough LA, Armstrong RW, Harris SR, Gregson JL, Field D. Development of a clinical measure of postural control for assessment of adaptive seating in children with neuromotor disabilities. Phys Tuer. 1991;71:981-993. [PubMed]

Fife SE. Reliability of a measure to assess outcomes of adaptive seating in children with neuromotor disabilities. Can J Rehabil 1993; 7: 11 -3.

Flatters I, Mushtaq F, Hill LJ, Holt RJ, Wilkie RM, Mon-Williams M. The relationship between a child's postural stability and manual dexterity. Exp Brain Res 2014;232(9):2907-2917

Pleiss B, Gressens P. Tertiary mechanisms of brain damage: a new hope for treatment of cerebral palsy? Lancet Neurol 2012; 11: 556-66.

Foster EC, Sveistrup H, Woollacott MH. Transitions in visual proprioception: a cross-sectional development study of the effect of visual flow on postural control. J Mot Behav 1996;28(2): 101-112.

Freud S. Infantile cerebrala.hmung, 1897 [Infantile cerebral paralysis]. Florida: University of Miami Press, 1968.

Fusi L, McParland P, Fisk N, Nicolini U, Wigglesworth J. Acute twin-twin transfusion: a possible mechanism for brain-damaged survivors after intrauterine death of a monochorionic twin. Obstet Gynecol 1991; 78: 517-20.

Gan SM, Tung LC, Tang YH, Wang CH. Psychometric properties of functional balance assessment in children with cerebral palsy. Neurorehabil Neural Repair 2008; 22: 745-53.

Gaspard N, Vanderhaeghen P. From stem cells to neural networks: recent advances and perspectives for neurodevelopmental disorders. Dev Med Child Neurol 2011; 53: 13-17.
Gesell A, Halverson HM, Thompson H, et al. The First Five Years of Life. New York, NY: Harper and Row; 1940

Gesell A. Infancy and Human Growth. New York, NY: Macmillan; 1928

Gewirtz JL, Pelaez-Nogueras M. B. F. Skinner's legacy to human infant behavior and development. Am Psychol 1992;47(1 l): 1411-1422

Girolami GL, Campbell SK. (1994) Efficacy of a neuro developmental treatment programmer to improve motor control in infants born prematurely. Pediatric Physical Therapy, 6, 175-84.

Gladstone M. A review of the incidence and prevalence, types and aetiology of childhood cerebral palsy in resource-poor settings. Ann Trop Paediatr 2010; 30: 181-96.

Goodman M, Rothberg AD, Houston-McMillan JE, Cooper PA, Cartwright JD, Van der Velde MA (1985) Effect of early neurodevelopmental therapy in normal and at-risk survivors of neonatal intensive care. The Lancet, 2, 1327-30.

Gorter, Jan Willem, et al. Use of GMFCS in infants with CP: the need for reclassification at 2 years or older. Developmental Medicine & Child Neurology. January, 2008, Vol. 51, 1, pp. 46-52 DOI: 10.1111/j.1469-8749.2008.03117.

Gough M. Continuous postural management and the prevention of deformity in children with cerebral palsy: an appraisal. Dev Med Child Neurol 2009; 51: 105-10.

Grether JK, Nelson KB, Cummins SK. Twinning and cerebral palsy: experience in four northern California counties, births 1983 through 1985. Pediatrics 1993; 92: 854-58.

Groen SE, de Blecourt AC, Postema K, Hadders-Algra M. General movements in early infancy predict neuromotor development at 9 to 12 years of age. Dev Med Child Neurol 2005;47(1 1): 731-738

Grunt S, Becher JG, Vermeulen RJ, Becher JG, Vermuelen RJ. Long-term outcome and adverse effects of selective dorsal rhizotomy in children with cerebral palsy: a systematic review. Dev Med Child Neurol 2011; 53: 490-98.

Gurfinkel VS, Lipshits MI, Mori S, Popov KE. Stabilization of body position as the main task of postural regulation. HumPhysiol. 1981;7(3):155-65.

Guzzetta, Francesco. Early brain injuries: infantile cerebral palsy. [book auth.] Francesco Romeo Guzzetta. Neurology of the Infant. Montrouge: Editions John Libbey Eurotext, 2009.
Haak P, Lenski M, Hidecker MJ, Li M, Paneth N. Cerebral palsy and aging. Dev Med Child Neurol 2009; 51 (suppl 4): 16-23

Hack M, Costello DW. Trends in the rates of cerebral palsy associated with neonatal intensive care of preterm children. Clin Obstet Gynecol. 2008;51:763-774.

Hadden KL, von Baeyer CL. Pain in children with cerebral palsy: common triggers and expressive behaviors. Pain 2002; 99: 281-88.

Hadders-Algra M, Carlberg EB. Postural Control: A key issue in developmental disorders.

Hadders-Algra M, Carlberg EB, editors. London: Mac Keith Press; 2008.
Hadders-Algra M. General movements: A window for early identification of children at high risk for developmental disorders. J Pediatr 2004; 145(2, Suppl)S12-S18

Hadders-Algra M. The neuronal group selection theory: promising principles for understanding and treating developmental motor disorders. Dev Med Child Neurol 2000;42(10):707-715

Hadders-Algra M. Typical and atypical development of reaching and postural control in infancy. Dev Med Child Neurol 2013;55(Suppl 4):5-8

Hadders-Algra M. Variation and variability: key words in human motor development. Phys Ther 2010;90(12): 1823-1837

Hadjipanayis A, Hadjichristodoulou C, Youroukos S. Epilepsy in patients with cerebral palsy. Dev Med Child Neurol 1997; 39: 659-63.

Hagberg B, Hagberg G, Beckung E, Uvebrant P. Changing panorama of cerebral palsy in Sweden. VIII. Prevalence an origin in the birth year period 1991-94. Acta Paediatr 2001; 90: 271-77.

Hagberg B, Hagberg G, Olow I. The changing panorama of cerebral palsy in Sweden. VI. Prevalence and origin during the birth year period 1983-1986. Acta Paediatr. 1993;82:387-393.

Hammal D, Jarvis SN, Colver AF. Participation of children with cerebral palsy is infl uenced by where they live. Dev Med Child Neurol 2004; 46: 292-98.

Hanzlik JR (1989) The effect of intervention on the free-play experience for mothers and their infants with developmental delay and cerebral palsy. Physical and Occupational Therapy in Pediatrics, 9(2), 33-51.

Harbourne RT, Deffeyes JE, Kyvelidou A, Stergiou N. Complexity of postural control in infants: linear and nonlinear features revealed by principal component analysis. Nonlinear DynPsychol Life Sci 2009; 13(1): 123-144

Hasson CJ, van Emmerik RE, Caldwell GE. Balance decrements are associated with age-related muscle property changes. J ApplBiomech 2014;30(4):555-562

Hayes RL (1998) Evidence-based practice: the Cochrane Collaboration and occupational therapy. Canadian Journal of Occupational Therapy, 65, 144-51.

Haywood, Kathleen M. and Getchell, Nancy. Life Span Motor Development. Campaign, Illinois: Human Kintetics, 2009. 0736075526.

Heba M Youssr El-Basatiny, AmrAlmaz Abdel-aziem: Effect of Trunk Exercises on Hedberg A, Carlberg EB, Forssberg H, Hadders-Algra M. Development of postural adjustments in sitting position during the first half year of life. Dev Med Child Neurol 2005;47(5):312-320

Hedberg A, Forssberg H, Hadders-Algra M. Postural adjustments due to external perturbations during sitting in I-month-old infants: evidence for the innate origin of direction specificity. Exp Brain Res 2004;157(1):10-17

Heineman KR, Middelburg KJ, Hadders-Algra M. Development of adaptive motor behaviour in typically developing infants. Acta Paediatr 2010;99(4):618-624

Heinen F, Desloovere K Schroeder AS, et al. The updated European Consensus 2009 on the use of Botulinurn toxin for children with cerebral palsy. Eur J Paediatr Neurol 2010; 14: 45-66.

Herdon WA, Troup P, Yngve DA, Sullivan JA (1987) Effects of neurodevelopmental treatment on movement patterns of children with cerebral palsy. Journal of Pediatric Orthopedics, 7, 395-400.

Heyrman L, Desloovere K Molenaers G, et al. Clinical characteristics of impaired trunk control in children with spastic cerebral palsy. Res Dev Disabil. 2013;34(1):327-34.

Heyrman L, Molenaers G, Desloovere K et al. A clinical tool to measure trunk control in children with cerebral palsy: the Trunk Control Measurement Scale. Res Dev Disabil. 2011; 32: 2624-2635.

Hidecker MJ, Paneth N, Rosenbaum PL, et al. Developing an validating the Communication Function Classification System for individuals with cerebral palsy. Dev Med Child Neurol 2011;53: 704-10.

Hinchcliffe, Archie. Children with Cerebral Palsy- A Manual for Therapists, Parents and Community workers. London: Sage Publication Ltd, 2007. 9780761935605.

Hjern, Anders and Thorgren-Jernec, Kristina. Perinatal complications and socio-economic differences in cerebral palsy in Sweden - a national cohort study. Stockholm: Centre of Epidemiology, National Board of Health and Welfare, 2008.

Hong Phi Pham, Anita Eidem, Gry Hansen et al Validity and Responsiveness of the Trunk Impairment Scale and Trunk Control Measurement Scale in Young Individuals with Cerebral Palsy, Physical & Occupational Therapy in Pediatrics, 00(00): 1-13, 2016.

Hopkins B, Ronnqvist L. Facilitating postural control: effects on the reaching behavior of 6-month-old infants. Dev Psychobiol 2002;40(2): 168-182

Hoyme HE, Higginbottom MC, Jones KL. Vascular etiology of disruptive structural defects in monozygotic twins. Pediatrics 1981;67: 288-91.

Hutton JL, Pharoah PO. Life expectancy in severe cerebral palsy. Arch Dis Child 2006; 91: 254-58.

Hvidtj0rn D, Grove J, Schendel D, et al. Multiplicity and early gestational age contribute to an increased risk of cerebral palsy from assisted conception: a population-based cohort study. Hurn Reprod 2010; 25: 2115-23.

Hvidtj0rn D, Grove J, Schendel DE, et al. Cerebral palsy among children born after in vitro fertilization: the role of preterm delivery-a population-based, cohort study. Pediatrics 2006; 118: 475-82.

Ibrahim SH, Bhutta ZA. Prevalence of early childhood disability in a rural district of Sind, Pakistan. Dev Med Child Neurol 2013; 55: 357-63.

Imms C, Reilly S, Carlin J, Dodd K Diversity of participation in children with cerebral palsy. Dev Med Child Neurol 2008; 50: 363-69.

Imms C. Children with cerebral palsy participate: a review of the literature. Disabil Rehabil 2008; 30: 1867-84.

Iwayama K. Eishima M. Neonatal sucking behaviour and its development until 14 months. Early Hum Dev 1997;47(1):1-9.

Jadad AR, Moher D, Klassen TP (1998) Guides for reading and interpreting systematic reviews II. Archives of Pediatrics and Adolescent Medicine, 152, 812-17.

Jadad AR, Moore RA, Carroll D, Jenkinson C, Reynolds JM, Gavaghan DJ, McQuay HJ (1996) Assessing the quality of reports of randomised clinical trials: is blinding necessary? Controlled Clinical Trials, 17, 1-12.

Jams T, Bart 0, Rabinovich G, et al. Effects of prone and supine positions on sleep state and stress responses in preterm infants. Infant Behav Dev 2011;34(2):257-263

Jarvis S, Glinianaia S, Torrioli M, et al, for the Surveillance of Cerebral Palsy in Europe (SCPE) collaboration of European Cerebral Palsy Registers. Cerebral palsy and intrauterine growth in single births: European collaborative study. Lancet 2003; 62: 1106-11.

Johnston MV, Fatemi A, Wilson MA, Northington F. Treatment advances in neonatal neuroprotection and neuro intensive care. Lancet Neurol 2011; 10: 372-82.
Joseph, K. S., et al. Does the risk of cerebral palsy increase or decrease with the increasing gestational age? Biomed Central. [Online] 23 December 2003. [Cited: 21 March 2012.] http://www.biomedcentral.com/1471-2393/3/8. doi: 10.1186/1471-2393-3-8.

Jun-Young Jeon a, Won-Seob Shin, Reliability and validity of the Korean version of the Trunk Control Measurement Scale (TCMS-K) for children with cerebral palsy, Research in Developmental Disabilities 35 (2014) 581-590.

Kan P, Gooch J, Amini A, et al. Surgical treatment of spasticity inchildren: comparison of selective dorsal rhizotomy and intrathecal baclofen pump implantation. Childs Nerv Syst 2008; 24: 239-43

Kanda T, Yuge M, Yamori Y, Suzuki J, Fukase H (1984) Early physiotherapy in the treatment of spastic diplegia. Developmental Medicine and Child Neurology, 26, 438-44.

Katalinic OM, Harvey LA, Herbert RD. Effectiveness of stretch for the treatment and prevention of contractures in people with neurological conditions: a systematic review. Phys Ther 2011; 91: 11-24.

Kennes, Janneke, et al. Health status of school aged children with cerebral palsy: information from a population-based sample. Developmental Medicine & Child Neurology. April, 2002, Vol. 44, 4, pp. 240-247 DOI: 10.1111/j.1469-8749.2002.tb00799.

Keshner EA (1981) Reevaluating the theoretical model underlying the neurodevelopmental theory. Physical Therapy, 61, 1035-1140.

King G, Law M, Hanna S, et al. Predictors of the leisure and recreation participation of children with physical disabilities: a structural equation modeling analysis. Child Health Care 2006; 35: 209-34.

Kirk S. Transitions in the lives of young people with complex healthcare needs. Child Care Health Dev 2008; 34: 567-75.

Klassen TP, Jadad AR, Moher D (1998) Guides for reading and interpreting systematic reviews I. Archives of Pediatrics and Adolescent Medicine, 152, 700-704.

Ko B, McEnery G. The needs of physically disabled young people during transition to adult services. Child Care Health Dev 2004; 30: 317-23.

Kolar, Pavel. Facilitation of Agonist-Antagonist Co-activation by Reflex Stimulation Methods. [book auth.] Craig Liebenson. Rehabilitation of the Spine. Baltimore, USA : Lippincott Williams & Wilkins, 2007.
Kong E. Early detection of cerebral motor disorders. In: Forssberg H, Hirschfeld H. eds. Movement Disorders in Children. Med. Sport Science. Basel, Ch: Karger; 1992: 80-85

Koy A, Hellmich M, Pauls KA, et al. Effects of deep brain stimulation in dyskinetic cerebral palsy: a meta-analysis. Mov Disord 2013; 28: 647-54.

Krageloh-Mann I, Cans C. Cerebral palsy update. Brain Dev 2009; 31: 537-44.

Krageloh-Mann I, Horber V. The role of magnetic resonance imaging in elucidating the pathogenesis of cerebral palsy: a systematic review. Dev Med Child Neurol 2007; 49: 144-51.

Kuperminc M, Stevenson R. Growth and nutritional disorders in children with cerebral palsy. Dev Dis Res Rev 2008; 14: 137-46.

Landis JR, Koch GG (1977) The measurement of observer agreement for categorical data. Biometrics, 33, 159-74.

Landy H, Nies B. The vanishing twin. New York, NY, USA: Parthenon Publishing Group, 1995.
Landy HJ, Keith LG. The vanishing twin: a review. Hum Reprod Update 1998; 4: 177-83.

Largo, R.H. Early motor development in preterm children. [book auth.] Geert J.P Savelsberg. Development of Coordination in Infancy. Amsterdam: Elsevier Science Publisher, 1993.

Law M, Baum C (1998) Evidence-based occupational therapy. Canadian Journal of Occupational Therapy, 65, 131-35.

Law M, Cadman D, Rosenbaum P, Walter S, Russell D, DeMatteo C (1991) Neurodevelopmental therapy and upper-extremity inhibitive casting for children with cerebral palsy. Developmental Medicine and Child Neurology, 33, 379-87.

Law M, Russell D, Pollock N, Rosenbaum P, Walter S, King G (1997) A comparison of intensive neurodevelopmental therapy plus casting and a regular occupational therapy programme for children with cerebral palsy. Developmental Medicine and Child Neurology, 39, 664-70.

Law MC, Darrah J, Pollock N, et al. Focus on function: a cluster, randomized controlled trial comparing child- versus context-focused intervention for young children with cerebral palsy. Dev Med Child Neurol 2011; 53: 621-29.

Levit K (1995) Remediating motor control and performance through traditional therapeutic approaches: neurodevelopmental (Bobath) treatment. In: CA Trombly, ed. Occupational therapy for physical dysfunction. 4th ed. Baltimore, MD: Williams and Wilkins, 446-62.

Levitt, Sophie. *Treatment of Cerebral Palsy and Motor Delay*. Oxford : Blackwell Publishing, 2010. 9781405176163.

Lewkowicz DJ, Hansen-Tift AM. Infants deploy selective attention to the mouth of a talking face when learning speech. Proc Natl Acad Sci U S A 2012;109(5):1431-1436

Lieve Heyrman, Guy Molenaers et al, A clinical tool to measure trunk control in children with cerebral palsy: The Trunk Control Measurement Scale, Research in Developmental Disabilities 32 (2011) 2624-2635.

Lieve Heyrman, Guy Molenaers, et al A clinical tool to measure trunk control in children with cerebral palsy:The Trunk Control Measurement Scale, Research in Developmental Disabilities 32 (2011) 2624-2635.

Little W. On the influence of abnormal parturition, difficult labours and asphyxia neonatorum on the mental and physical condition of the child, especially in relation to deformities. In: Phillips J, Boulton P, eds. Transactions of the Obstetric Society of London. London: Obstetrical Society of London, 1862; 3: 293.

Lobo MA, Kokkoni E, de Campos AC, Galloway JC. Not just playing around: infants' behaviors with objects reflect ability, constraints, and object properties. Infant Behav Dev 2014;37(3):334-351

Lowes LP, Sveda M, Gajdosik CG, Gajdosik RL. Musculoskeletal development and adaptation. In: Campbell S K Palisano RJ, Orlin MN. 4th ed. Physical Therapy for Children. St. Louis, MO: Elsevier; 2011: 175-204

Lundy CT, Doherty GM, Fairhurst CB. Botulinum toxin type Ainjections can be an effective treatment for pain in children with hip spasms and cerebral palsy. Dev Med Child Neurol 2009; 51: 705-10.

Mac Keith, Ronald C., Mackenzie, Ian C. K. and Polani, Paul E. The Little Club- Memorandum on Termonology and Classification on "Cerebral Palsy". Developmental Medicine & Child Neurology. September, 1959, Vol. 1, 5, pp. 27-35.

MacLennan A A template for defining a causal relation between acute intrapartum events and cerebral palsy: international consensus statement. BMJ 1999; 319: 1054-59.

Majnemer A, Shevell M, Law M, et al. Participation and enjoyment of leisure activities in school-aged children with cerebral palsy Dev Med Child Neurol 2008; 50: 751-58.

Majnemer A Measures for children with developmental disabilities: an ICF-CY approach, 1st edn. London, UK: Mac Keith Press, 2012.

Martin, Suzanne and Kessler, Mary. *Neurologic interventions for physical therapy.* St. Louis : Saunders Elsevier, 2007. 0721604277.

Maryam Oskoui ,Franzina Coutinho, Jonathan Dykeman, Nathalie Jette. An update on the prevalence of cerebral palsy: a systematic review and meta-analysis. Dev Med Child Neurol. 2013; 55: 509-519.

Maudsley G, Hutton JL, Pharoah PO. Cause of death in cerebral palsy: a descriptive study. Arch Dis Child 1999; 81: 390-94.

Mayo NE (1991) The effect of physical therapy for children with motor delay and cerebral palsy: a randomised clinical trial. American Journal of Physical Medicine and Rehabilitation, 70, 258-67.

McGraw M. The Neuromuscular Maturation of the Human Infant. New York, NY: Hafner; 1963
McIntyre S, Taitz D, Keogh J, Goldsmith S, Badawi N, Blair E. A systematic review of risk factors for cerebral palsy in children born at term in developed countries. Dev Med Child Neurol 2013; 55: 499-508.

McMaster University Health Sciences Centre Department of Clinical Epidemiology and Biostatistics (1981a) How to read clinical journals: I. Why to read them and how to start reading them critically. Canadian Medical Association Journal, 124, 555-58.

McMaster University Health Sciences Centre Department of Clinical Epidemiology and Biostatistics (1981b) How to read clinical journals: V. To distinguish useful from useless or even harmful therapy. Canadian Medical Association Journal, 124, 1156-62.

McPherson RJ, Juul SE. Erythropoietin for infants with hypoxic-ischemic encephalopathy. Curr Opin Pediatr 2010; 22: 139-45.

Michael J. Healthcare for all: report of the independent inquiry into access to healthcare for people with learning disabilities London, UK: Department of Health, 2008.

Michelsen SI, Flachs EM, Uldall P, et al. Frequency of participation of 8-12-year-old children with cerebral palsy: a multi-centre cross-sectional European study. Eur J Paediatr Neurol 2009; 13: 165-77.

Michelsen SI, Uldall P, Hansen T, Madsen M. Social integration of adults with cerebral palsy. Dev Med Child Neurol 2006; 48: 643-49.

Michelsen SI, Uldall P, Kejs AMT, Madsen M. Education and employment prospects in cerebral palsy. Dev Med Child Neurol 2005; 47: 511-17.

Miller, Freeman. Cerebral Palsy. New York: Springer Science, 2005. 0-387-2437-7.
Minear, W.L. Special Article: A Classification of Cerebral Palsy. Pediatrics. 1956, 18, pp. 841-852.

Moher D, Cook DJ, Eastwood S, Olkin I, Rennie D, Stroup DF (1999) Improving the quality of reports of meta-analyses of randomised controlled trials: the QUOROM statement. The Lancet, 354, 1896-1900.

Moher D, Jadad AR, Klassen TP (1998) Guides for reading and interpreting systematic reviews III. Archives of Pediatrics and Adolescent Medicine, 152, 915-20.

Moll LR, Cott CA The paradox of normalization through rehabilitation: growing up and growing older with cerebral palsy. Disabil Rehabil 2013; 35: 1276-83.

Moore CM, McAdams AJ, Sutherland J. Intrauterine disseminated intravascular coagulation: a syndrome of multiple pregnancy with a dead twin fetus. J Pediatr 1969; 74: 523-28.

Moreno-De-Luca A, Ledbetter DH, Martin CL. Genetic [corrected] insights into the causes and classification of [corrected] cerebral palsies. Lancet Neurol 2012; 11: 283-92.

Morris C, Bartlett D. Gross Motor Function Classification System: impact and utility. Dev Med Child Neurol 2004: 46; 60-65.

Morris, C., Kurinczuk, J.J. and Rosenbaum, P.L. Who best make the assessment? Professionals' and families' classifications of gross motor function in cerebral palsy are highly reliable. Archives of Disease in Childhood. 2006, Vol. 91, 8, pp. 675-679 DOI: 10.1136adc.2005.090597.

Morris, Christopher and Bartlett, Doreen. Gross Motor Function Classification System: impact and utility. Developmental Medicine and Child Neurology. January, 2004, Vol. 46, 1, pp. 60-65 DOI: 10.1111/j.1469-8749.2004.tb00436.x.

Morris, Christopher, et al. Reliability of the Manual Ability Classification System for children with cerebral palsy. Developmental Medicine & Child Neurology. December, 2006, Vol. 48, 12, pp. 950-953 DOI: 10.1111/j.1469-8749.2006.tb01264.x.

Morris, Christopher, Galuppi, Barbara E. and Rosenbaum, Peter L. Reliability of family report for the Gross Motor Function Classification System. Developmental Medicine & Child Neurology. July, 2004, Vol. 46, 7, pp. 455-460DOI:10.1017/S00121622040000751.

Morris, Christopher. Definition and classification of cerebral palsy: Historical perspective. Developmental Medicine & Child Neurology. February, 2007, Vol. 49, Supplement s2, pp. 3-7

Moster, Dag, et al. Cerebral Palsy Among Term AndPostterm Births. The Journal of the American Medicine Association, JAMA September I, 2010, Vol. 127, 9, pp. 976-982

Mutch, Leslie, et al. Cerebral Palsy Epidemiology: Where are We Now and Where are We Going? Developmental Medicine & Child Neurology. June, 1992, Vol. 34, 6, pp. 547-551.

National Perinatal Epidemiology Unit. Oxford register of early childhood impairments. Oxford, UK: National Perinatal Epidemiology Unit, 2002.

NICE. Guideline 145. Spasticity in children and young people with non-progressive brain disorders. Manchester, UK: National Institute for Health and Clinical Excellence, 2012.

NICE. Report IP318-2. Interventional procedure overview of selective dorsal rhizotomy for spasticity in cerebral palsy. London UK: National Institute for Health and Clinical Excellence, 2009.

Nieuwenhuijsen C, Donkervoort M, Nieuwstraten W, Stam HJ, Roebroeck ME, and the Transition Research Group South West Netherlands. Experienced problems of young adults with cerebral palsy: targets for rehabilitation care. Arch Phys Med Rehabil 2009;90: 1891-97.

Niznik TM, Turner D, Worrell TW. Functional Reach as a Measurement of Balance for Children with Lower Extremity Spasticity. Phys OccupTherPediatr 1996; 15: 1-16.

Nordmark, E., Hagglund, G. and Lagergren, J. Cerebral Palsy in southern Sweden II. Gross motor function and disability. Acta Paediatrica. November, 2001, Vol. 90, 11, pp. 1277-1282 DOI:10.1111/j.1651-2227.2001.tb01575.x.

Nystrom P. The infant mirror neuron system studied with high density EEG. Soc Neurosci 2008;3(3-4):334-347

O'Callaghan ME, Maclennan AH, Gibson CS, et al, and the Australian Collaborative Cerebral Palsy Research Group. Fetal and maternal candidate single nucleotide polymorphism associations with cerebral palsy: a case-control study. Pediatrics 2012; 129: e414-23.

O'Shea TM, Klinepeter KL, Goldstein DJ, Jackson BW, Dillard RG. Survival and developmental disability in infants with birth weights of 501 to 800 grams, born between 1979 and 1994. Pediatrics. 1997;100: 982-986

Oberg GK, Campbell SK, Girolami GL, Ustad T, J0rgensen L, Kaaresen PI. Study protocol: an early intervention program to improve motor outcome in preterm infants: a randomized controlled trial and a qualitative study of physiotherapy performance and parental experiences. BMC Pediatr2012;12:15

Odding, Else, Roebroeck, Marij E. and Stam, Hendrik J. The epidemiology of cerebral palsy: Incidence, impairments and risk factors. Disability and Rehabilitation. February, 2006, Vol. 28, 4, pp. 183-191 DOI: 10.1080/09638280500158422.

Oeffinger D, Bagley A, Rogers S, et al. Outcome tools used forambulatory children with cerebral palsy: responsiveness and minimum clinically important differences. Developmental Medicine &Child Neurology 2008;50:918-925.

Oeffinger, D.J., et al. Gross Motor Classification System and outcome tools for assessing ambulatory cerebral palsy: A multicenter study. Developmental Medicine & Child Neurology. May, 2004, Vol. 46, 5, pp. 311-319 DOI: 10.1111/j.1469-8749.2004.tb00491.x.

Office CDC Epidemiology Program. Economic costs associated with mental retardation, cerebral palsy, hearing loss, and vision impairment-United States, 2003. MMWR Morb Mortal Wkly Rep. 2004;53:57-59.

Ohrvall, Ann-Marie. *MACS- a classification ofmanual abilityfor children with cerebralpalst. A study ofvalidity and reliability (Thesis).* Sweden: Karolinska Institute, 2005.
Oliver M. Theories in health care and research: theories of disability in health practice and research. BMJ 1998; 317: 1446-49.

Opheim A, Jahnsen R, Olsson E, Stanghelle JK. Walking function, pain, and fatigue in adults with cerebral palsy: a 7-year follow-up study. Dev Med Child Neurol 2009; 51: 381-88.

Oudgenoeg-Paz O, Riviere J. Self-locomotion and spatial language and spatial cognition: insights from typical and atypical development. Front Psychol2014;5:521-527

Paine RS (1962) On the treatment of cerebral palsy: the outcome of 177 patients, 74 totally untreated. Pediatrics, 47, 605-16.

Palisano R, Rosenbaum P, Walter S, et al. Development and reliability of a system to classify gross motor function in children with cerebral palsy. Dev Med Child Neurol. 1997;39:214-223.

Palisano R, Rosenbaum P, Walter S, Russell D, Wood E, Galuppi B Development and reliability of a system to classify gross motor function in children with cerebral palsy. Dev Med Child Neurol 1997; 39: 214-23.

Palisano RJ (1991) Research on the effectiveness of neurodevelopmental treatment. Pediatric Physical Therapy, 3, 143-48.

Palisano RJ, Hanna SE, Rosenbaum PL, et al. Validation of a model of gross motor function for children with cerebral palsy. Phys Ther. 2000;80:974-985.

Palisano, Robert J., et al. Stability of the Gross Motor Function Classification System Developmental Medicine &Chukde Neurology. June, 2006, Vol. 48, 6, pp. 424-428 DOI:10.1111/j.1469-8749.2006.tb01290.x. 97

Palisano, Robert, et al. Development and reliability of a system to classify gross motor function in children with cerebral palsy. Developmental Medicine & Child Neurology. April, 1997, Vol. 39, 4, pp. 214-223 DOI: 10.1111/j .1469-8749.1997.tb07414.x.

Palisano, Robert, et al. Gross Motor Function Classification System- Expanded and Revised. www.motorgrowth.canchild.ca. [Online] 2007. [Cited: 23 March 2012.] http ://motorgrowth. canchil d ca/en/GMFC Sfresources/GMFC S-ER. pdf.

Palmer FB, Shapiro B K Wachtel RC, Allen MC, Hiller JE, Harryman SE, Mosher BS, Meinert CL, Capute AJ (1988) The effects of physical therapy on cerebral palsy: a controlled trial in infants with spastic diplegia. New England Journal of Medicine, 318, 803-808.

Paneth N, Kiely J. The frequency of cerebral palsy: a review of population studies in industrialised nations since 1950. Clin Dev Med 1984; 87: 46-56.

Panteliadis, Christos P. and Strassburg, Hans-Michael. Cerebral Palsy- principles and management. New York :Thieme, 2004. 3131400218.

Park CH, Elavsky S, Koo KM. Factors influencing physical activity in older adults. J ExercRehabil 2014; 10(1):45-52
Parkes J, White-Koning M, Dickinson HO, et al. Psychologica problems in children with cerebral palsy: a cross-sectional European study. J Child Psychol Psychiatry 2008; 49: 405-13.

Parkinson KN, Dickinson HO, Arnaud C, Lyons A, Colver A, and the SPARCLE group. Pain in young people aged 13 to 17 years with cerebral palsy: cross-sectional, multicentre European study. Arch Dis Child 2013; 98: 434-40.

Parkinson KN, Gibson L, Dickinson HO, Colver AF. Pain in children with cerebral palsy: a cross-sectional multicentre European study. Acta Paediatr 2010; 99: 446-51

Patel, Dilip R. Basic Concepts of Developmental Diagnosis. [book auth.] Dilip R. Patel, et al. Neurodevelopmental Disabilities- Clinical care for children and young adults. New York : Springer Verlag, 2011.

Payne, V. Gregory and Isaacs, Larry D. Human Motor Development- A lifespan approach. New York: McGraw-Hill, 2011. 9780078022494.

Peacock, Judith. Cerebral Palsy- Perspective on disease and illness. s.l. : Life Matters, 2000. 0736802800.

Pearson PH (1982) 'The results of treatment': the horns of our dilemma. Developmental Medicine and Child Neurology, 24, 417-18.

Penelope Butler et al , Refinement, Reliability and Validity of the Segmental Assessment of Trunk Control (SATCo), Pediatr Phys Ther. 2010; 22(3): 246-257.

Pennington L, Virella D, Mj0en T, et al. Development of The Viking Speech Scale to classify the speech of children with cerebral palsy. Res Dev Disabil 2013; 34: 3202-10.

Penta, M., et al. The ABILHAND questionnaire as a measure of manual ability in chronic stroke patients. Rasch-based validation and relationship to upper limb impairment. Stroke. July, 2001, Vol. 32, 7, pp. 1627-1634 DOI: 11.1161./01.STR.32. 7.1627.

Petra marsico, Elena mitteregger, The Trunk Control Measurement Scale: reliability and discriminative validity in children and young people with neuromotor disorders, Developmental Medicine & Child Neurology 2017, 59: 706-712.

Petterson B, Nelson KB, Watson L, Stanley F. Twins, triplets, and cerebral palsy in births in Western Australia in the 1980s. BMJ 1993;307: 1239-43.

Pharoah PO, Buttfi eld IH, Hetzel BS. Neurological damage to the fetus resulting from severe iodine deficiency during pregnancy. ancet 1971; 1: 308-10.

Pharoah PO, Cooke RW. A hypothesis for the aetiology of spastic cerebral palsy-the vanishing twin. Dev Med Child Neurol 1997; 39: 292-96.

Pharoah PO, Cooke T, Johnson MA, King R, Mutch L. Epidemiology of cerebral palsy in England and Scotland, 1984-9.Arch Dis Child Fetal Neonatal Ed 1998; 79: F21-25.

Pharoah PO, Cooke T, Rosenbloom I, Cooke RW. Trends in birth prevalence of cerebral palsy. Arch Dis Child. 1987;62:379-384

Pharoah PO, Cooke T. Cerebral palsy and multiple births. Arch Dis Child Fetal Neonatal Ed 1996; 75: F174-77.

Pharoah PO, Homabrook RW. Endemic cretinism of recent onset n New Guinea. Lancet 1974; 2: 1038-40.

Pharoah PO. Cerebral palsy in the surviving twin associated with infant death of the co-twin. Arch Dis Child Fet Neonatal Ed 2001; 84: F11 1-16.

Pharoah PO. Prevalence and pathogenesis of congenital anomaliesn cerebral palsy. Arch Dis Child Fetal Neonatal Ed 2007; 92: F489-93.

Pharoah POD, Dundar Y. Monozygotic twinning, cerebral palsy and congenital anomalies. Hum Reprod Update 2009; 15: 639-48.

Pharoah POD. Causal hypothesis for some congenital anomalies. Twin Res Hum Genet 2005; 8: 543-50.

Piaget J. The Origins ofIntelligence in Children. New York, NY: International Universities Press; 1952

Piek, Jan P. Infant motor development. Stanningley : Human Kinetics, 2006. 9780736002264.
Piper MC, Kunos VI, Willis D, Mazer BL, Ramsay M, Silver KM (1986) Early physical therapy effects on the high-risk infant: a randomised controlled trial. Pediatrics, 78, 216-24.

Piper MC, Mazer B, Silver KM, Ramsay M (1988) Resolution of neurological symptoms in high-risk infants during the first two years of life. Developmental Medicine and Child Neurology, 30, 26-35.
Platt MJ, Cans C, Johnson A, et al. Trends in cerebral palsy among infants of very low birthweight (<1500 g) or born prematurely (<32 weeks) in 16 European centres: a database study. Lancet 2007; 369: 43-50.

Pountney TE, Cheek L, Green E, Mulcahy C, Nelham R. Content and criterion validation of the Chailey Levels of Ability. Physiotherapy 1999; 85: 410-16.

Pountney TE, Mulcahy CM, Clarke SM, Green EM. The Chailey Approach to Postural Management.North Chailey: Chailey Heritage Clinical Services; 2004.

Puscavage, April and Hoon, Alec. Spasticity/Cerebral Palsy. [book auth.] Harvey S. Singer, et al. Treatment of Pediatric Neurologic Disorders. Boca Raton : Taylor & Francis Group LLC, 2005.

Quinton M. Making the Difference in Babies: Concepts and Guidelines for Baby Treatment. Albuquerque, NM: Clinician's View; 2002

Ramstad K, Jahnsen R, Skjeldal OH, Diseth TH. Characteristics of recurrent musculoskeletal pain in children with cerebral palsy aged 8 to 18 years. Dev Med Child Neurol 2011; 53: 1013-18.

Rankin J, Cans C, Game E, et al. Congenital anomalies in children with crebral palsy: a population-based record linkage study.Dev Med Child Neurol 2010; 52: 345-51.

Reddihough DS, King J, Coleman G, Catanese T. Effi cacy of programmes based on Conductive Education for young children with cerebral palsy. Dev Med Child Neurol 1998; 40: 763-70.

Reddihough, Dinah S. and Collins, Kevin J. The epidemiology and causes of cerebral palsy. Australian Journal of Physiotherapy. March, 2007, Vol. 49, 1, pp. 7-12.

Reddihough, Dinah. Measurement tools: new opportunities for children with cerebral palsy. Developmental Medicine & Child Neurology. July, 2006, Vol. 48, 7, pp. 558 DOI: 10.1111/j.1469-8749.2006.tb01312.x.

Reid SM, Carlin JB, Reddihough DS. Survival of individuals with cerebral palsy born in Victoria, Australia, between 1970 and 2004. Dev Med Child Neurol 2012; 54: 353-60.

Reid SM, Johnson HM, Reddihough DS. The Drooling Impact Scale: a measure of the impact of drooling in children with developmental disabilities. Dev Med Child Neurol 2010; 52: e23-28.

Report of the Australian cerebral palsy register, birth years 1993-2006. Sydney, NSW, Australia: Cerebral Palsy Research Institute, 2013.
Roberton, Don M. and South, M.J. Practical Peadiatrics. Elsevier :s.n., 2007. 9780443102806.

Roebroeck ME, Jahnsen R, Carona C, Kent RM, Chamberlain MA Adult outcomes and lifespan issues for people with childhood-onset physical disability. Dev Med Child Neurol 2009; 51: 670-78.

Roebroeck ME, Jahnsen R, Carona C, Kent RM, Chamberlain MA.Adult outcomes and lifespan issues for people with childhood-onsetphysical disability. Dev Med Child Neurol 2009; 51: 670-78.

Rosenbaum P, Paneth N, Leviton A, et al. A report: the definition and classification of cerebral palsy April 2006. Dev Med Child Neurol Suppl 2007; 109: 8-14.

Rosenbaum P. Family and quality of life: key elements in intervention in children with cerebral palsy. Dev Med Child Neurol 2011; 53 (suppl 4): 68-70.

Rosenbaum P. The definition and classification of cerebral palsy: are we any further ahead in 2006? NeoReviews. 2006;17: e569- e574

Rosenbaum, Peter L., et al. Development of the Gross Motor Classification System for cerebral palsy. Developmental Medicine & Child Neurology. April, 2008, Vol. 50, 4, pp. 249-253 DOI:10.1111/j.1469-8749.2008.02045.x.

Rosenberg W, Donald A (1995) Evidence-based medicine: an approach to clinical problem solving. British Medical Journal, 310(6987), 1122-26.

Rothberg AD, Goodman M, Jacklin LA, Cooper PA (1991) Six-year followup of early physiotherapy intervention of very low birth weight infants. Pediatrics, 88, 547-52.

Rothman JG (1978) Effects of respiratory exercises on the vital capacity and forced expiratory volume in children with cerebral palsy. Physical Therapy, 58, 421-25.

Russell D, Rosenbaum P, Gowland C, et al. Gross Motor Function Measure: A Measure of Gross Motor Function in Cerebral Palsy. 2nd ed. Hamilton, Ontario, Canada: Institute for Applied Health Sciences, McMaster University; 1993.

Russell D, Rosenbaum P, Wright M, et al. Gross motor function measure (GMFM-66 and GMFM-88) user's manual. London: MacKeith Press, 2002.
Russell DJ, Avery LM, Walter SD, et al. Development and validation of item sets to improve efficiency of administration of the 66-item gross motor function measure in children with cerebral palsy. Developmental Medicine & Child Neurology 2010;52:e48-e54.

Sackett DL (1989) Rules of evidence and clinical recommendations on the use of antithrombotic agents. Chest, 95 (2, Suppl), 2S-4S.

Sacrey LA, Whishaw IQ. Development of collection precedes targeted reaching: resting shapes of the hands and digits in 1-6-month-old human infants. Behav Brain Res 2010;214(1): 125-129

Salokorpi T, Sajaniemi N, Rajantie I, Hallback H, Hamalainen T, Rita H, Von Wendt L (1998) Neurodevelopment until the adjusted age of 2 years in extremely low birth weight infants after early intervention - a casecontrol study. Pediatric Rehabilitation, 2(4), 157-63.

Sanger TD, Delgado MR, Gaebler-Spira D, Hallett M, Mink JW, and the Task Force on Childhood Motor Disorders. Classification and definition of disorders causing hypertonia in childhood. Pediatrics 2003; 111: e89-97.

Santos GL, Bueno TB, Tudella E, Dionisio J. Influence of additional weight on the frequency of kicks in infants with Down syndrome and infants with typical development. Braz J Phys Ther 2014; 18(3):237-246

Scherzer AL, Mike V, Ilson J (1976) Physical therapy as a determinant of change in the cerebral palsied infant. Pediatrics, 58, 47-52.

Sellier E, Surman G, Himmelmann K, et al. Trends in prevalence of cerebral palsy in children born with a birthweight of 2500 g or over in Europe from 1980 to 1998. Eur J Epidemiol 2010; 25: 635-42.

Shaffer SW, Harrison AL. Aging of the somatosensory system: a translational perspective. Phys Ther 2007 ;87(2): 193-207

Shatrov JG, Birch SC, Lam LT, Quinlivan JA, McIntyre S, endz GL. Chorioamnionitis and cerebral palsy: a meta-analysis. bstet Gynecol 2010; 116: 387-92.

Shields N, Loy Y, Murdoch A, Taylor NF, Dodd KJ. Self-concept of children with cerebral palsy compared with that of children without impairment. Dev Med Child Neurol 2007; 49: 350-54.

Shikako-Thomas K, Lach L, Majnemer A, Nimigon J, Cameron K, Shevell M. Quality of life from the perspective of adolescents with cerebral palsy: "I just think I'm a normal kid, I just happen to have a disability". Qual Life Res 2009; 18: 825-32.

Shulz KF, Chalmers I, Hayes RJ, Altman DG (1995) Empirical evidence bias. Journal of the American Medical Association, 273, 406-12.

Shumway-Cook A, Woollacott MH. Motor Control: Translating Research into Clinical Practice. 4th ed. Philadelphia, PA: Lippincott Williams and Wilkins; 2011

Sigurdardottir S, Indredavik MS, Eiriksdottir A, Einarsdottir K, Gudmundsson HS, Vik T. Behavioural and emotional symptoms of preschool children with cerebral palsy: a population-based study. Dev Med Child Neurol 2010; 52: 1056-61.

Simpson DM, Gracies JM, Graham HK, et al, and the Therapeutics and Technology Assessment Subcommittee of the American Academy of Neurology. Assessment: Botulinum neurotoxin for the treatment of spasticity (an evidence-based review): report of the Therapeutics and Technology Assessment Subcommittee ofth American Academy ofNeurology. Neurology 2008; 70: 1691-98.

Simpson EA, Murray L, Paukner A, Ferrari PF. The mirror neuron system as revealed through neonatal imitation: presence from birth, predictive power and evidence of plasticity. Philos Trans R Soc Lond B Biol Sci 2014;369(1644):20130289

Sindhu F, Dickson R (1997) Literature searching for systematic reviews. Nursing Standard, 11(41), 40-42.

Smith LB, Thelen E. Development as a dynamic system. Trends Cogn Sci 2003;7(8):343-348
Soll RF. Prophylactic synthetic surfactant for preventing morbidity and mortality in preterm infants. Cochrane Database Syst Rev. 2000;2

Stanley F, Alberman E. Birthweight, gestational age and the cerebral palsies. Clin Dev Med 1984; 87: 57-68.

Stanley FJ, Watson L. The cerebral palsies in Western Australia: trends, 1968 to 1981. Am J Obstet Gynecol. 1988;158:89-93

Stanley FJ, Watson L. Trends in perinatal mortality and cerebral palsy in Western Australia, 1967 to 1985. BMJ 1992; 304: 1658-63.

Stanley, Fiona J. The aetiology of cerebral palsy. Early human development. February, 1994, Vol. 36, 2, pp. 81-88 DOI:10.1016/0378-3782(94)90035-3.

Steinbok P, Reiner AM, Beauchamp R, Armstrong RW, Cochrane DD (1997) A randomised clinical trial to compare selective posterior rhizotomy plus physiotherapy with physiotherapy alone in children with spastic diplegia cerebral palsy. Developmental Medicine and Child Neurology, 39, 178-84.

Strauss D, Brooks J, Rosenbloom L, Shavelle R. Life expectancy in cerebral palsy: an update. Dev Med Child Neurol 2008; 50: 487-93.

Strauss D, Cable W, Shavelle R. Causes of excess mortality in cerebral palsy. Dev Med Child Neurol 1999; 41: 580-85.

Strax TE, Luciano L, Dunn AM, Quevedo JP. Aging and developmental disability. Phys Med Rehabil Clin N Am 2010; 21: 419-27.

Sullivan P, Morrice J, Vernon-Roberts A, Grant H, Eltumi M, Thomas A. Does gastrostomy tube feeding increase the risk of respiratory morbidity? Arch Dis Child 2006; 91: 478-82.

Sundermier L, Woollacott MH. The influence of vision on the automatic postural muscle responses of newly standing and newly walking infants. Exp Brain Res 1998;120(4):537-540

Surveillance of Cerebral Palsy in Europe. Surveillance of cerebral palsy in Europe: a collaboration of cerebral palsy surveys and registers. Dev Med Child Neurol 2000; 42: 816-24.

Taft LT (1972) 'Are we handicapping the handicapped?' Developmental Medicine and Child Neurology, 14, 703-704.

Taub E, Uswatte G, Mark VW. The functional significance of cortical reorganization and the parallel development of CI therapy. Front Hum Neurosci2014;8:396

Taylor MC (2000) Evidence-based practice for occupational therapists. Oxford: Blackwell Science. Tickle-Degnen L (1999) Organising, evaluating, and using evidence in occupational therapy practice. American Journal of Occupational Therapy, 53, 537-39.

Tecklin, Jan S. Pediatric Physical Therapy. Baltimore : Lippincott Williams &wilkins, 2008. 07817533996.

Thelen E, Corbetta D, Kamm K, Spencer JP, Schneider K, Zemicke RF. The transition to reaching: mapping intention and intrinsic dynamics. Child Dev 1993;64(4):1058-1098

Thelen E. Developmental origins of motor coordination: leg movements in human infants. Dev Psychobiol 1985;18(1): 1-22

Thelen E. Self-organization in developmental processes: Can system approaches work? In: Guner M, Thelen E, eds. Systems and Development. Minnesota Symposium on Child Psychology. Hillsdale, NJ: Erlbaum; 1998:77-117

Thelen, Esther. Motor Development- A new synthesis. American Psychologist. February, 1995, Vol. 50, 2, pp. 79-95.

Tickle-Degnen L (2000a) Gathering current evidence to enhance clinical reasoning. American Journal of Occupational Therapy, 54, 102-105.

Tickle-Degnen L (2000b) Teaching evidence-based practice. American Journal of Occupational Therapy, 54, 559-60.

Trunk control, Balance and Mobility Function in Children with Hemiparetic Cerebral Palsy.2015;4(5):236-243.

Ulrich BD. Opportunities for early intervention based on theory, basic neuroscience, and clinical science. Phys Tuer 2010;90(12):1868-1880

United Cerebral Palsy, http://www.ucp.org/uploads/media_ items/cerebral-palsy-fact-sheet.original.pdf, accessed March 2011

United Nations. Convention on the rights of the child. NewYork,NY, USA: United Nations, 1989
Valvano JS, Long T (1991) Neurodevelopmental treatment: a review of the writings of the Bobaths. Pediatric Physical Therapy, 3, 125-29.

Van Balen LC, Dijkstra LJ, Hadders-Algra M. Development of postural adjustments during reaching in typically developing infants from 4 to 18 months. Exp Brain Res 2012;220(2): 109-119

Van der Heide JC, Begeer C, Pock JM, et al. Postural control during reaching in preterm children with cerebral palsy. Dev Med Child Neurol. 2004 Apr;46(4):253-66.

Van der Heide JC, Pock JM, Otten B, Stremmelaar E, Hadders-Algra M. Kinematic characteristics of postural control during reaching in preterm children with cerebral palsy. Pediatr Res. 2005 Sep;58(3):586-93.

Van Der Slot WM, Nieuwenhuijsen C, Van Den Berg-Emons RJ, et al. Chronic pain, fatigue, and depressive symptoms in adults with spastic bilateral cerebral palsy. Dev Med Child Neurol 2012; 54: 836-42.
Van Sant AF (1991) Neurodevelopmental treatment and pediatric physical therapy: a commentary. Pediatric Physical Therapy, 3, 137-41.

Vargus-Adams J. Health-related quality of life in childhood cerebral palsy. Arch Phys Med Rehabil 2005; 86: 940-45.

Vereijken B. The complexity of childhood development: variability in perspective. Phys Ther 2010;90(12): 1850-1859

Vidailhet M, Yelnik J, Lagrange C, et al, and the French SPIDY-2 Study Group. Bilateral pallidal deep brain stimulation for the treatment of patients with dystonia-choreoathetosis cerebral palsy: a prospective pilot study. Lancet Neurol 2009; 8: 709-17.

Vieira DC, Tibana RA, Tajra V, et al. Decreased functional capacity and muscle strength in elderly women with metabolic syndrome. Clin Interv Aging 2013;8: 1377-1386

Vogtle LK. Social participation and quality of life in adults with cerebral palsy. NDT Network 2012;19:24-29

Von Hofsten C, Ronnqvist L. The structuring of neonatal arm movements. Child Dev 1993;64(4):1046-1057

Von Zweck C (1999) The promotion of evidence-based occupational therapy practice in Canada. Canadian Journal of Occupational Therapy, 66, 208-13.

Wallace PS, Whishaw IQ. Independent digit movements and precision grip patterns in 1-5-month-old human infants: hand-babbling, including vacuous then self-directed hand and digit movements, precedes targeted reaching. Neuropsychologia 2003;41(14):1912-1918

Wang B, Chen Y, Zhang J, Li J, Guo Y, Hailey D. A preliminary study into the economic burden of cerebral palsy in China. Health Policy. 2008;87:223-234

Watson N, Shakespeare T, Cunningham-Burley S, Barnes C. Life as a disabled child: a qualitative study of young people's experience and perspectives. Edinburgh, UK: Department of Nursing Studies, University of Edinburgh, Economic and Social Science Research Council, 1999.

Weiss, Lawrence G. and Oakland, Thomas, Aylward, Glen. Bayley III- Clinical Use and Interpretation.

Westcott S, Dusing P. Motor control: developmental aspects of motor control in skill acquisition. In: Campbell SK, Palisano RJ, Orlin MN, eds. Physical Therapy for Children. 4th ed. St. Louis: Elsevier; 2011:87-150

White MA, Paper KE. The slump test. Am J OccupTher. 1992;46:271-274.

WHO. International classifi cation of functioning, disability and health. Geneva, Switzerland: World Health Organisation, 2001.

Wilkins, Robert H. and Brody, Irwin A. Neurological Classics. Park Ridge, Illinois : The American Association of Neurological Surgeons, 1997. 1879284499.

Winter S, Autry A, Boyle C, Yeargin-Allsopp M. Trends in the prevalence of cerebral palsy in a population-based study. Pediatrics. 2002; 110: 1220 -1225

Wong A, Pei Y-C, Lui T. Comparison between botulinum toxin type A injections and selective posterior rhizotomy in improving gait performance in children with cerebral palsy. J Neurosurg Pediatr 2005; 102: 385-89.

Wood E, Rosenbaum P. The gross motor function classification system for cerebral palsy: a study of reliability and stability over time. Dev Med Child Neurol. 2000;42:292-296.

Wood, Ellen and Rosenbaum, Peter. The Gross Motor Classification System for Cerebral Palsy: a study of reliability and stability over time. Developmental Medicine & Child Neurology. May, 2000, Vol. 42, 5, pp. 292-296.

Woolfson L. Family well-being and disabled children: a psychosocial model of disability-related child behaviour problems. Br J Health Psychol 2004; 9: 1-13.

Woollacott M, Debu B, Mowatt M. Neuromuscular control of posture in the infant and child: is vision dominant? J Mot Behav 1987;19(2):167-186

World Health Organization. ICF-CY, International classificationof functioning, disability, and health: children & youthversion. Geneva: World Health Organization, 2007.

World Health Organization. International Classification of Impairments, Disabilities, and Handicaps. Geneva: WHO; 1980.

Wright T, Nicholson J (1973) Physiotherapy for the spastic child: an evaluation. Developmental Medicine and Child Neurology, 15, 146-63.
Wu YW, Croen LA, Vanderwerf A, Gelfand AA, Torres A R Candidate genes and risk for CP: a population-based study. Pediatr Res 2011; 70: 642-46.

Yang H, Einspieler C, Shi W, et al. Cerebral palsy in children: movements and postures during early infancy, dependent on preterm vs. full term birth. Early Hum Dev 2012;88(10): 837-843

Yeargin-Allsopp M, Van Naarden Braun K, Doemberg NS, Benedict RE, Kirby RS, Durkin MS. Prevalence of cerebral palsy in 8-year-old children in three areas of the United States in 2002: a multisite collaboration. Pediatrics 2008; 121: 547-54.

<u>References for the Appendix</u>

Atkinson, J., 1984. How does Infant Vision change in the first three Months of Life. In: Prechtl, H.F.R. (Ed.), Continuity of Neural Functions from Prenatal to Postnatal Life. Clinics in

Developmental Medicine 94, Spastics International Medical Publications, Oxford, pp. 159-178.
Bly, L., Whiteside, A., 1997. Facilitation Techniques Based on NDT principles. Therapy Skill Builders, San Antonio.

Bly, L., 1999. Baby Treatment Based on NDT Principles. Therapy Skill Builders, U.S.A.. XV-XVIII, 1-9.

Bobath, B., Bobath, K., 1964. The Facilitation of Normal Postural Reactions and Movements in the Treatment of Cerebral Palsy. Physiotherapy, London.

Bobath, B., 1967. The Very Early Treatment of Cerebral Palsy. Developmental Medicine and Child Neurology. 9, 373-390.

Bobath, B., Bobath, K., 1984. The Neuro-Developmental Treatment. In: Scrutton, D., and al., 1984. Management of the Motor Disorders of Children with Cerebral Palsy. Clinics in

Developmental Medicine 90, Spastics International Medical Publications, Oxford, pp. 6-18.
Bobath, B., 1990. Adult Hemiplegia: Evaluation and Treatment. Heinemann Medical Books, Oxford, pp. IX- 19.

Boehme, R., 1988. Improving Upper Body Control. Therapy Skill Builders, U.S.A., pp. 1-18.

Bryce, J., 1972. Facilitation of Movement-the Bobath Approach. Physiotherapy. 58, 403-408.

Finnie, N.R., 1968. Handling the Young Child with Cerebral Palsy at Home. Butterworth-Heinemann, Oxford.

Finnie, N.R., 1997. Handling the Young Child with Cerebral Palsy at Home. Butterworth-Heinemann, Oxford. 3rdEd.

Gramsbergen, A, 1997. Regression of Polyneuronal Innervation in the Human psoas muscle. Early Human Development. 49, 49-61.

Gramsbergen, A, Hadders-Algra, M., 1998. Development of Postural Control. Neuroscience & Biobehavioral Reviews. 22, 463-595.
Hadders-Algra, M., 1996. The assessment of General Movements is a valuable technique for the detection of brain dysfunction in young infants. A review. Acta Paediatrica. Suppl 416, 39-43.

Hirschfeld, H., 1992. Postural Control: Acquisition and Integration during Development. In: Forssberg, H., Hirschfeld, H. (Eds.), Movement Disorders in Children. Medicine and Sport Science 36, Karger, Basel, pp. 199-208.

Hochleitner, M., 1977. Vergleichende Untersuchung von Kindem mit zerebraler Bewegungsstorung mit und ohne neurophysiologischer Frtihtherapie. Osterreichische Artztezeitung. 32, 18, 1108-1113.

Hochleitner, M., 1986. Das Bobath-Konzept. Der Kinderartzt. 17, 539.

Keller, . Z., 1997. Oral and Communication Problems in Multiple Handicapped Children (Speech-Language, Emotional,

Social, Educational Aspects). In: Book of Abstracts. The First World Congress of the Neuro-Developmental Treatment Concept; 1997 June 13-16; Ljubljana, Slovenia, pp. 39.

Kong, E., 1965. Fruherfassung und Fruhbehandlung angeborener Schaden im Sinne einer bestmoglichen Rehabilitation. Praxis. 54, 44, 1270.

Kong, E., 1966. Very Early Treatment of Cerebral Palsy. Developmental Medicine and Child Neurology. 8, 2, 198- 202.

Kong, E., 1972. Fruhtherapie zerebraler Bewegungsstorungen. Die Medizinische Welt. 23, 446-448.

Kong, E., 1974. Erfahrungen mit der Fruhtherapie. Padiatrische Fortbildungskurse for die Praxis. 40, 132-137.

Kong, E., 1974. Erfahrungen mit Langjahriger Therapie spatbehandelter Kinder. Padiat. Fortbildk. Praxis. 40, 104-126.

Kong, E., 1982. Anderung der Situation der zerebralenBewegungsstorungen beeinflusst <lurch Pravention und Fruhtherapie. Padiatrische Fortbildungskurse for die Praxis. 53, 1-9.

Kong, E., 1986. Die Bedeutung der sensomotorischen Erfahrungen. Schweizerisches Bund der Therapeuten cerebraler Bewegungsstorungen. Mitteilungs Blatt No. 25. pp. 3-8.

Kong, E., 1990. Langjahrige Erfahrungen mit der Frtihtherapie. Die Kinderartzt. 10, 1419-1420.

Kong, E., 1990. Fruherfassung cerebraler Bewegungsstorungen. Der Kinderartzt. 8, 1119-1123.

Kong, E., 1990. Therapieerfolge bei spaterem Therapiebeginn von CP-Kindem. Der Kinderartzt. 21, 1569-1570.

Kong, E., 1991. Geschichte und Entwicklung des Bobath-Konzeptes. Der Kinderartzt. 22, 705-710.

Kong, E., 1992. The Bobath Concept-Evolution and Application. In: Forssberg, H., Hirschfeld, H. (Eds.), Movement Disorders in Children. Medicine and Sport Science, 36, Karger, Basel, pp. 80-86.

Kong, E., 1999. Frtihdiagnose und Fruhtherapie der zerebralen Bewegungsstorungen. Ein Erfahrungsbericht. Kinderartzliche Praxis. 4, 222-234.

Leeuwenburg-Grijseels, E., van der Weerd, C., 1997. Experiences with Feeding Problems in early Treatment of CP and non CP Children. In: Book of Abstracts. The First World Congress of the Neuro-Developmental Treatment Concept; 1997 June 13-16; Ljubljana, Slovenia, pp. 41.

Mayston, M.J., 1992. The Bobath Concept- Evolution and Application. In: Forssberg, H., Hirschfeld, H. (Eds.), Movement Disorders in Children. Medicine and Sport Science, 36, Karger, Basel, pp. 1-6.

Meek, M.M., 1997. Adaptation of Oral MotorNeuro Developmental Treatment Techniques with other Paediatric Syndromes. In: Book of Abstracts. The First World Congress of the Neuro-Developmental Treatment Concept; 1997 June 13-16; Ljubljana, Slovenia, pp. 42.

Michaelis, R., Niemann, G., 1995. Entwicklungsneurologie und Neuropadiatrie. Hippokrates, Stuttgart, pp. 38-40.

T. Dolenc Veli-kovi}, M. Veli-kovi} Perat BASIC PRINCIPLES OF THE NEURO DEVELOPMENTAL TREATMENT Medicina 2005;42(41): 112-120

Muller, H.A., 1997. Glimpses of the Development of Pre- Speech/Speech Therapy and its Place in the NDT (Bobath) Concept. In Retrospect and Prospect. In: Book of Abstracts. The First World Congress of the Neuro- Developmental Treatment Concept; 1997 June 13-16; Ljubljana, Slovenia, pp. 43.

Mueller, H.A., 1999. Speech. In: Finnie N.R. (Ed.), Handling the Young Child with Cerebral Palsy at Home. Butterworth- Heinemann, Oxford, pp. 112-117.
Mutch L., Alberman E, Hagberg B, Kodama K, Veli-kovi} Perat M. 1992. Cerebral Palsy Epidemiology: Where are We Now and Where are We Going? Developmental Medicine and Child Neurology. 34. 547-551.

Nathan, P.W., 1990. Foreword to the First edition. In: Bobath, B. Adult Hemiplegia: Evaluation and Treatment. Heinemann Medical Books, Oxford, pp. VII-VII.

Nelson, C., 1996. Postural Development and Vision. In: Padula, W.V. (Eds.), Neurotmetic Rehabilitation. Optometric Extension Program Foundation Inc., U.S.A., pp. 28-37.

Peiper, A, 1963. Cerebral Function in Infancy and Childhood. Consultants Bureau, New York, pp. 147-210.

Papou{ek, H., Papou{ek, M., 1984. Qualitative Transitions in Integrative Process during the first Trimester of Human Postpartum Life. In: Prechtl, H.F.R. (Ed.), Continuity of Neural Functions from Prenatal to Postnatal Life. Clinics in Developmental Medicine 94, Spastics International Medical Publications, Oxford, pp. 220-244.

Prechtl, H.F.R., 1984. Continuity and Change in Early Neural Development. In: Prechtl, H.F.R. (Ed.), Continuity of Neural Functions from Prenatal to Postnatal a Life. Spastics International Medical Publications, Oxford, pp. 1-15.

Prechtl, H.F.R., 1988, Development of Postural Control in Infancy. Neurobiology of Early Infant Behaviour. In: Von Euler, C., Forssberg, H., Lagercrantz, H., (Eds.), Proceedings of International Wallenberg Symposium at the Wenner-Gren Center, Stockholm, August 28-September 1, 1988, M Stockton Press, Stockholm, pp. 59-67.

Prechtl, H.F.R., 1997. Spontaneous Motor Activity as a Diagnostic Tool. Functional Assessment of the Young Nervous System. Early Human Development. 50, pp. 1-147.

Prechtl, H.F.R., Einspieler, C., Cioni, G., Bos, AF., Ferrari, F., Sontheimer, D., 1997. An early marker for neurological deficits after perinatal brain lesions. The Lancet. 349, 1361-1363.

Purves, D., 1994. Neural Activity and the Growth of the Brain. Cambridge University Press, Cambridge, pp. 44-68.

Quinton, M.B., 1986. The Importance of the Body Image in our daily Lives and in Therapy. Schweizerischer, Bundder Therapeuten cerebraler Bewegungsstorungen, Mittteilungsblatt.25, pp. 9-17.
Quinton, M.B., 1997. Structure of NDT Baby Treatment. In: Book of Abstracts. The First World Congress of the Neuro-Developmental Treatment Concept; 1997 June 13-16; Ljubljana, Slovenia, pp. 44-45.

Quinton, M.B., Nelson, C.A, 2002. Concepts&Guidelines for Baby Treatment. Clinician's view, Albuquerque, New Mexico.

Rohlfs, B.P., 1999. Erfahrungen mit dem Bobath-Konzept. Georg Thieme Verlag, Stuttgart. 52. Scherzer, AL., Tschamuter, I., 1982. Early Diagnosis and Therapy in Cerebral Palsy. Pediatric Habilitation 3, Marcel Dekker, New York, pp. 205-256.

Steding-Albrecht, U., 2003. Das Bobath-Konzept im Alltag des Kindes. Georg Thieme Verlag, Stuttgart.

Touwen, B., 1978. Variability and Stereotipy in normal and deviant development. In: Apley, J. (Ed.), Care of the Handicapped Child. Clinics in Dev Med, 67; 99-110.

Weisz, B., 1938. Studies in Equilibrium Reactions. J Nerv and Ment Dis, 88; 153-162.

Zador, J., Les Reactions d' Equilibre chez l'Homme. Basic principles of the neurodevelopmental treatment, Medicina 2005;42(41): 112-120

APPENDIX

OVER VIEW OF NDT APPROACH

1. Rationale

NDT is an integrated approach dealing with the quality of patterns of coordination of movement and not only with the problems of individual muscle function. The approach involves the whole person, not only his sensory-motor dysfunctiona but also problems of development, perceptual-cognitive impairment, emotional, social and functional problems of the daily life as well (Bobath, 1990). The concept of NDT is based upon the recognition of the following facts:

a   A brain lesion results in the appearance of stereotyped abnormally coordinated.

b   Movement patterns, which will abnormally affect a great number of muscle groups in extensor and/or flexor synergies. In the beginning these abnormal patterns are changeable but as time goes on, they may increase with stimulation, effort and stress.

c   Tonic postural activity (particularly associated reactions) reinforces the abnormal movement patterns which contribute to the development of contractures and deformities.

d   A brain lesion interferes with the development of normal postural control in relation to gravity.

e   Instead of normal postural tone, one can find abnormal tone: too high (spasticity), too low (hypotonicity) or fluctuating (athetosis).

f   Instead of normal reciprocal interaction, we find excessive co-contraction, or sudden inhibition of antagonists resulting in the lack of ability to make a graduated movement.

g   Instead of normal automatic movement patterns of righting, equilibrium and protective reactions, we find a few static and stereotyped postural patterns of tonic reflexes.

h   The abnormal sensory-motor development interferes with the child's whole development (sensory, perceptual- cognitive, psychological).

i.   Associated sensory and/or perceptual deficits can be primary (due to brain damage) but frequently they are secondary to the physical disability, which prevents the child from exploring himself the environment. He does not develop the same concept of his body, as does a normal child.

j.   Abnormal sensory-motor experiences will result in an abnormal body awareness and abnormal body image, which can be reinforced by parents' inexperience and inability to deal with their child's disability (Bobath, 1984; Kong, 1986; Quinton, 1986; Bobath, 1990).

Evolution of the NDT concept and its application

In 1942, while she was handling a patient with hemiplegia, Mrs. Bobath discovered that by preventing him from moving into an abnormal pattern of activity by his spasticity, a more normal movement and a more normal functional activity became possible for the patient through her handling (Kong, 1991; Rohlfs, 1999).

By observing the patient's reactions to her handling, she became aware of three important facts:

a. It is impossible to superimpose normal movement patterns on abnormal ones; the abnormal patterns need to be suppressed (inhibited)

b. The importance of sensory-motor experience - we do not learn a movement but the "sensation of movement"

c. By moving the proximal part of the body it is possible to influence and to change the movements of the distal parts.

Mrs. Bobath was influenced by the work of Knott, Kabat and Voss and recognized the importance of Proprioceptive stimulation to build up tone in patients with low and unstable postural tone. From Rood and Goff she learned of the importance of tactile stimulation in order to obtain movements of hands, feet, mouth and tongue (Bobath, 1984; 1990, Kong 1991).

Inhibitory control

"Reflex inhibiting postures" (**R.I.P.**) Influenced by animal experiments of Sherrington and Magnus who found out that identical stimulus in different positions elicited different reactions, i.e. different movement patterns, she placed and held the patient in "reflex inhibiting postures" to break up the abnormal postural and movement patterns. First, she used a pattern opposite to the patient's total pattern, which she modified later into an individually adapted mixed pattern of a better-coordinated flexion and extension.

Active adaptation of the child being held in **R.I.P.** resulted in a change of activity of the whole body due to the normalization of postural tone. The child was held in a series of postures, which controlled his whole body.

Unfortunately, except in a few very young children, no spontaneous carry over into movement and function occurred, as the child had never previously experienced the sensation of normal movements. This made normal active and spontaneous movements impossible. The treatment was too static and was not continued in this way (Bobath, 1984; Kong, 1991; Mayston, 1992).

The concept of inhibition remained except that its application was changed later on. Inhibition is the process of intervention that reduces dysfunctional muscle tone. It breaks up the abnormal excessive flexion or extension (Bobath, 1984; Quinton, 1986; Boehme, 1988). The concept of stimulation of low tone was developed gradually and the dangers of each were recognized (Bobath, 1984).

Inhibition combined with stimulation and facilitation

After preparing and obtaining a more normal postural tone the patient needs to learn to move in many different combinations of more normal movement patterns.

Mrs. Bobath looked for possibilities of how to transmit F the patient in order to enable them to experience normal sensations of functional movements they had either lost or never developed.

Only by feeling a near normal active movement with minimal effort can the patient learn how to perform it. The therapist's task is to make this possible.

Then the Bobaths recognized the importance of postural reactions (righting and equilibrium reactions) from the work of Magnus, Peiper, Weisz and Zador. The various postural reactions are coordinated in definite patterns, which are common to all of us. Although they occur automatically they are active movements. All voluntary and skilled functional activity with its complex and selective patterns of coordination is performed on the basis of automatic postural reactions.

The motor patterns of normal postural reactions develop in the child gradually during the first few years of life (Weisz, 1938; Zador, 1938; Peiper, 1963; Bobath, 1990). The Bobaths realized the importance of understanding normal development in order to be able to understand abnormal development and how to treat it. A good working knowledge of normal and abnormal development, and an awareness of their effect on the developing body image is one of the most important professional qualities of a NDT therapist (Quinton, 1997).

The Bobaths recognized that during normal development, in the beginning there is the influence of tonic reflexes which later disappear and are suppressed by the development of righting reactions. These are later overlapped and integrated into balance reactions and voluntary movements. This knowledge helped them toward a more dynamic treatment - the facilitation of sequences of righting reactions, equilibrium reactions, supporting reactions and other automatic reactions (Kong, 1991).

Dynamic treatment with control from key points

Mrs. Bobath found a way of using "key points of control" (body parts, mainly proximal - head, shoulders, pelvis) from which abnormal patterns could be controlled (inhibited), and the strength and distribution of postural tone could be influenced while at the same time normal movement patterns could be facilitated or a specific technique of stimulation could be used. From the key point of control the therapist is able to control and guide the movement of the whole body. The child could be facilitated to react actively where not actually held or controlled (Bobath, 1984).

Facilitation is the process of intervention, which uses the improved postural tone in a goal-directed activity. The patient is active and the therapist is guiding and controlling the activity. Facilitation makes movement easier but in the treatment, it also means "making it possible" and "making it have to happen". The therapist should make movements easy for the child, enjoyable and safe, so that he likes to move and feels an urge to do so (Bobath, 1964; Bryce, 1972; Boehme, 1988; Bly and Whiteside, 1997; Rohlfs, 1999).

Inhibitory control is used with facilitation. It is accomplished simultaneously with the least amount of physical intrusion. As the therapist uses techniques that reduce the dysfunctional tone, the patient makes more efficient movement adaptations. This happens spontaneously because the patient is actively involved in functional movement and automatic postural reactions while the therapist is handling him. The treatment is done by "handling" and based on the close interplay between the patient and the therapist. The therapist is guided by the patient's reaction to his handling (Bobath, 1984; Boehme, 1988).

One of the greatest problems in the treatment of children with cerebral palsy is to obtain good balance reactions. It has a detrimental effect on movement when they are insufficient or absent. It is easier to obtain them if we start the treatment early because we are able to follow the normal developmental overlap of righting by the equilibrium reactions (Bobath, 1984).

The treatment should not follow rigidly the developmental milestones. In normal development children develop many activities simultaneously. There is a big variability and inconsistency in normal development (Touwen, 1978). Normal basic movement patterns which belong together at any developmental level should be transmitted through repetition to the child and enable him to perform various different activities (Bobath, 1984; Kong, 1992; Quinton, 1997).

During the treatment it is necessary to reduce the therapist's control, handing it over gradually to the child and allowing him the control of his own movements. Much guided control and repetition of the required reactions may be necessary to assure their quality (Bobath, 1984; Quinton, 1997).

Treatment in functional situation

Not all movements obtained through treatment are spontaneously carried over into the activities of daily life. There is a need for a direct transition of treatment to functional skills, which is the only way to influence also the quality of prehension and manipulation. The treatment incorporates systematic preparation to improve specific functions in the present and to prepare specific functions needed in the near future.

Such an approach demands a thorough analysis of each task to be prepared for the child to perform, which should be related to the assessment of the needs of the individual child, finding out what interferes with or what is missing from each part of the task, looking chiefly at the quality and not just the quantity of the child's performance. The treatment in functional situations allows the child to repeat and experience normal movements in many different ways (Bobath, 1984; Mayston, 1992).

This treatment approach makes it possible for occupational and speech therapists each to play an important part in the team. Nancy Finnie and Helen Muller did this pioneer work respectively (Finnie, 1968; Muller, 1997). Occupational therapy based on NDT concept can improve the quality of eyes/hand function, sensation and perception, which are each so essential in all functional activities (Finnie, 1968, 1997; Boehme, 1988; Kong, 1991).

A better postural control obtained through NDT influences the quality of breathing, phonation, eating and drinking, which are important factors in the development of comprehensible speech (Keller, 1997; Leeuwenburg-Grij seels, 1997; Meek, 1997; Mueller, 1999).

Parent participation, education and guidance

A child's development occurs within a permanent interaction with his environment, that is the mother in the beginning. She handles the child in a pattern of her social cultural environment and intuitively adapts her handling to the child's behavior and developmental achievements (Papou{ek and Papou{ek, 1984). When there is a retarded or abnormal development she will intuitively adapt to protect her child (Bobath, 1967).

In treatment It is essential to establish adequate mutual child-mother reciprocity, interaction and communication, and a mutual mother-therapist relationship. Guiding and training the parents in home management is of the greatest importance (Finnie, 1968, 1997; Bobath, 1984). No amount of treatment can be effective unless the progress, which the child makes during the treatment, is carried over into his everyday life and activities.

With the cooperation of parents and teachers there is a better chance of obtaining a carryover of a more normal movement into everyday activities and thus avoid frustration and overloading of the child and parents with treatment. We have to respect the situation of the family and their individual abilities. We practice with them so that they can feel and learn how to continue a treatment programmed at home and how to handle the child in order to help him with his own movements during the day.

We have to help them to understand why their child cannot perform some movements. They have to understand the child's problems and possibilities to solve them and what they can do to help. Parent training takes time, is difficult and needs good communication between the therapist and the parents.

Team approach

The child's whole development depends largely on his ability to move and explore his environment. All his problems are related and in order to understand them an overall approach is needed. Everyone concerned with the child's treatment and management should work closely together and have the same understanding of what is being done and of its aim It should be a common effort rather than each one working in isolation.

The NDT concept today

The basic principles of NDT remain the same. By the inhibitory control of abnormal movement patterns and simultaneous facilitation of automatic postural reactions (righting and equilibrium reactions) with the therapist's hands combined with different techniques of stimulation, we reduce the dysfunctional abnormal postural tone to facilitate and transmit to the child a variety of sensory-motor experiences in functional and goal directed activities.

The therapist controls proximal key points of control (head, shoulders, trunk, pelvis) to achieve a good for each child individually adapted, a mobile control of the posture. In the early treatment we can facilitate righting and equilibrium reactions close to the sequences of normal development. In an older child we have to compromise, and find and transmit the essential basic patterns, which are needed to improve the child's activities in the present and near future.

The treatment is, therefore, adapted to the needs of the individual child. The child's abilities and disabilities are carefully assessed and the child is handled and treated in a specialized way, observing and controlling his responses. There is a necessity for a constant interaction with assessment and reassessment during the treatment (Bobath, 1987; Mayston, 1992).

Early treatment based on NDT principles

The characteristic syndromes of cerebral palsy are the result of abnormal sensory-motor development and appear gradually. If we start to treat a child in the period when abnormal patterns of posture and movement are already fully established and habitual, we can achieve only limited results and we cannot avoid deformities and orthopedic surgical interventions (Kong, 1974; Hochleitner, 1977; 1986; Kong, 1990).

Elizabeth Kong, pediatrician in Switzerland, did the pioneer work in the field of early detection and early treatment. Inspired by the idea of the Irish therapist Eirene Collis, who first recognized the need for early detection and treatment, and supported by new advances in developmental and child neurology, she recognized the advantages and importance of the NDT Bobath concept as an appropriate approach to early treatment (Kong, 1965; Kong, 1966; Bobath, 1967; Kong, 1982; Scherzer, Tscharnuter, 1982; Kong, 1999).

The English physiotherapist Mary Quinton, working side by side with Elizabeth Kong in Bern, adapted and further developed the techniques for early treatment of babies based on the NDT-Bobath concept (Quinton, 1986; 1997). There are many infants who show apparently abnormal motor behavior during the first months of life. Most of them overcome it spontaneously.

Substantial improvement in obstetrics and perinatal care during the last decades have resulted in a decrease in perinatal mortality, in a significant change of panorama of cerebral palsy and in an increase in the number of surviving neonates at risk of developmental disorders. It is of great importance that these babies are longitudinally followed and checked by experienced paediatricians not only during the first months but during the whole first year of life (Kong, 1966; 1990).

The observation and evaluation of the quality of an infant's spontaneous motor behaviour introduced by Heinz Prechtl, has become the most reliable diagnostic tool in detecting potential cerebral palsy (Prechtl, 1997; Prechtl at all, 1997). The age of three months (corrected in preterm infants) has proved to be a stage from which early abnormal signs may either be disappearing or increasing. A growing dominance of abnormal movement patterns from the third month onward is an absolute indication for NDT.

If abnormal spontaneous general movements are accompanied by abnormal sucking-swallowing and/or visual problems, we have to introduce NDT earlier on (Kong, 1990). Early NDT is considered to be the treatment which starts before or at the age of two to three months (corrected age), that is in the period of fidgety character of general movements before anti-gravity voluntary movements emerge. The functional aim of fidgety movements is probably the calibration of the proprioceptive system (Prechtl, personal communication). In the fidgety period there is also a change from perineuronal to mononeuronal innervation (Purves, 1994; Gramsbergen, 1997).

If fidgety movements are absent or of abnormal quality, it is a predictive sign of developmental disorder (Prechtl, 1997). Not every baby treatment is early treatment. Early treatment is considered to be the treatment that starts as soon as brain lesion as abnormal movement patterns are observed and begin to be predominant.

The importance, advantages and possibilities of early treatment

The sensory side of the sensory-motor experience and its influence on the body image standing, walking, prehension and manipulation in human infants require a certain level of postural control (Gramsbergen, Hadders-Algra, 1998). The normal baby gradually develops the dynamic chain of sequences of righting reactions and balance reactions in relation to gravity, the repetition of which lays down with increasing precision these finely integrated sensory-motor experiences.

These in time become automatic and form the basis for the learning of future skills. The resulting body image that evolves from this variation of sensory motor experiences will be normal. On the other hand, the development of babies with brain dysfunction, the abnormal sensory-motor experiences with their resulting habit patterns and limited development of righting and balance reactions, will result in an abnormal body image and an inadequate sensory-motor base for the later learning of movement skills.

With the early treatment we have the chance to integrate active normal sensory-motor experiences before abnormal movement patterns have become a habit. These are the babies who without help only develop abnormally, their body image playing a large part in this process. This is where we can help (Quinton, 1986; 1997, Bly, 1999).

The importance of righting reactions and midline orientation

In the third month ("fidgety" period) there is an orientation to the midline head control in relation to the body (Prechtl, 1988) under the influence of righting reactions (head - body righting, active vertical midline), which enables the visual system to be integrated and interrelated into the postural control coupling of the visual system (Nelson, 1996; Quinton, 1997).

Competition of patterns in normal and abnormal development

These righting reactions (only evident when the neck is posteriorly lengthened and there is a chin-sternum tuck) will compete with tonic activities and Moro reflex, which thrust the neck and head into extension. This competition remains normal providing that postural tonic extensor activities are slowly but surely suppressed during the third to the fifth month of life so that the normal head control and midline symmetry may be established. If this does not occur, Moro reaction and postural tonic activity will become dominant and influence all future development in an abnormal way.

In the same way of competition, the asymmetric tonic neck reflex (ATNR) may start to become dominant. In early treatment by activating and repeating the dynamic sequences of righting reactions we have the possibility of laying down more normal pathways which will compete with and inhibit the otherwise continuing development of the abnormal. Of course, the outcome depends on the initial brain damage. If we can find and release the righting reactions, there is always hope for improvement (Quinton, 1997).

The importance of handling the baby and the baby mother interaction in early treatment One of the most common criticisms of NDT is that there is too much handling of too many hands on the child. It is natural that a baby during his first months of life is picked up, carried, put down, dressed, undressed and so on. There is a natural interplay between baby and mother, between her way of supporting a baby and his growing ability of "putting himself right" by righting and controlling the position of his head and trunk.

It seems improper to ask the mother to take her hands off her baby. To teach the mother special ways of handling her baby is the most important aspect of early treatment. Only if she helps in this way can the baby acquire a variety of necessary sensory-motor patterns of postural adjustment. Repetition is so important. It has a dual effect not only upon his motor development but also upon the gradual formation of a more normal body image, which underlies his future development and learning of skills (Bobath, 1967; Quinton, 1986; 1997).

Prevention of contractures and deformities

Contractures and deformities are not present in the baby, except for possible congenital dislocation of one or both hips or congenital clubfoot not due to a brain lesion. There may be very early signs of threatening deformities such as shortening of neck extensors due to dominant tonic extensor activity or persistent asymmetry with shortening of one side of the trunk and pelvic obliquity because of the dominance of ATNR with a tendency to hip dislocation and scoliosis due to the dominance of abnormal patterns in competition with the normal ones. Early treatment can in most cases prevent the development of major contractures and deformities and frequent early orthopaedic surgical intervention in children with cerebral palsy.

The limits of the outcome of early treatment

Extensive brain lesion will limit the outcome of early treatment. In babies with additional severe sensory loss, perceptual impairment, and severe mental retardation the treatment result is very limited. Children with severe Proprioceptive and temporo-spatial perception problems perceive only to a small degree normal reaction transmitted through treatment. Their motor progress is slow. They need some additional specific perceptual training.

Severely mentally retarded children do not make spontaneous use in daily life of what they have experienced during treatment. Children with hemiplegia will always continue to favour their better side even if their disabled side becomes mobile and automatic activities can be obtained. If we cannot establish mutual cooperation with the family, for whatever reasons, the effect of early treatment may be reduced and limited (Kong, 1990).

Quality of treatment

Treatment results depend a great deal on the quality of treatment. Besides a good theoretical background, good working knowledge and professional skills of the therapist, there are some very important points that add to the quality of the treatment. Therapy should be a mutual communication between the child and the therapist as a two-directional, positive experience of giving, receiving and responding to one another, coupled with anticipation and pleasure, always advancing together. The baby/child should always be respected. If he is getting what he needs, he will accept and follow.

If something is always refused, there is a reason that needs to be explored and dealt with. It is essential to obtain active automatic normal reactions in the treatment, to be able to prepare and to wait for these reactions, to adapt the treatment continuously to the momentary situation of the child and to withdraw control gradually so that the child can repeat and initiate by himself in order to be able to take over the control. Careful challenge within the therapy is necessary to make a treatment interesting for the child. The child and his parents will refuse dull, monotonous and uninteresting treatment.

The adaptation of the therapy to the individual personality, interests and potentials of the child will contribute much to the motivation of the child. The involvement and realistic expectation of the therapist in obtaining improvements are an important motivation for parents. It is essential that the doctor and the therapist clearly explain to the parents the essence and aims of the treatment not just in words but also to encourage them to feel the movements they aim to transmit to the child on and within their own bodies, as well as to perform them on a doll. This way they will understand more fully what their baby or child requires (Quinton, 1986; Quinton 1997).

Duration of treatment

It is necessary to continue therapy until the desired result is secured, i.e. equilibrium reactions are obtained while standing and walking in order to free the hands for function. Later on these children need a longitudinal follow up because sometimes they deteriorate, especially during puberty, in the quality of their postural control with a tendency to develop a kyphotic or scoliotic deformity. With a residual disability, even a slight one, it is worthwhile to continue treatment in a reasonable way until or into adulthood. Functional abilities and the quality of life will further improve. The amount of treatment should be individually adapted according to problems and priorities with strong emphasis on the child's control of its own movements (Kong, 1999).

Appendix - 2 - GMFCS

GMFCS-E&R
Gross Motor Function Classification System
Expanded and Revised

GMFCS• E&R© Robert Palisano, Peter Rosenbaum, Doreen Bartlett, Michael Uvingston, 1007
CanChildCentre for ChildhoodDisabilityResearch, McMasterUniversity

GMFCS© Robert Palisano, Peter Rosenbaum, Stephen Walter, Dianne Russell, Bien Wood, Barbara Galuppi, 1997
CanChildCentre for ChildhoodDisabilityResearch, McMasterUniversity
(Reference: Dev Med Child Neurol 1997;39:214-223)

INTRODUCTION & USER INSTRUCTIONS

The Gross Motor Function Classification System (GMFCS) for cerebral palsy is based on self-initiated movement, with emphasis on sitting, transfers, and mobility. When defining a five-level classification system, our primary criterion has been that the distinctions between levels must be meaningful in daily life. Distinctions are based on functional limitations, the need for hand-held mobility devices (such as walkers, crutches, or canes) or wheeled mobility, and to a much lesser extent, quality of movement. The distinctions between Levels I and II are not as pronounced as the distinctions between the other levels, particularly for infants less than 2 years of age.

The expanded GMFCS (2007) includes an age band for youth 12 to 18 years of age and emphasizes the concepts inherent in the World Health Organization's International Classification of Functioning, Disability and Health (ICF). We encourage users to be aware of the impact that environmental and personal factors may have on what children and youth are observed or reported to do. The focus of the GMFCS is on determining which level best represents the child's or youth's present abilities and limitations in gross motor function. Emphasis is on usual performance in home, school, and community settings (i.e., what they do), rather than what they are known to be able to do at their best (capability). It is therefore important to classify current performance in gross motor function and not to include judgments about the quality of movement or prognosis for improvement

The title for each level is the method of mobility that is most characteristic of performance after 6 years of age. The descriptions of functional abilities and limitations for each age band are broad and are not intended to describe all aspects of the function of individual children/youth. For example, an infant with hemiplegia who is unable to crawl on his or her hands and knees, but otherwise fits the description of Level I (i.e., can pull to stand and walk), would be classified in Level I. The scale is ordinal, with no intent that the distances between levels be considered equal or that children and youth with cerebral palsy are equally distributed across the five levels. A summary of the distinctions between each pair of levels is provided to assist in determining the level that most closely resembles a child's/youth's current gross motor function.

We recognize that the manifestations of gross motor function are dependent on age, especially during infancy and early childhood. For each level, separate descriptions are provided in several age bands. Children below age 2 should be considered at their corrected age if they were premature. The descriptions for the 6 to 12 year and 12 to18 year age bands reflect the potential impact of environment factors (e.g., distances in school and community) and personal factors (e.g., energy demands and social preferences} on methods of mobility.

An effort has been made to emphasize abilities rather than limitations. Thus, as a general principle, the gross motor function of children and youth who are able to perform the functions described in any particular level will probably be classified at or above that level of function; in contrast, the gross motor function of children and youth who cannot perform the functions of a particular level should be classified below that level of function.

Body support walker - A mobility device that supports the pelvis and trunk. The chHd/youth is physically positioned in the walker by another person.

Hand-held mobility device - Canes, crutches, and anterior and posterior walkers that do not support the trunk during walking.

Physical assistance-Another person manuaUy assists the child/youth to move.

Powered mobility - The child/youth actively controls the joystick or electrical switch that enables independent mobility. The mobility base may be a wheelchair, scooter or other type of powered mobility device.

Self-propels manual wheelchair - The child/youth actively uses arms and hands or feet to propel the wheels and move.

Transported - A person manually pushes a mobility device (e.g., wheelchair, stroller, or pram) to move the child/youth from one place to another.

Walks - Unless otherwise specified indicates no physical assistance from another person or *any* use of a hand-held mobility device. An orthosis (i.e., brace or splint) may be worn.

Wheeled mobility - Refers to any type of device with wheels that enables movement (e.g., stroUer, manual wheelchair, or powered wheelchair}.

GENERAL HEADINGS FOR EACH LEVEL

LEVELi   -   Walks without Limitations

I.EVELO   -   Walks with Limitations

LEVEi.iii   -   Walks Using a Hano-Held Mobility Device

LEVEi.iV   -   Sett-Mobility with Limitations; *May* Use Powered Mobility

LEVEL V   -   Transported in a Manual Wheelchair

DISTINCTIONS BETWEEN LEVELS

Distinctions Between Levels I and U - Compared with children and youth in Level I. children and youth in Level II have limitations walking long distances and balancing; may need a hand-held mobility device when first learning to walk; may use wheeled mobility when traveling long distances outdoors and in the community; require the use of a railing to walk up and down stairs; and are not as capable of running and jumping.

Distinctions Between Levels II and 111- Children and youth in Level II are capable of walking without a hand-held mobility device after age 4 (although they may choose to use one at limes). Children and youth in Level III need a hand-held mobility device to walk indoors and use wheeled mobility outdoors and in the community.

Distinctions Betw een Levels III and IV - Children and youth in Level III sit on their own or require at most limited external support to sit, are more independent in standing transfers, and walk with a hand-held mobility device. Children and youth in Level IV function in sitting (usually supported) but self-mobility is limited. Children and youth in Level IV are more likely to be transported in a manual wheelchair or use powered mobility.

Distinctions Between Levels IV and V - Children and youth in level V have severe limitations in head and trunk control and require extensive assisted technology and physical assistance. Sett-mobility is achieved only if the childtyouth can learn how to operate a powered wheelchair.

Gross Motor Function Classification System - Expanded and Revised (GMFCS- E & R)

BEFORE 2ND BIRTHDAY

LEVEL I: Infants move in and out of — and sit with both hands free to manipulate objects. Infants crawl on hands and knees, pull to stand and take steps holding on to furniture. Infants walk between 18 months and 2 years of age without the need for any assistive mobility device.

LEVEL II: Infants maintain floor — but may need to use their hands for support to maintain balance. Infants creep on their stomach or crawl on hands and knees. Infants may pull to stand and take steps holding on to furniture.

LEVEL III: Infants maintain floor — the kif both is — Infants roll and creep forward on their stomachs.

LEVEL IV: Infants have head control but trunk support is required for floor sitting. Infants can roll to supine and may roll to prone.

LEVEL V: Physical impairments limit voluntary control of movement. Infants are unable to maintain antigravity head and trunk postures in prone and sitting. Infants require adult assistance to roll.

BETWEEN 2ND AND 4TH BIRTHDAY

LEVEL I: Children floor sit with both hands free to manipulate objects. Movements in and out of floor — and standing are performed without adult assistance. Children walk as the preferred method of mobility without the need for any assistive mobility device.

LEVEL II: Children floor sit but may have difficulty with balance when both hands are free to manipulate objects. Movements in and out of — are performed without adult assistance. Children pull to stand on a stable surface. Children crawl on hands and knees with a reciprocal pattern, cruise holding onto furniture and walk using an assistive mobility device as preferred methods of mobility.

LEVEL III: Children maintain floor sitting often by "W-sitting" (sitting between flexed and internally rotated hips and knees) and may require adult assistance to assume sitting. Children creep on their stomach or crawl on hands and knees (often without reciprocal leg movements) as their primary methods of self-mobility. Children may pull to stand on a stable surface and cruise short distances. Children may walk short distances indoors using a hand-held mobility device (walker) and adult assistance for steering and turning.

LEVEL IV: Children floor sit when placed, but are unable to maintain — and balance without use of their hands for support. Children frequently require adaptive equipment for — and standing. Self-mobility for short distances (within a room) is achieved through rolling, creeping on stomach, or crawling on hands and knees without reciprocal leg movement.

LEVEL V: Physical impairments restrict voluntary control of movement and the ability to maintain antigravity head and trunk postures. All areas of motor function are limited. Functional limitations in sitting and standing are not fully compensated for through the use of adaptive equipment and assistive technology. At level V, children have no means of independent movement and are transported. Some children achieve self-mobility using a powered wheelchair with extensive adaptations.

BETWEEN 4TH AND 6TH BIRTHDAY

LEVEL I: Children get into and out of, and sit in, a chair without the need for hand support. Children move from the floor and from chair — to standing without the need for objects for support. Children walk indoors and outdoors and climb stairs. Emerging ability to run and jump.

LEVEL II: Children sit in a chair with both hands free to manipulate objects. Children move from the floor to stand and from chair — to standing but often require a stable surface to push or pull up upon with their arms. Children walk without the need for a hand-held mobility device indoors and for short distances on level surfaces outdoors. Children climb stairs holding onto a railing but are unable to run or jump.

LEVEL III: Children sit on a regular chair but may require pelvic or trunk support to maximize hand function. Children move in and out of chair sitting using a stable surface to push on or pull up with their arms. Children walk with a hand-held mobility device on level surfaces and climb stairs with assistance from an adult. Children frequently are transported when traveling for big distances or outdoors on uneven terrain.

LEVEL IV: Children sit on a chair but need adaptive — for trunk control and to maximize hand function. Children move in and out of chair sitting with assistance from an adult or a stable surface to push or pull up on with their arms. Children may at best walk short distances with a walker and adult supervision but have difficulty turning and maintaining balance on uneven surfaces. Children are transported in the community. Children may achieve self-mobility using a powered wheelchair.

LEVEL V: Physical impairments restrict voluntary control of movement and the ability to maintain antigravity head and trunk postures. All areas of motor function are limited. Functional limitations in sitting and standing are not fully compensated for through the use of adaptive equipment and assistive technology. At level V, children have no means of independent movement and are transported. Some children achieve self-mobility using a powered wheelchair with extensive adaptations.

C

Level I: Children walk at home, school, outdoors, and in the community. Children are able to walk up and down curbs without physical assistance and stairs without the use of a railing. Children perform gross motor skills such as running and jumping but speed, balance, and coordination are limited. Children may participate in physical activities and sports depending on personal choices and environmental factors.

Level II: Children walk in most settings. Children may experience difficulty walking long distances and balancing on uneven terrain, inclines, in crowded areas, confined spaces or when carrying objects. Children walk up and down stairs holding onto a railing or with physical assistance if there is no railing. Outdoors and in the community, children may walk with physical assistance, a hand-held mobility device, or use wheeled mobility when traveling long distances. Children have at best only minimal ability to perform gross motor skills such as running and jumping. Limitations in performance of gross motor skills may necessitate adaptations to enable participation in physical activities and sports.

Level III: Children walk using a hand-held mobility device in most indoor settings. When seated, children may require a seat belt for pelvic alignment and balance. Sit-to-stand and floor-to-stand transfers require physical assistance of a person or support surface. When traveling long distances, children use some form of wheeled mobility. Children may walk up and down stairs holding onto a railing with supervision or physical assistance. Limitations in walking may necessitate adaptations to enable participation in physical activities and sports including self-propelling a manual wheelchair or powered mobility.

Level IV: Children use methods of mobility that require physical assistance or powered mobility in most settings. Children require adaptive seating for trunk and pelvic control and physical assistance for most transfers. At home, children use floor mobility (roll, creep, or crawl), walk short distances with physical assistance, or use powered mobility. When positioned, children may use a body support walker at home or school. At school, outdoors, and in the community, children are transported in a manual wheelchair or use powered mobility. Limitations in mobility necessitate adaptations to enable participation in physical activities and sports, including physical assistance and/or powered mobility.

Level V: Children are transported in a manual wheelchair in all settings. Children are limited in their ability to maintain antigravity head and trunk postures and control arm and leg movements. Assistive technology is used to improve head alignment, seating, standing, and and/or mobility but limitations are not fully compensated by equipment. Transfers require complete physical assistance of an adult. At home, children may move short distances on the floor or may be carried by an adult. Children may achieve self-mobility using powered mobility with extensive adaptations for seating and control access. Limitations in mobility necessitate adaptations to enable participation in physical activities and sports including physical assistance and using powered mobility.

Level I: Youth walk at home, school, outdoors, and in the community. Youth are able to walk up and down curbs without physical assistance and stairs without the use of a railing. Youth perform gross motor skills such as running and jumping but speed, balance, and coordination are limited. Youth may participate in physical activities and sports depending on personal choices and environmental factors.

Level II: Youth walk in most settings. Environmental factors (such as uneven terrain, inclines, long distances, time demands, weather, and peer acceptability) and personal preference influence mobility choices. At school or work, youth may walk using a hand-held mobility device for safety. Outdoors and in the community, youth may use wheeled mobility when traveling long distances. Youth walk up and down stairs holding a railing or with physical assistance if there is no railing. Limitations in performance of gross motor skills may necessitate adaptations to enable participation in physical activities and sports.

Level III: Youth are capable of walking using a hand-held mobility device. Compared to individuals in other levels, youth in Level III demonstrate more variability in methods of mobility depending on physical ability and environmental and personal factors. When seated, youth may require a seat belt for pelvic alignment and balance. Sit-to-stand and floor-to-stand transfers require physical assistance from a person or support surface. At school, youth may self-propel a manual wheelchair or use powered mobility. Outdoors and in the community, youth are transported in a wheelchair or use powered mobility. Youth may walk up and down stairs holding onto a railing with supervision or physical assistance. Limitations in walking may necessitate adaptations to enable participation in physical activities and sports including self-propelling a manual wheelchair or powered mobility.

Level IV: Youth use wheeled mobility in most settings. Youth require adaptive seating for pelvic and trunk control. Physical assistance from 1 or 2 persons is required for transfers. Youth may support weight with their legs to assist with standing transfers. Indoors, youth may walk short distances with physical assistance, use wheeled mobility, or, when positioned, use a body support walker. Youth are physically capable of operating a powered wheelchair. When a powered wheelchair is not feasible or available, youth are transported in a manual wheelchair. Limitations in mobility necessitate adaptations to enable participation in physical activities and sports, including physical assistance and/or powered mobility.

Level V: Youth are transported in a manual wheelchair in all settings. Youth are limited in their ability to maintain antigravity head and trunk postures and control arm and leg movements. Assistive technology is used to improve head alignment, seating, standing, and mobility but limitations are not fully compensated by equipment. Physical assistance from 1 or 2 persons or a mechanical lift is required for transfers. Youth may achieve self-mobility using powered mobility with extensive adaptations for seating and control access. Limitations in mobility necessitate adaptations to enable participation in physical activities and sports including physical assistance and using powered mobility.

D

CHAPTER 7

Conclusion

This study tried analyze the effect of NDT on improving the segmental trunk control of cerebral palsy children falling under GMCS score 3 and 4. 80 subjects were recruited into the study and were randomly allotted into two groups namely group A (conventional group) and group B (experimental group treated using NDT). Four outcome measures were used namely GMFM, SATCO, TCMS and CP-QOL. The intervention was provided for a period of 4 weeks.

(1) From the analysis of the results of the study it is clearly understood that both conventional physiotherapy and NDT have brought about significant improvement in all the outcome measures.

(2) The NDT intervention used with a segmental approach in group B have brought about a superior improvement than the conventional intervention.

(3) Further except the quality of life all other parameters have shown a faster and sustained improvement following the NDT intervention compared to the conventional physiotherapy.

(4) Thus, it is concluded from this study that NDT with a segmental approach is a better intervention tool in bringing about improvement in gross motor function, segmental trunk control, static and dynamic balance in cerebral palsy children with GMFCS scale 3 and 4.